Journalism in the Digital Age

Journalism in the Digital Age

Theory and Practice for Broadcast, Print and On-line Media

John Herbert

Focal Press

OXFORD   AUCKLAND   BOSTON   JOHANNESBURG   MELBOURNE   NEW DELHI

Focal Press
An imprint of Butterworth-Heinemann
Linacre House, Jordan Hill, Oxford OX2 8DP
225 Wildwood Avenue, Woburn, MA 01801-2041
A division of Reed Educational and Professional Publishing Ltd

A member of the Reed Elsevier plc group

First published 2000

British Library Cataloguing in Publication Data
Herbert John
  Journalism in the digital age: theory and practice for
  broadcast, print and on-line media
  1. Journalism   2. Journalism – Technological innovations
  3. Journalism – Practice   4. Digital communications
  I. Title
  070.4

Library of Congress Cataloguing in Publication Data
Herbert, John
  Journalism in the digital age: theory and practice for
  broadcast, print and on-line media/John Herbert
  p. cm.
  Includes bibliographical references and index.
  ISBN 0-240-51589-7 (alk. paper)
  1. Journalism – Data processing.   2. Telecommunication – Technological
  innovations.   3. Broadcast journalism – Data processing.   4. Interactive
  multimedia.   5. Electronic publishing.   I. Title
  PN4784.E5 H47
  070.4'0285 21–dc21   99–045337

Composition by Genesis Typesetting, Rochester, Kent
Printed and bound in Great Britain by MPG Books Ltd, Bodmin, Cornwall

Contents

We find that if any sentence takes more than two lines, when it gets to the end most people have forgotten how it began, including the person speaking it

Jonathan Lynn and Anthony Jay
Yes, Prime Minister, 1978

I want fearless honesty about every government triumph

Jonathan Lynn and Anthony Jay
Yes, Prime Minister, 1978

It is not the English habit, as a rule, to accord distinction to journalists

John Le Carré
The Honourable Schoolboy, 1977

Events, dear boy, events

Harold Macmillan
quoted in Hayward, A. (1997). *Politics*. Macmillan. p. 387.

All the journalists had left, and a great peace settled over the town

Evelyn Waugh
Scoop, 1938

There's nothing to replace being there. I mean, that's what journalism is all about

Helen Thomas
UPI White House Bureau chief, 1999

Preface

Unlike Shakespeare's seven, the journalist has three ages: learning, practising and managing. Any practical theory of journalism must be about all three. It must be firmly based on the needs of journalism, not on some other discipline. That's what this book is about; it is an attempt to produce the basis of a practical theory of journalism, which integrates the *study of* with the *practice in* broadcast and print journalism. But it's more than that, because we are now firmly in the digital age when the whole journalistic process is changing. Gathering is digital; sending is digital. The whole newsroom process is digital.

Journalism is all about news and information. Journalists discover news and report it. Journalism consists of gathering facts, deciding how to assemble them and making important decisions about which facts to include and which to omit. It is about talking to people, being curious, thinking clearly, and being able to translate difficult ideas into simple ones so that everyone can understand them. Journalism is about analysing and interpreting events; knowing how government, politics, business, industry and modern society work; and being able to make interesting stories out of all kinds of events. Journalism therefore consists of practical skills and a wide intellectual foundation, which gives credibility to the reporting. However, journalism is different from other disciplines because integration of the practical and the theoretical builds the discipline of journalism. The theoretical has to be seen always in conjunction with the practical skills. Law and ethics, for example, are not separate entities as far as journalists are concerned; they infuse all their news gathering, reporting and communicating and are integrated with the practical skills. All the intellectual theory is integrated into, not separated from, the journalism skills.

Such a practical theory will help journalists to enlarge their understanding, test various theories and work out their own solutions to problems in gathering and reporting news, as well as developing their own creative skills. It will also help to develop important transferable skills that will be useful throughout life, not just in journalism. These include communication, self-assertion and confidence, leadership, co-operation and teamwork, independence, autonomy and self-assessment. Journalists also need the interpersonal skills of influencing others, listening and negotiation; the organizational skills of time and project management and problem solving; and, of course, IT. But again, none of this is in isolation; it is all part of a practical theory.

A practical theory of journalism has eight vital aims. It must provide:

1 The ability to understand what makes a good story; to find the best angle and communicate it with interest and enthusiasm to readers, listeners and viewers
2 Experience of the various theories involved in gathering, writing and reporting news
3 A critical understanding of journalism through an informed, analytical and creative approach to professional practice
4 Transferable skills through written, interpersonal and verbal activities within theoretical and practical frameworks
5 The capacity for rational analysis and argument
6 An understanding of the increasing sophistication and technological advances in the journalism profession
7 A sense of social consciousness towards journalism, and an ethical self-responsibility
8 An awareness of the latest technology such as new computer newsroom technology and satellite communications.

Print and broadcast journalists must be able to:

- understand the basic vocabulary of news and journalism
- understand contending theories in journalism studies
- acquire information from various printed and electronic sources
- use information, concepts and theories to formulate arguments
- analyse problems and formulate responses to them

- present information and arguments orally, and discuss fluently with others
- create information and arguments as well written, interesting and accurate news stories
- work in a team
- have a practical news writing and reporting ability
- have a knowledge of the legal and ethical implications of news
- know about new technology and computer-assisted reporting
- use the latest editing and production techniques to create pleasing, interesting and inventive print and broadcast page layouts, bulletins and programmes
- appreciate the various methodological issues and problems of journalism
- understand contemporary theories and theoretical approaches to the practice of journalism
- read, understand and critically assess contemporary contributions to journalism research
- report in specialist and general areas of journalism.

None of these can be achieved without a finely tuned approach to journalism theory and practice.

Therefore, a practical theory of journalism provides

- a broad scope of basic knowledge
- professional reporting and writing ability
- independent thinking and sense of judgement.

The important intellectual (and therefore theoretical) requirements for journalists are a wide range of knowledge about the society in which they live and work, its economics, politics, sociology, history, international relations, and an appropriate foundation in professional skills. These are the foundations on which an integrated practical theory of journalism is based.

There is more, specifically related to broadcast journalism. A national survey in the United States in 1994 found the most common reasons for employing a new reporter in broadcast newsrooms were: self-motivation, journalism skills, dedication, news judgement, on-air presence, personality, voice quality, physical appearance, broadcast news experience and audition tape quality (Hilt and Lipschultz, 1994).

This is a text book aimed at academics, journalists and journalist managers. It is an attempt to integrate the 'how' and the 'why'; to look at the whole rather than individual parts. It is also an attempt to stop the argument – usually unproductive and carried out by academic non-journalists – which says that all that is needed is the theory (usually communication theory), and the rest will take care of itself. It won't. Journalism has its own theoretical foundation upon which is built journalism practice. In this way I have tried to integrate the foundations and elements of journalism practice, principles and management into one practical theory. This book aims to put under one cover all the basic information that student journalists need for their undergraduate or postgraduate studies and it will also be helpful in later life as they progress in their work. It aims to present ideas and various methodologies for journalism educators, whether they are working in universities or within the industry, and also to be a guide for those journalists who have gone from being working reporters to working management. They too need help, and sympathy.

Because it covers all aspects of print and broadcast journalism, there will be the need to look at more detailed books on specific subjects. Others in this series will provide this additional detail: Andrew Boyd's *Broadcast Journalism*, Anthony Davis's *Magazine Journalism Today* and Brendan Hennessey's *Writing Feature Articles,* F. W. Hodgson's *Modern Newspaper Practice* and *New Subediting: Apple-Mac, QuarkXPress and After*, Nicholas Bagnall's *Newspaper Language* and Harris and Sparks's *Practical Newspaper Reporting* were all of immense help to me in writing this present book.

J.H.

Acknowledgements

This is a book that distils almost 30 years of experience in journalism in several countries, and everyone with whom I've worked in these countries needs a thank you. My media and academic friends in Australia, Singapore, New Zealand, the United Kingdom, the US and Hong Kong will find some thoughts throughout this book which will certainly be familiar. For that, thank you. I hope I have given ideas back in return. For the three years leading up to the handover to China I was in Hong Kong. Inevitably, some of the flavour of that historic and disturbing time found its way into this book, particularly on matters concerning censorship and freedom of the press. Many thanks to my Hong Kong friends and colleagues from whom I learnt so much about the local situation, and about the way journalism is practised and taught there. To all my students, I would also like to give sincere thanks. The best way of learning is by teaching. They taught me a lot. I hope they have learnt at least a little from me in return. Since I was teaching the future journalists of Hong Kong, their worries became my worries. I will always remember their dedication, courage and enthusiasm for the cause of journalism; without them this book would not have been written. To Tim Hamlett, long-suffering and patient listener to my various thoughts as they tumbled forth, who ever patiently waited for the final edited version, many thanks. I am particularly grateful for his help with the print style guide, which owes much to him and his elegance of style. Thanks also to other Hong Kong colleagues, Dr Judith Clarke and Professor Chen Yu Hsi, who were always willing to listen and give of their experiences, and to

Acknowledgements

Jenny Welham, Beth Howard and Margaret Denley of Focal Press, who shepherded the book through its various stages of publication so kindly and efficiently. But most of all, my greatest thanks go to my wife Margaret, who has been reader, critic and ideas-person throughout the whole writing process. This book would not have been written without her.

Finally, of course, although so many have wittingly or unwittingly helped my thought processes over the years, they provided only the good bits. The mistakes, as always, are mine alone.

1 Journalism in the digital age

In Britain in 1999 there were 10.6 million people on-line, and the numbers are growing. That is about 18 per cent of the population. In the United States it is 27 per cent and rising.

The broadsheet newspapers have been on-line for several years. In 1999, the two largest selling newspapers in the world, the British *Sun* and *Mirror* went on-line. The *Sun* jumped on the bandwagon with a website called CurrantBun.com, whilst the *Mirror* has a site called ic24.co.uk, which stands for *I see 24 hours a day*. The *Sun* believes that the Internet is no longer for nerds and boffins, it is for ordinary people like you and us. Its aim is to prove that the Internet is fun, cheeky and dead easy to use.

The effect the digital age is having on journalism is also starkly seen in the way photos can now be in the paper within minutes of being taken. In the old days it would take hours, if not days.

In the pre-digital age, getting a photo back to the newsroom would mean fast cars, film being hurled onto passing trains, boats and planes, and time-consuming processes in the darkroom. All it takes now is a digital camera, a mobile phone and a laptop computer. Once the photo is taken on the digital camera, the camera disk is plugged into the laptop, which takes about a minute to read the disk and its images; it then downloads the images onto the laptop screen (another 20 seconds). The computer is hooked up to the mobile phone, and the images are beamed to the newsroom – all in about 2 minutes. The picture editor in the newsroom or newsagency then spends about 2 minutes checking the quality of the images and adding a caption before sending them instantaneously down an Integrated Services Digital Network (ISDN) line to wherever they need to go (sometimes to newsagency offices around the world). Images made this way can also be manipulated, so they can be used to design a website, be presented on a television set or beamed via satellite anywhere where they can be downloaded. Some digital cameras also come with an inbuilt microphone to enable recording of a running commentary on the pictures, which can be played back with the pictures.

Newspaper editors can also use the system in reverse. They can use the Internet to look through the camera viewfinder, and advise the photographers what shots they want from thousands of miles away. The digital age is changing journalism forever. Now, anyone with access to the Internet can order on-line personalized news services that deliver to their computer only the kinds of stories that interest them. Major news organizations update their overseas news on the Internet every hour. In other words, the digital age of journalism makes available to customers the news they want when they want it.

Digital age journalism is now also interactive. Until recently it was a one-way process, and we had to trust the editors, reporters and photographers and take what they gave us. That is no longer the case. Discussion and debate over all kinds of issues is enhanced by the digital age.

The digital age means that journalism is taking on a new style of writing and editing. Traditional journalistic writing was based on linear storytelling, often called the inverted pyramid (discussed later in this book). This provided the reader, listener or viewer with a summary lead and details in descending order of importance. It works well on the printed page, but not on the computer screen. Hypertext now enables journalists to write on-line stories that are multi-dimensional. The journalist can structure the story differently, and it allows readers to pick their own path through the story. Perhaps one reader will click onto a sidebar or to a set of definitions of technical terms; another to a related feature about a particular fact in the main body of the story. Every story published on-line can be read in many ways, and entirely as the reader wishes. The links are built on association of ideas, which is a very different approach to the way traditional journalism is compiled, logically and analytically.

The computer also allows journalists to find facts in a very different way. Searching for facts is now easy. However, this form of computer reporting means the journalist must still check the facts, and not take them as gospel because the computer says they are right. Anyone can put anything on the Internet. Luciano Floridi (1995) argues that the

Internet 'resembles a huge library where every half hour a new load of books is dumped at the doors and every day they change the position of the books on the shelves'.

The digital age means that information is drifting away from governments into the hands of journalists. It also means new opportunities for the modern journalist. Word processing was one of the first products of digitization to enter the newsroom, and spreadsheets and databases for storing and analysing data followed. Later, the Internet revolutionized news sources and information search strategies.

Databases are like old-fashioned card files. If you're looking for specific information, such as a particular person, for example, it is easy. You might want to know statistical facts, and the computer database via the Internet will do it for you. Spreadsheets consist of rows and columns, with a cell on each junction. These cells contain text, figures and formulas. A spreadsheet is more powerful than a pocket calculator because it not only does the calculations, but will tell you what they mean as well. For example, when writing a story about the government budget, the journalist can enter a suggested change in the spreadsheet and the computer will instantly calculate the consequences for the total budget.

The databases and connected networks on the Internet are invaluable for journalists. All kinds of documents, news and information can be found easily. This changes the task of the journalist in the digital age. Instead of finding and disclosing information, the task is now fighting through the information glut and selecting the most important information. It is therefore important to know how to find what you are looking for, and you need time to sift through the information to find exactly what you want.

Taking part in discussion lists and news groups is one of the best ways to remain informed about news stories and to update yourself easily. A basic research tool is e-mail, and home pages of journalists are also good sources. Everyone is a journalist in the digital age!

The digital age journalist has to become a specialist who knows how to search for information on the web and turn it into news. Readers do not have this training or ability. The great on-line opportunity, says Katherine Fulton, is finding ways to inform people more deeply and save time.

The question is whether people will turn to journalists or to someone else in 10 or 20 years, when they need a better information filter. Journalists, who have already lost so much authority and standing in the culture, are going to have to re-earn their right to both.

At its simplest level, news gathering consists of three stages: getting the idea; finding the information; writing the story. Using the Internet for reporting allows the journalist in the digital age to locate and gather the information. Selecting, verifying and writing is still personal and creative, and needs training, knowledge and experience.

FURTHER READING

Floridi, L. (1995). Internet: which future for organised knowledge, Frankenstein or Pygmalion? Paper delivered at the first UNESCO Philosophy Forum, Paris, March. (seen at: www.unleyhs.schools.sa.edu.au/issues/floridi.html)

Fulton, K. (1996). A tour of our uncertain future. *Columbia Journalism Review*, March/April. (seen at: www.crj.org/html)

Granato, L. (ed.) (1998). *Newsgathering on the Net*. Macmillan.

Ross, S. (1997). Columbia Journalism School survey of online media (seen at: www.mediasource.com/study/CONT.HTM).

2   A questioning profession

Journalism is a simple profession. It is all about asking questions. The questions – of people, about events – provide the facts, and it is the facts that make the news. Without the facts, there is no news. So the profession of journalists is focused, in the end, on knowing the right question to ask; being able to ask it in the most knowledgeable and open way, and then being able to communicate it in the most interesting, creative and forceful manner. In order to ask that question the profession requires much knowledge and ability, and it is asking the question despite pressures not to, that protects freedom. Journalism is the ultimate expression of democracy and freedom. Governments and politicians realize this and constantly try to legislate against total journalism freedom, and this is particularly bad in broadcast journalism. The relationship between journalism and democracy is a complex one. How and to what degree do the news media contribute to democratic practices and structures? And how do democratic processes shape the news of the day, the institutions themselves and their practices and routines?

News is a living, changing thing, showing at any one time only a snapshot of reality. For this reason, journalism is often called *the first draft of history*. Of course, this definition is easier to understand for print journalists than for broadcast journalists. In print there is time to think about the facts before publishing, whereas in broadcasting there is never this luxury. Broadcast journalism depends on an uncontrolled succession of events which in themselves make news, hour by hour, day by day. Each part of the jigsaw is put together hour by hour, and is seldom complete from the start. Each bulletin adds or detracts from the knowledge that is available.

Since the 1989 English translation of Jurgen Habermas's *The Structural Transformation of the Public Sphere*, a growing body of theoretical literature has attempted to put this journalism–democracy question within a proper public relationship. In a true democracy, everyone has the right to know and to discuss what is going on round them. Their elected representatives may try to set legal restraints on the right to know. The judiciary measures one public interest against another and does not hesitate to say 'publish' when the defenders of concealment and strict confidentiality fail to make their case. There are many examples. In Australia, a High Court judge refused to injunct as a breach of confidence a book that reprinted diplomatic cables between Canberra and Djakarta, because the government failed to show that the public interest required restrictions on material that might cause diplomatic embarrassment and political criticism. News exists to serve the right to know. Prior restraint of reporting is usually a drastic interference with freedom of speech and should occur only when there is a risk of grave injustice (Denning, 1982: 264). Lord Denning, the famous English judge said *The remedy is to take action afterwards. The liberty of the press is indeed essential to the nature of a free state, but this consists of laying no previous restraints on publication.* The European Court of Human Rights says *there must be a social need sufficiently pressing to outweight the public interest in freedom of expression* (Denning: 265).

News is important. No effort must be spared to get it right, not only to the satisfaction of professional journalists but also to the general public. This importance makes journalists close guardians of the freedom of speech and the right to know. They are therefore suspicious of the motives of their critics. Both journalists and their critics have to avoid stereotypes. One is the image of the unfeeling and neurotically questioning reporter, whether a seasoned campaigner or one newly arrived from the country with three years of flower shows, Rotary dinners and magistrates courts behind them. The other stereotype is that of the critic who conceals behind fair words a desire to use journalism for any purpose that is not truly journalistic, whether idealistic or sinister. But underlying all this is the need for the journalists of the future to be vividly aware of the need for the greatest professionalism in their work.

Professionalism is central to the role of the journalist as the watchdog of democracy and freedom. Professionalism as a journalistic concept has been around for a long time, yet there are many ideas about what professionalism really means in journalism. Shoemaker and Reese (1991) warn that the term professionalism must be used with caution. Although most journalists are not sure exactly what professionalism means, all journalists should think of themselves as professionals.

While journalists must believe in the neutral, unbiased approach to news, they should do so within the parameters of the three main roles with which they involve themselves in their professional job: they are disseminators of news and information, interpreters of news and information and adversaries of the newsmakers and politicians to test the case and arrive at the truth.

Journalists from both democratic and non-democratic political systems will agree on their role as disseminators of news. They will have more difficulty in reconciling the other two roles, interpreters of events and, most difficult of all, adversaries of newsmakers. It is this last, the adversarial role of the professional journalist, that causes most trouble in both democracies and non-democracies, and it is precisely this adversarial role that marks the free democracy from the restricted one.

However, professionalism has two dimensions: the universal and the specific. Professionalism in any society, under any conditions, implies some general, universal principles. At the same time, professionalism cannot exist in a social vacuum. It is a relative concept, determined by different historical and cultural traditions and defined by specific political, economic and social contexts. The journalism practised in any country is deeply embedded in national culture and history. Common to both groups, professionals and lay people, is a firm conviction from everyone that bent news is bad news, no matter in which direction the bending takes place.

Journalism has come a long way since the Gutenberg Bible of 1455, which was itself the result of new technology; in this case movable type and mechanical printing. Since then, new technology has been at the forefront of journalism developments. Journalism has grown up alongside the telegraph, telephones, satellites and newsagencies. Satellite delivery of copy to printers is now commonplace. Newspaper copy, complete with layouts, is sent by satellite from central editorial offices to remote printing plants, which makes delivery times even faster and global. Computerization is making even greater changes. Software such as Pagemaker and QuarkXPress now allows journalists and editors to do much of the work at their desks on their own computers. Journalists can now carry round with them their own personal newsroom. The technological revolutions of radio in the early 1920s and television in the 1950s transformed the news industry as dramatically as the computer and Internet are doing today. The electronic newsroom, modems and satellite phones have transformed the working life of the journalist. Technological change in television has affected work practices in the broadcast news profession. Video is now universal, and two-person or even one-person reporting teams using lightweight cameras can file by cable or satellite from just about anywhere. Satellites and computers are changing the way reporters collect and write their information. They are also changing dramatically the whole editing and transmission process with digital computer editing and storage. The tapeless newsroom is almost here. Convergence is the new buzzword, in which all forms of communication affect the way audiences receive their information. Journalists now communicate instantly all over the world through cyberspace. At their fingertips are the Internet, electronic bulletin boards, e-mail, the ability to access information from all kinds of public and private sources, electronic databases as sources of information, and the use of database programs, spreadsheets and statistical packages to interpret information. Official electronic databases have sprung up throughout the world's bureaucracies and large corporations. Databases as sources of information are reliable, easy to access, and often on tap 24 hours a day, 7 days a week. Newspapers in the UK are starting down this path, and some European media users are already proficient at it. More than seventy-five per cent of American newspapers now subscribe to news related databases. These services offer, among other things, full texts of major newspapers and hundreds of magazines and journals that can be searched on a particular topic to get background information, story angles and names of sources: information otherwise not available. Ninety per cent of papers with a circulation of 100 000 or more have at least one database for reporting.

In the US, computer analysis is being used to investigate everything from property taxes to drunken driving records and campaign funding. The Internet's bulletin board on computer-assisted reporting has spawned other bulletin boards dealing exclusively with access to state government records. Computer access to government data and the technique of using a computer program to analyse them is a dramatic breakthrough for journalists, not only because it allows reporters to dig deeper and faster than before and find patterns not possible by traditional means but also because the tool can be value-neutral. It can replace anecdotal tales or interpreted statistics with the record itself. By dealing directly with the unadorned numbers of a database, reporters can bypass the spin doctors and vested-interest parties who previously not only supplied the information but also selected and interpreted it. Reporters borrowing the tools of the social scientist and the statistician must become experts in analysing and interpreting the data. This requires new skills, and a new educative process at our universities. It also requires specialized knowledge of social science and statistics.

Future journalists will have to be comfortable using database software like Foxpro and the variants of dBase, and with spreadsheets like Quattro Pro and Excel. The Internet itself, that huge worldwide linking of computer networks that grew out of the need for research scientists to communicate with one another across continents, is responsible for a shift to computer-assisted journalism, simply because it provides journalists with an additional constantly available source. These databases, used properly, ensure that journalists know what questions to ask and which answers are meaningful. They make it possible for journalists and researchers to get background and data.

There is no question that journalists with database computer skills are increasingly in demand. Reporters using computers for data retrieval have won the American Pulitzer prize for 6 years in a row from 1989 to 1995. Computer-assisted reporting is one of the top needs for the future. The need will become even greater as the cost of equipment drops and databases become available through more on-line services.

Computer assisted reporting (CAR) includes the use of computers by reporters for gathering and processing information in every phase of news story development: obtaining story ideas from the computer databases, on-line services, networks and bulletin boards; collecting and analysing information from government and private databases; verifying information received from people via on-line sources and databases; and creating databases at the newspaper to analyse statistical information for stories and graphics. Already, broadcasters and reporters are walking around with their small laptops and satellite sky phones, available everywhere in the world and linked by their personal laptop to their offices, or direct into the printing or broadcasting process. Notebooks are museum pieces.

The use of computers by journalists is not new. In the 1970s, there were video display terminals (VDTs) and electronic pagination software as major technological changes occurred in the newspaper industry worldwide. In broadcasting, various forms of software allow broadcast journalists to input their stories in formats such as the Basys system. Basys, and other systems like it, are now in use throughout the world in many of the major broadcast newsrooms. The system keeps as much information as possible in the computer, and receives all the newsagencies' reports and incoming telex messages from reporters and correspondents around the world. Items can be assembled into a program, and the computer calculates running times. Any changes can easily be put into the program running time, and the computer will recalculate the timings. Split-screen editing allows the original story to appear beside the subbed version. The computer system also produces scripts formatted for TV, with text on the right and video and graphics on the left. Systems such as this also access other computer archives for rapid recall of cuttings electronically, and commercial databases, which keep the contents of newspapers and magazines on file. Portable computers, increasingly used by newspaper journalists the world over, allow reporters to type their stories on location and feed them into the newsroom computer by phone. They can also be attached to mobile phones. The adoption of VDT technology changed writing, editing and production processes. At the same time, electronic pagination systems transferred much of the production work to the journalists' desks. Journalism has moved from the pre-computer age into a digital age that is computer-reliant in all aspects of journalist resources and production. The knowledge and proficiencies needed by young journalists have not simply changed as the pace of change accelerates; they have expanded. Now, reporters must not only be good writers with a mastery of fundamental news gathering techniques and a thorough understanding of the law, but also be able to guide a desktop computer on a clear course through the information world.

The widespread computer capability that allows journalists access to thousands of on-line databases is only a few years old. As a result, the full potential of the technology may not yet be realized by individual journalists and their information sources. Newspaper librarians, who have traditionally served as reference points for reporters, are more likely to serve as gateways to the electronic databases. There may also be a new type of 'boffin' journalist in future cyberspace newsrooms whose job is to work on the computer and achieve journalistic results as well as update journalist databases.

There is another problem: the translation of computer data into good writing. Creativity can't be taught by computer. Creativity probably can't be taught at all. However, journalists need to be able to write in a style that is creative, readable, clear and non-clichéd. Interesting writing is dependent on skills, background education and deadline constraints. Computers can't (yet) teach these factors. In fact, computers can actually be a disadvantage in achieving good, clear, logical, fresh, creative journalistic writing. Students and practising journalists faced with a large amount of information on their computer screens from newsagencies or raw data tend to go for the easiest option, and simply cut and paste without any original consistent style. Just as the use of databases has proliferated, so has the use of computers by reporters and editors to analyse data. The importance of this is great; more and more reporters will be able to access public documents and information and analyse the data for themselves. No longer will they have to rely on the traditional sources or spokespeople. They won't need official attribution. The reporter can deal with the record itself, examining the information in a politically and economically neutral way. That will in turn redefine news in real terms, not in terms of others' agendas.

For most of the twentieth century, journalism has been dominated by a production process of the 1880s. Broadcasting began to have an impact only in the 1970s. The changes brought about first of all by radio news and then by television became irreversible in the 1980s, as style and news values changed as a result of broadcast techniques. These spilled over into the print media. The new forms of information collection and dissemination – the Internet and satellites – are having a new and even more profound effect. By the 1990s, journalism had become a mixture of tradition and a new digitized future. Even the basic tools of ink and paper were changing as there was increasing reliance on satellite links, satellite phones, portable computers and electronic imaging. Now these new forms require a new approach, a new converging professionalism that is local and global at the same time.

The public have a right to respect and believe their journalists. At present, that is not always the case. Journalists, as a profession, are almost at the bottom of the pile. If people have a low opinion of journalists, it's much easier for governments to curtail press freedom. Only if the press is trusted is press freedom safe. Journalists have therefore a very great responsibility. On their shoulders rests the future of the freedom of the press. Journalists have to find the best ways of gathering the facts, and the best ways of communicating those facts in language that is stylish, accurate and instantly understood. They must also lead the way in integrity, honesty and tenacity. They have to be ethical. Journalists of the future must take their responsibilities seriously; know about their profession; have competency in the technical and practical skills; and have a *thinking* approach based on credible, rigorous, academic research that is at all times based on reality. A major role for future journalists is to reverse the 'sleaze factor'. Just as Watergate in the United States and the Thalidomide breakthrough in the London pre-Murdoch *Sunday Times* brought for a few shining hours a new respect for journalism, the increased sensationalism of tabloid journalism in recent years has brought increasing disrespect for journalism in many quarters. This is particularly the case as tabloid journalism becomes more prevalent. However, this is not new; there was tabloid-like sensationalism in the news as far back as the sixteenth century. The human fascination with crime, sex and gossip wasn't invented by Murdoch. It seems to transcend time and space (Erlich, 1996). What these critics forget is this: freedom of the press is the freedom to make mistakes. So this tabloid journalism, with all its excess, is a proof of the existence of press freedom, and must be tolerated.

Technology and the beginning of regular commercially-licensed sound broadcasting in the 1920s caused a major media revolution. It ended the print monopoly and opened the doors to the more immediate and pervasive electronic media. Now technology is causing a new media revolution, and changing fundamentally the meaning of media. Media no longer simply means the traditional forms of newspapers, television, radio, books and magazines. In this age of digital technology it also includes cable television, telephone and computer companies. However, even that is changing. These separate media, as they develop, are converging. Newspapers now sell database information, books are repackaged on floppy disks and encyclopaedias on CD-ROM, and telephone and cable television companies are developing on-demand delivery systems for movies and other programmes from video storehouses. The old models no longer apply. A new information age is under way, the product of a communication revolution based on computers, satellites and digitization. All three new technologies are converging to produce a global communication web that will soon cover the whole world. Convergence is the buzzword of the on-line digital world, and is shorthand for bringing together telecommunications, computers and content, texts, images and audio. It is all now considered to be content. Technological evolution is piercing the barriers between industries, and convergence is the result. In a convergent world, all forms of content become digitized and can be delivered through a single communication mechanism to a single spot or a single consumer. The digital age will also bring with it the next phase of this convergence: interactivity. Readers, viewers and listeners will be able to interact with the media and its content. All three technologies are now so common that it can easily be forgotten how new they really are, and how they are changing the way journalists communicate.

The first communication satellite was launched just over 30 years ago. Digitization, the convergence of text, sound and picture into a simple binary language represented by zeros and ones, is a product of the 1980s. Most long-distance phone calls are now transmitted in this way. Computers can convert any combination of text, sound or pictures into packets of data that can be sent anywhere by satellite. Included in this development of convergent technology is a huge growth in the speed with which information is transmitted, the capacity of the systems to transmit and receive the information, and the amount of information available for transmission. As Williams and Pavlik (1994, p. 81) said in their book *The People's Right to Know*:

In the ways that mechanical printing presses and ink-on-paper publishing have defined the present era, it now appears likely that personal electronic presses and multimedia publishing will define the new.

The new communication technology, from live news via satellite to the smallest music-playing Walkman™, is affecting the culture of even the most isolated parts of the world. For journalists, it is the increase in global news flow caused by the rapid increase in technology and convergence of the media that is having a great effect on the way news is collected and reported. The big four western newsagencies, Associated Press (AP), United Press International (UPI), Reuters and Agence France-Press (AFP) are the heart of the world's news systems, pumping basic information from their headquarters to newsrooms throughout the world, whether English-speaking or not. Less well known, but for the broadcast journalist just as important, are the television news film organizations. Reuters Television, which was once

Visnews, is the largest. It feeds television pictures to 260 client broadcasters around the world. Worldwide Television News (WTN) was originally a British organization set up by Independent Television News as a rival to Visnews, which was partly owned by the BBC at the time. Now, WTN is owned by the American Broadcasting Corporation (ABC). These agencies provide about 80 per cent of their material from either the US or UK. Significantly, they are all based in London, where the decisions are made about what is covered and how, and to which countries stories are sent. The American commercial news networks, ABC, CBS and NBC, also market their news abroad, and Cable News Network (CNN) has become a world-wide news network of great importance. CNN is sold in 140 countries, and its signal is available to anyone with a satellite dish almost everywhere. The BBC's World Service Television began operating in 1991, and is a competitor to CNN. It is expanding rapidly, particularly in countries such as Asia and Africa, where the British accent and news formats are familiar. New global and regional networks are springing up all over the world. In Britain and parts of Europe, Rupert Murdoch's satellite Sky news channel broadcasts news from the American networks.

Satellites aren't the only globalizers. Newspapers are also becoming global through satellite distribution, allowing regional and local printing to occur. The *International Herald Tribune*, the *Wall Street Journal* and *USA Today*, as well as the British *Financial Times* and the *Guardian*, are now printed and distributed internationally. The phenomenon of globalization is not solely Western, although it might look that way. China prints its *People's Daily* and an English language newspaper, *China Daily*, around the world. An international edition of *Al Ahram*, the Egyptian daily, is printed in London and New York. The major Hong Kong Chinese newspapers, *Mingpao* and *Singtao*, are published in Britain, the United States and Australia, as well as elsewhere. These and other newspapers are now also available in whole or in various parts on the Internet.

Journalism is in a state of upheaval because of this convergence of technology. It would be good to be able to predict that, as part of this international upheaval, journalism would become even freer. This journalistic freedom and language is becoming an even more important topic because of the globalization of communication. However, government control of the media is not showing any signs of diminishing. Globalization puts honest, or dishonest, journalism in the full glare of international publicity. Government monopoly and control is becoming even more difficult. Consider the use of fax machines and computer bulletin boards in China, satellite dishes and short-wave radio everywhere. Today, journalists send their news through a complex web of telecommunications that includes satellites, optical fibre cables and copper wire.

This media globalization is also being affected by media convergence. Legislation is therefore a huge problem for those countries wanting to control the flow of information from outside and from within; legislation which will have to deal at the same time with the globalization and convergence issues. Convergence is occurring because of rapid technological development, and is a by-product of the proliferation of celestial hardware. Historically the Asia–Pacific region has had an underdeveloped broadcast base, in programming, technology, and certainly in news. Things are now changing rapidly. This region is now the fastest developing base for convergent and global technology in the world. The current expansion is about 10 per cent a year. The number of households with at least one TV set has increased by 70 per cent in the last 5 years, and the potential audience is about two billion. In 1991, two satellite operations provided transnational services in the Asia–Pacific region, Intelsat and Indonesia's Palapa. Today there are more than nine satellite systems covering the region, and more are coming. Soon there could be as many as 900 satellite transponders serving the region. Trans-border broadcasting is forcing governments to review their domestic broadcasting policies and embrace a degree of liberalization thought impossible a few years ago. At the same time, there is legitimate concern that local cultures may be destabilized by the flood of foreign signals that now rain down on the countries of the region. These social effects can have far-reaching consequences, as they link globalization with cultural imperialism. In fact, cultural imperialism is not something that only affects developing countries. It affected Europe in the late 1980s, when cross-border satellite television started and public broadcasting lost its monopoly, as the member nations of the European Community have to ensure freedom of satellite television reception and cannot restrict retransmissions on their territory of any EC broadcasts that meet certain minimum conditions.

Asia is currently arriving at the point where Europe found itself 10 years ago: trans-border globalization. Take Star TV, for example. When it began operating in 1991, it immediately opened a new horizon for information flow in the Asian region. Or, as Rupert Murdoch himself put it: *Advances in the technology of telecommunications have proved an unambiguous threat to totalitarian regimes everywhere. . . . Satellite broadcasting makes it possible for information-hungry residents of many closed societies to bypass state-controlled television channels.* Star now claims over 220 million regular viewers in 12 nations, and has stimulated a flood of other transnational satellite TV services, including many US cable channels, a range of new region-based commercial services and even channels from some Asia–Pacific public service broadcasters, including the Australian Broadcasting Corporation, NHK from Japan, and the Indian state broadcaster Doordarshan (Yu, 1995).

After Star, the region moved beyond the old model of broadcasting (a state-owned network complemented by one or two highly regulated commercial services) to a region where the world's most powerful media interests are all challenging one another for huge audience attention. As reception technology develops, the size of the dish and the cost of associated electronics drop dramatically. The reception footprint is getting bigger and regulatory distinctions are becoming blurred; for instance, between high-powered DBS and mid-powered satellites, which operate under different rules but are still capable of delivering a proper service to individual homes. Dishes are already available which are only about 60 cm in diameter for even mid-powered satellites. This diameter is decreasing even further, and it won't be long before someone in a car will be able to put a DBS aerial up and drive across the Australian Nullabor Plain with ABC radio all the way, unfading, unchanging, in perfect digital quality.

The international converging media structure is three-pronged: programming of various types for various media (symphonies to sitcoms to faxes); communication links (copper wire, fibre-optic cable, satellite and terrestrial broadcast); and end-user devices (cellular and wired telephones, television, desktop and mobile computers, intelligent communicators, CD players, fax machines, and who knows what else that hasn't yet been thought of, but is probably just around the corner!). They will all interact with programs and data at home, at work or in the field. Media convergence is all about encoding or reformatting new or existing information into several different products for transmission over a variety of telecommunication vehicles to satisfy different customer needs. Media's convergence can be seen in the growing number of specialized information services giving data of every sort and in different formats (on-line, CD-ROM, digital tape, fax etc.).

Newspapers are a bit slow, but they are also jumping onto the convergence bandwagon. Some newspapers are scared of this new convergent revolution, but then that's nothing new. History has shown that when new media developments occur, existing media elements not only remain but become stronger in their own right. When radio was invented, newspapers thought broadcast news spelt the end of the line for them. It didn't. People realized that newspapers were needed as well. When television came along, everyone thought radio was dead. It isn't. Similarly, as the media converges into something new, print and broadcasting will remain, possibly fulfilling a different need but still there as part of the ever-widening range of choices. The worst mistake journalists or academics can make is to believe that convergence will throw out all existing individual elements and replace them with a single new composite system. It won't. People will still do what they've always done since the time of Caxton; it's just that they'll do more of it, differently. Look at the Internet and the web to see how quickly newspapers are developing this new medium. Many newspapers now allow users to customize their own newspaper. It is possible to specify the areas to be read, and it puts them all into a personal, customized version. And it's free.

As the telephone, television and media systems converge, something else is happening: the Internet, which is not part of the broadcasting media, is converging with these more traditional media forms. In the latest Internet developments, it is now possible to receive from broadcasting organizations their news bulletins in text, audio and, in some cases, video as well. Convergence is occurring because the potential of broadcast and cable systems is only now being realized. Cable systems alone will deliver a world superhighway, not only able to carry about 200 channels but also to integrate telephony and a whole new range of broadband services.

Convergence, together with these rapidly developing technologies, is making it extremely difficult for governments to develop regulatory policy fast enough. Current press and broadcast laws are only valid within the borders of the state concerned, although this may change.

Any future regulation will have to safeguard the essential freedoms associated with free flow of information.

The regulatory framework already exists in many Asian countries to restrict foreign media imports. In South Korea, for example, only 20 per cent of television programming can be imported, while in Vietnam the figure is about 30 per cent. Singapore's own satellite broadcasting service (SCV) carries mostly domestically produced programming in Mandarin, English and Malay. In Malaysia, local production is likewise being encouraged by tax incentives and subsidies. In Taiwan, the picture looks rather different. Broadcasting law has been liberalized, and government authority to control media has ended. Legalization of home satellite dishes has opened the door to foreign programming, allowed rapid growth in the industry and rendered state monopoly of television irrelevant (Lee and Wang, 1995).

A good and practical defence against transnational television (and radio) is not heavy regulation, but local broadcast development to encourage better local quality production values, a rapid growth of local broadcasters to provide a more attractive local choice, and better technical infrastructure. In order to do this it is probably necessary to regulate lightly through some kind of Broadcast Authority (such as exists in Australia and Singapore), which would also introduce a local content clause of some kind together with a greater emphasis on self-regulation. International broadcasters cannot be local. All they can do is provide a transnational approach, which in fact also means a view of events and cultural entertainment as seen by the host broadcaster. Somehow the localness of news and information services must be preserved as an essential prerequisite of public service broadcasting. Exactly the same applies in this new international plethora of satellite and cable services. There is always the possibility for some kind of self-regulation, but control of transnational services throughout the world still remains in the hands of the huge multi-national corporations, and these of course often find their way back eventually to the United States. And in the United States the urge to go transnational is stronger than ever, not just within the major network players, but also within the lesser known and more 'propagandist' areas of broadcasting.

As the Internet converges with the broadcast media, regulation may have to deal with a number of additional problems. For instance, violations of intellectual property rights, government eavesdropping, computer break-ins, electronic libel and freedom of on-line speech continue to be important issues needing resolution. Unauthorized access to protected computers, distribution of illegal child pornography and unrestricted distribution of copyrighted software have tarnished the image of this cyberspace heaven, and will probably need rationalization through regulation of some kind or other.

Television programmes tend to reflect the values of the country of origin. Even if non-political in character, they are never value-free. They may be valued as good, bad or indifferent artistically, but the real point is that they do not foster local values but the values of some other culture. Nations with tender new communications systems can be dominated by the strong ones. For some small nations there may be other problems. Under international regulations, all nations have certain rights to pieces of the frequency spectrum. These are like property rights in outer space. What is given by regulation can be lost if the regulation collapses, and their positions in space can be taken by a stronger, more predatory country, culture or ideology. The prospect of every person with his or her own satellite dish, receiving television programmes from anywhere in celestial space, is making nations everywhere search for defensive alternatives. Faced with losing control over the television signals entering their countries, and thereby over the whole structure of their broadcast communications, they have three options. They can impose restrictive laws, set up external barriers in the market place by establishing technical standards incompatible with those of other countries and making it uneconomical to try to overcome them, or give financial incentives to the domestic market to allow it to compete and beat the international broadcasters – the local option.

The strategy for the future, which will protect the local society and its culture, is to multiply the choices from within. The history of the BBC shows how this can work. In the 1950s, popular commercial programming from Luxembourg, complete with hit tunes and breezy chatter, competed with the long-standing radio monopoly of the British Broadcasting Corporation with its staid and high-brow image. Later, it was followed by the pirate stations from ships offshore, such as Radio London, Radio Caroline and Radio Luxembourg. Rather than lose its appeal to younger British listeners altogether, the BBC had to revamp its image and its programming to produce the popular Radio One.

That, and the introduction of commercial radio into the UK, brought the audiences back to British rather than off-shore programming.

Some governments, of course, argue that rather than make their own programmes more palatable and easier to watch, it is economically and technically preferable to pass programming through a new kind of filter. In China, that filter is decreed to be a professionally controlled cable system. With cable, the principle of a national filter is retained even as the choices of programmes multiply. The market can be rigged to inhibit the spread of satellite reception directly by individuals. The trick is not actually to ban direct reception, but to discourage it by technological standards and an economic structure that makes cable cheaper for the consumer. Cable can then be regulated because it is always, somehow, a public franchise. Any form of regulation that aims at more viewing and listening options, by whatever technology, should first strengthen the local programme base. Regulation should be aimed at providing a service to the overall public, rather than allowing direct competition for the sake of making money. Some degree of government involvement may well be needed to provide ground rules and give some bridging financial help. In theory, the more international broadcasting the better. Greater viewer choice is theoretically a good thing, but only if there is real choice, enriching the viewer, rather than programmes manufactured for largest audiences at lowest cost, or everyone running a soap opera at the same time every day. The danger is that a multiplication of television options may homogenize the localness of the output, and eventually make it disappear.

In the broadest sense, the terms multimedia and convergence mean a marriage of technology and commerce, with advances in one propelling the other. As the technologies of communications, media and computers change into a host of devices and delivery mechanisms that can liberate information and potentially satisfy any demand for knowledge or entertainment, the old rules for separate technology-driven markets no longer apply. Industry convergence is a regulator's nightmare, because it changes control. Regulators and governments will have to revisit underlying policy objectives. Traditionally, telecommunications was defined as private information and broadcasting, and the press was defined as public information. That line has disappeared with the emergence of interactive, transactional, transnational information and entertainment services. Simply keeping old regulations in place in the face of the new convergence of media simply won't work. The drive of any regulation of the onrush of media convergence and the resulting broadcast policy that must eventuate should be to put national identities and cultures first; not to create, by deregulation or a do nothing and hope it all goes away model, a synthetic international culture with a harmonized American media model for everyone, everywhere. Each country should have government support for services that bolster the strong national cultures and identities of the region.

Today, the printed word changes to the visual image, the computer screen becomes a cinema theatre, the telephone changes into a combination of TV and computer. Multimedia is the future. The journalists of the future, and their audience, will probably be answering their television sets and watching their telephones.

FURTHER READING

Akwule, R. (1992). *Global Telecommunications*. Focal Press.

Breen, M. (ed.) (1998). *Journalism Theory and Practice*. MacLeay Press.

Crissell, A. (1998). *An Introductory History of British Broadcasting*. Routledge.

Denning, Lord (1980). *The Due Process of Law*. Butterworth.

Denning, Lord (1982). *What Next in the Law?*. Butterworth.

Franklin, B. (1997). *Newszak and News Media*. Arnold.

Granato, L. (ed.) (1998). *Newsgathering on the Net*. Macmillan.

Gross, L. S. (1996). *The International World of Electronic Media*. McGraw-Hill.

Hodgson, F. W. (1993). *Modern Newspaper Practice*. Focal Press.

Inglis, A. F. (1991). *Satellite Technology: An Introduction*. Focal Press.

Johnston, C. (1995). *Winning the Global TV News Game*. Focal Press.

Seymour-Ure, C. (1997). *The British Press and Broadcasting since 1945*. Blackwell.

Van Ginneken, J. (1998). *Understanding Global News*. Sage.

3 Working in a digital age newsroom

News is a cultural discipline. Choosing it an intellectual skill; collecting it a profession

Anthony Smith
The Shadow in the Cave, 1974

THE NEWSROOM

Newsrooms are complex places, places of creative conflict, of fast decision-making; where egotistical individuality and competition sit side by side with teamwork and high speed production values. They are also becoming increasingly complex technologically.

Newspaper newsroom organization

Newsrooms tend to be personal – and management of them tends to be personal. But they need to be managed, and reporters need to be able to work in them freely and creatively. Managers need to be able to control the creative process without squashing it. Management control comes from the top (the board) and is exercised through a number of executive or working directors, each responsible for separate departments in the newspaper. It is essential for there to be communication between these separate departments, not constant fighting over who gets the biggest share of the resources and favours. The senior executive of the newspaper has a two-fold job; letting the boardroom know what is happening in the newspaper departments, and offering specialist advice for formulating policy at departmental and board level. The difference between a news organization and other companies is the way in which control is exercised and the precise limits of that control, which is organized at an administrative but not at a content level.

The directors of the newspaper exercise control by initiating and imposing budgets and taking decisions, within the overall policy guidelines, on such things as:

- expenditure on capital equipment
- preparing trading statements
- statistics
- controlling departmental activities.

They also exercise control by making the main and senior appointments in their area and to the whole newspaper. These directors and the managing director are usually the final court of appeal in departmental disputes. Budgeting and financial forecasting by departmental directors are helped by daily checks and reports from line managers. Below the director level comes the senior management, which might include a general manager who is involved more with the mechanical production and administration and with the overall problems of the workforce, never with editorial matters. The production side of a newspaper has a complex series of middle management jobs:

- a production manager
- a deputy production manager
- usually several assistants
- a night production manager.

They are important because they control the main mechanical workforce, and it is here that problems of quality and work flow are most likely to arise, and where quality control is vital. This requires constant physical managerial presence.

Other managers and departments will probably include:

- advertising and circulation
- personnel
- publicity and promotions.

Below senior management comes middle management. Their job is to ensure that their departments are properly manned, and that work is completed to schedule and to the required quality. Managers and their deputies are responsible for normal appointments, budget control, duty rostering and work planning.

Below middle management, and reporting to it, are the line managers. Their job is mainly quality control, organizing the actual work on the job, and making sure there is someone competent on the job at all times. They are the first point of contact when job problems arise.

In a newspaper, the editor is the person who counts most, and it is the editor alone who can control content. Editors traditionally run the editorial function as a separate department of the newspaper, but their responsibility is usually the greatest of all department heads. The administration side of the newsroom is usually delegated to a deputy editor or a managing editor. Editors pride themselves on having great independence, and use it for the good of the newspaper and newsroom.

Although the editor is such an important person in the hierarchy of any news gathering organization, newspapers must have editorial delegation and good communication. The daily work is delegated to executives such as:

- the news editor
- the features editor
- the picture editor.

Editors usually exert overall control by means of an 'inner cabinet' of the deputy editor, night editor and the various assistant editors. Communication occurs at the daily news meeting, where everyone finds out what everyone else is doing.

Newspapers are a very high-cost industry. The biggest single cost is newsprint, at between 28 and 33 per cent of the operating costs. Newsprint costs have reduced as new methods of providing it have risen. All other news costs have increased constantly, the main increases being in salaries. Good newspapers keep a balance between advertising and editorial content. Managers and editors have to fight over this target, which ideally should be about 40 per cent advertising to 60 per cent editorial. This will give a reasonable profit margin.

Radio newsroom organization

Newsrooms in newspapers, radio and TV used be very similar, all based on an old-style print news organization. The structure and job titles were sometimes different; sometimes not. Radio newsrooms, however they are organized, contain:

- news gatherers (reporters)
- news processors (subeditors etc.)
- news managers (section editors etc.).

There is also sport, features and, of course, in most radio organizations there is, separately, current (public) affairs. Because radio is an immediate medium, the normal newspaper newsroom organization was found to be too slow. Nevertheless, checking and rechecking still remain vital, although in radio every reporter and producer is expected to be able to gather, collect and write the story and, in most cases, read the story on air. In radio, it is essential to have a good voice that can broadcast. Radio newsrooms are small because they are simple. They operate round-the-clock. They need a good reporter, with a good sense of news, a good voice, and a telephone. That's all. Compare it with TV, and it is obvious why radio is so immediate and will never be replaced by the Internet or any other form of transmission for news and information. Radio newsrooms can exist on the smallest number of staff, and with the smallest amount of equipment. That's why it is so exciting. That's why it is so difficult.

Behind any radio news output lies the combined efforts of dozens of news editors, sub-editors, reporters and experts. There is no guarantee that the titles will be uniform from organization to organization, but the people are there, sifting news, writing it, preparing it for broadcast, presenting it. As titles and jobs change between organizations, there is no point in being too specific about job titles. A news editor in one place may be called something entirely different in another place.

Of prime importance at the start of any shift is the reading-in period. This is the 15 minutes or so used by the news editor and the rest of the news-desk staff to read the copy and bulletins of the previous shift so as to know precisely what has been covered. The copy taster and news editor also glance through the spiked copy (rejected newsagency reports which, before computers, were actually put on a spike on the copy taster's and news editor's desk. Today, of course, it is all in the computer, but still the word spiked survives). This gives an idea of the sort of things that have been coming in from reporters and newsagencies.

It is important that newsagency material coming into the newsroom is rewritten in the local radio house style. Newsagencies tend to write in print style, and this needs to be changed so that it sounds right for radio.

As much as it offends personal pride, every news editor (and journalist for that matter) has his or her own ideas about good writing and good news sense. So don't be hurt when the next shift comes in and tears apart everything that's been done, rewriting furiously, throwing away stories and resurrecting others. That's journalistic life! It also illustrates the subjectivity of news values and style.

Radio technology

Although it only needs a telephone, the technology in radio is moving at a fast rate and is very complex. Radio is going digital in many ways:

- digital recording for reporters to use in the field
- digital editing for reporters to use in the newsroom or in the field
- computers to edit stories, and on which stories can be received
- satellite phones to contact base
- laptop computers for use anywhere.

The important thing in radio is to remember that a reporter does it all: collects, edits and presents. The reporter decides on what inserts to use, edits the inserts and puts them into the latest digital storage space, then presents the news and the inserts in a studio, using digital replay equipment. Radio also invented and uses extensively touch screen studio operations.

Therefore, although radio is simple, its reporters require an operational and technical ability that no other reporters need. In radio, reporters are totally in control. This means great satisfaction; it also means if something goes wrong, everyone knows whose fault it is!

Communication in the newsroom

Journalists can be great communicators with their readers, viewers or listeners. They can also be the worst communicators with one another in the newsroom.

An editor briefs or discusses a story with a reporter: that's communication. Communication is not just about sending messages (the e-mail problem versus actually talking). Many things can happen between the time a message is sent and the time it is received. Newsroom people colour the instructions by their perceptions of the editor, and if they think the editor is no good, they won't respect his or her ideas.

People each have their own style of communicating. Some are blunt, to the point, direct; others are vague and reporters have to work out what they're trying to say. Some are compulsive memo (e-mail) writers, some are talkers and others are meetings people. Each method has its particular place (memos for complicated 'on the record' matters, etc.). If speed is the main thing, a conversation is the best way to communicate. The interpersonal communication process is influenced by the way newsrooms operate and are organized. Decentralization in newsrooms means a high degree of participation between editors and staff members. Messages can go direct from editor to reporter, and not through the many different layers of hierarchy. This reduces the opportunity for message distortion – the more layers an oral message goes through, the more likely it is that the message will become garbled. Remember: communication is expectation. We perceive what we expect to perceive, we see largely what we expect to see, and we hear largely what we expect to hear.

Newsroom communication takes two forms:

1 Communication between individuals
2 Organizational communication that flows up or down through the various levels of authority (Giles, 1995).

Communication between individuals takes place in meetings, via memos and notice boards, and during conversations in the passageway, one-to-one discussions, phone calls, lunch or a drink after work. This is how individuals communicate within the newsroom structure. Managers spend about 80 per cent of their time in oral communication, more often listening than talking. Newsroom communication is quick and casual. Managers decide what to share and what to hold back. Negative or discouraging information might be held back; however, if the manager/editor does not keep staff informed, there will be gossip. Newsrooms are great places for gossip.

The manager/editor is a filter, stopping the flow of unnecessary information to the staff and giving them only what's necessary. Managers are gatekeepers, and so are secretaries. The manager/editor is a go-between, linking various parts of the newsroom or other departments with the newsroom. Sometimes, the editor is the spokesperson for the newsroom, their defender. Staff respect the editor's opinions and he or she sometimes has sources they don't have to make better informed decisions. Editors who hide between piles of paper are bad editors and bad managers. The editor is too busy, the editor isn't interested, the editor doesn't want to know new ideas or opinions, the editor doesn't care; these are all things to watch if you hide between piles of paper and are not approachable.

Employees want a continuous flow of knowledge about the company and its goals, but prefer it to come from their immediate superior. Good newspaper communication needs:

- a keen interest at all levels in what is happening in the newspaper profession
- an understanding of the art of communication – both speaking and listening – and a determination to practice the art.

This way you build a friendly, tightly knit, enthusiastic management team. Good newsroom communication makes employees think their ideas are valued and that the editors care about their feelings and attitudes.

Newsroom creativity

The best stories come from free newsroom discussion. Stifle the discussion, and you stifle the stories. People often feel least free to speak out in the workplace because of the fear of managerial retaliation. Most people feel it is moderately likely that their manager may make things more difficult for them if they speak out. The ability to speak one's mind is important in solving problems confronting contemporary managers.

Freedom of expression encourages creativity in journalists. Creativity is about freedom. By definition, creativity springs from within us all, not from outside. It needs freedom to flourish. Creativity does not flourish in an authoritative, hierarchical workplace, but in open, unstructured surroundings in which the individual can create order from chaos, without being directed closely how to do it. Creators have a high tolerance for complexity and ambiguity. Imposed order means little creativity. Freedom to explore issues and all the options for solutions to problems is a necessary condition for the creative individual.

It has been proved that co-operation and the free flow of ideas among the various functional areas of a newsroom enhance creativity. It is crucially important to provide both managers and employers with the freedom to think and question, and to encourage them to form independent judgements and take responsibility for changing the way newsrooms work. The big problem for newsroom creativity is managerial timidity, which provides an unforgivable sameness to the news output. There's no creativity, willingness to initiate or risk taking.

Newsroom managers have many problems. They are constantly forced to adapt to changing circumstances and to the accelerated pace of technological revolution. They are also faced with declining readership and circulation, newsroom changes, staff problems, ownership changes and increased competition. The solution is better managerial use of their own employees and their own creativity. Managers who allow freedom of expression from journalists also benefit themselves from their staff experiences and insights. Employees are a vast source of new information, and change in an organization requires the stimulus of new information. *We've always done it this way* is a major reason why creativity in newsrooms doesn't happen. Good newsroom management innovates (takes creative ideas and produces something new from them). If journalists don't feel they can express their own ideas, then the new ideas that are necessary for creativity won't occur. Managers can't think of everything. The result will be a sameness, blandness, a conformity to established practices and ways of acting and thinking. The result is a decrease in creativity and ideas for new stories and different angles.

Employees have a right of free speech in a newsroom. Free expression in the newsroom does not undermine authority; it simply allows democracy in the decision-making process. If the employees are involved in the decision-making process, they then feel it is their decision, and will be better motivated to carry it out. There is no harm or loss of face in asking people what they think. Good management should always allow staff, and themselves, to question existing customs, conventions, processes and institutions. Journalists are always asking, WHY? The same applies to newsroom management. Dissent is a vital newsroom tool. This is the doctrine of dissent: good newsroom management creates an open market place into which all viewpoints can be placed. By tolerating varied opinions, an organization is better able to reach common decisions that will meet the needs and aspirations of its members. This is all about individualism, and in some societies individualism is not considered a 'good' attitude. However, for creativity and journalism, individualism is better than collectivism.

Freedom of expression also means the manager is respecting individual staff members' views. As a matter of basic human respect, people owe it to one another to listen to others' views. They don't have to agree; they only have to listen. The philosopher Thomas Emerson says: *suppression of belief, opinion and expression is an affront to the dignity of man, a negation of man's essential nature.* The newsroom manager who recognizes the value of individual self-worth and self-esteem and the management role in enhancing these values is also one who is likely to foster a culture of freedom and free expression, and thereby provide organizational stability by accommodating and acknowledging whatever interests exist.

Newsroom politics

This is simply power in action. Political newsroom behaviour is increased by a scarcity of resources, by decisions or goals that are ambiguous, and by change. Editors can increase their power by building alliances. The best kind of management leadership in a newsroom occurs when the editor uses skills and human insight to enhance the development of individual abilities. The pace of management requires a leadership style that includes shifting gears as situations change, forming creative viewpoints, acting quickly on simple problems, setting up mechanisms for feedback, and using social skills, rewards and punishments to control the newsroom organization.

Newsrooms and power

Power is a great motivator. We need to control or have influence over others in the newsroom. Managers have a high need for power, and this is important since managers have to influence the behaviour of others. Some employees are motivated by a desire for personal power. They want to dominate. Employees with a highly developed sense of power often assume leadership roles in newsrooms. Clever editors use such people for their own ends. They put them on a planning committee, where they can be influential.

Newsroom journalists attach value to their work. In a newsroom, a strong work ethic produces a goal of accomplishing more, which then causes employees to work longer hours. So good newsroom managers develop ways of translating goals into performance.

Good editors clearly define the goal for their reporters (without making them feel they have no room to be creative). When an editor asks a reporter to do a specific story, they should then discuss together the specific goals required, the kind of questions and the kind of headline that might occur, so the reporter will have a clear understanding of the assignment. If the goal is made more difficult, the reporter will usually try harder to achieve it successfully. The editor says that a reporter can't become a specialist until he or she improves the way the story is organized. The reporter accepts this as a goal and starts to work towards it. The good editor will keep a watchful eye on this improvement, and reinforce the goal by occasionally asking how things are going. Journalists are independent workers and independent thinkers. This independence is part of the creative work approach. It is therefore important for a good editor to make reporters feel they are part of the decision-making process in setting goals for the future. Good editors don't say: *this is how you'll do it*. Their attitude is: *how do you think you can do it better, and how can I help?* The reporter owns the decision-making process, and therefore has more motivation to make it work.

Feedback is important. It keeps reporters on target, and encourages them to make greater effort. Reporters can improve their writing if the editor keeps offering suggestions and observations. Creative managers find it very easy to criticize; they find it much harder to be constructive, with some words of praise or encouragement before the criticism. Newsrooms are full of strong egos, so peer competition is part of the furniture, and competition makes performance better. Individuals have to accept the goals set for them. Never use the weapon of fear in trying to motivate creative workers like journalists;

it has the opposite effect. The focus of motivation should always be on achievement.

Newsroom stress

There's a lot of stress in newsrooms. Some is good; the stress of a big story and working for a long time covering it. That's great excitement. Other kinds of stress aren't so good.

Giles (1995) says stress in newsrooms is a major cause of:

- absenteeism
- high staff turnover
- low productivity
- unrest and unhappiness
- low morale
- family break-ups
- substance abuse
- health problems.

Good management can and should eliminate many of these problems. Stress results from undue demands on the body. If it is pleasant, the body adapts. If it is disagreeable, the body doesn't adapt, and the results can be unpleasant. Any effect on the body sets into motion a chain of events that includes a rise in blood pressure, heightened senses, increased energy and other physical reactions from adrenaline action. Signs of stress include the following:

- digestion stops
- blood is shunted to the brain
- muscles tense for action
- the heart pounds
- blood pressure increases
- skin becomes cool and clammy
- the adrenal glands give out a hormone, adrenaline, which increases heart action, supplies extra glucose to fuel the muscles and relaxes and enlarges the airways to allow more air to reach the base of the brain. We are now ready to deal with the stressful situation.

When stress occurs, we respond by flight or fight. We cope by fighting (confronting the editor over a decision we disagree with); fleeing (withdrawing and passively accepting the decision); or adapting (adjusting to the new situation and making the best of it pragmatically). The secret is to maintain a balance, and when this balance is disturbed for any length of time, we have physical or emotional or mental health problems. The first reaction to stress of any kind is alarm. We get frightened. After the initial shock, we either fight, flee or adapt. If the stress continues, we get tired of fighting the problem. Our defences wear away and we experience stress-related illnesses or symptoms. The basic element of stress is tension, which can occur due to:

- inner conflict (neurosis)
- external factors (problems in the newsroom, goals etc.)
- the need to be creative (we, working in creative areas, need a special environment to work as creative people). There can be great tension from performing, writing and reporting a long, complicated story or analysing a difficult newsroom management situation.

Stress can be good. It can be a crucial part of creativity, and can contribute to production and satisfaction. Stressful energy can be channelled into achievement. We can be stressed because of:

1 The environment: when it's good, we're OK; when it's bad, we're stressed. This can be at the office, or at home, or because of personal relationships.
2 Vulnerability: this determines the effect of stress on an editor or newsroom employee. It depends on the individual; the personality, physical and psychological makeup, and preparation for unexpected events.

Indicators to check your vulnerability to stress include:

1 Your response to life changes. Sickness (colds, rashes, stomach upsets) may follow major changes in life.
2 Your personality. There's a link between personality and heart attack, but stress can also be a major influence.

In general, people divide into two types: Type A and Type B:

1 Type A people:

- have a chronic sense of time urgency
- are constantly involved in deadline projects
- have a persistent desire for recognition and advancement

33

- have excessive competitive drive
- are only interested in work
- take on too many responsibilities – *only I can handle this*
- are fast speaking, fast living, fast playing.

2 Type B people:

- are serious but easygoing
- are able to enjoy leisure
- have no high drive feelings.

Most journalists and creative people are usually Type A. Newsroom stress is caused by excessive workload and unrealistic deadlines; by disparity between executives' goals and levels of achievement; by the political climate at work or within the company; and by lack of feedback on job performance. Editors find the worst sources of stress to be demands on their time, and overall responsibility for the production of the newspaper. Political pressures also build stress. The deadlines are always with them, and they are always responsible, even on days off. Editors are never completely free. Editors are their own worse critics (so are all creative people), and they are never satisfied with their own or others' output. This causes internal stress and tensions. There is also the stress of maintaining professional standards and accuracy and credibility of the newspaper. Executive stress is common in editors and newspaper managers. This is partly as a result of recognizing the creativity of journalists and reporters, and that creative people have a different approach to work and control. They have to be managed differently, and lightly. Reporters are independent, and therefore do not take kindly to being managed or told what to do; they see it as an infringement of their freedom to report. Change can produce stress; so can new technology and learning about it. Some people can handle stress well; others can't. Newsroom people like the stress of working to deadlines, the urgency of handling news and managing people who are stimulating and challenging. The editors and managers who have health problems are usually those who have problems with the boss. The key is to keep stress in balance. As stress increases, so do efficiency and performance, but only to a certain level. When stress goes beyond that level, performance and efficiency decrease.

There are a number of ways to keep stress levels in check. Keep calm. Tell yourself to keep calm and enjoy the situation. Encourage staff members to take exercise, to keep a balance in their lives, to relax, take scheduled days off and vacations. Regular exercise that involves at least 30 minutes sustained effort three times a week helps the body combat the physical effects of stress. Substance abuse is often a newsroom problem. It's also a general creative problem. Alcoholism is a major problem, although things are changing. Time management is essential to reduce stress. Analyse what needs to be done; set priorities; determine the best and most effective way to do a job; focus on the most important aspects of the job; eliminate time wasters. Make enough time to accomplish tasks, handle requests and do things requested by the editor.

NEWSROOM MANAGEMENT ROLES

Newsrooms, unlike most other organizations, depend on personalized, charismatic leadership for success. Newsroom employees tend to become committed to the editor/manager rather than to the organization. Newsroom management is often based on professional journalism codes, ethics and commitment to deadlines. Managers must realize that this is the way journalists work, and allow them to do so. Managers also need to remember that there are significant differences between workers in various media fields. For example, advertising grew out of the need to make money for the advertisers. Radio and TV grew out of the entertainment industry. Newspapers have grown over the centuries from institutional clashes, fighting political/government entities, business organizations, religious groups and military structures.

Newspapers and journalists are all about dissent, and that philosophy carries over into the management of a newsroom and of creative newsroom personnel. It needs a particularly strong leadership. Hence it is traditional that there is conflict between news departments and the rest of the organization. The traditional centralized hierarchical alignment of different departments should stop at the newsroom door. The newsroom is different, with a separate professional ethic from all other divisions of the news organization. In a highly organized hierarchy, there is a militaristic assumption that staff will obey once the decision is made. In journalism, it's different. If that assumption should extend to journalists, then the professional news as we know it will sooner or later become discredited, not only with its staff but with its audience.

News employees tend to be sceptical, untrusting and suspicious, even of colleagues within their own news organization. It's a historical condition, and is expected of them by other professionals in their own field. The editorial office of a newspaper is a subculture within the larger newspaper culture. A newspaper ultimately should be a reflection of some personality who is willing to become identified with and take a stand for what the product is and what the product is not. Newsrooms have leaders and they also have managers. The best is when they have both in the same person . . . the manager/leader.

Good editorial management means working through and with others to accomplish organizational goals, while the broader concept of leadership involves using influence to establish an atmosphere conducive to achievement. Some editors have instinctive management gifts. They can plan, organize staff, direct and control, but they lack true leadership. They are administrators, not managers. They can't influence their staff towards strong dedicated performance of quality. Editors/managers supervise, lead and manage.

The management ladder

At the top is the editor or executive editor. The editor reports to the publisher, board of directors and managing director.

Managers have three categories:

- Top
- Middle
- Supervisory (first level).

Top management

Top managers are most influential. They make policy. The editor or executive editor is the person who is most influential in this area of management, and is responsible for the overall news management, news policy and style. The editor also co-operates with other members of the top management team: the advertising director, circulation director, production director, personnel director and promotions director.

Middle management

Middle management is usually headed by the managing editor – the person who is the day-to-day boss of the news operation. Middle managers supervise the work of other managers.

First level managers

In newspapers there are various supervisory editors: political, finance, city, sports, chief artist, graphics editor, photo editor. Their main tasks include the supervision and direction of reporters, copy editors, photographers, artists etc.

All three levels of management carry out the basic management functions of:

- planning
- organizing
- staffing
- directing
- controlling.

All newsroom managers have authority: the right to make decisions. All newsroom staff members have some authority; photographers make decisions about which pictures to shoot, and reporters make decisions about how to write a story. Authority does not come with the title. Just because someone has the title, it does not mean they have authority and that people recognize it. It has to be earned. Newsroom authority is the recognition that members have the right to direct the work of the people on the staff who report to them.

They also have responsibility (the obligation to direct work of the staff) and accountability (which ties together authority and responsibility). In a newsroom, everyone answers to someone. That's accountability.

As a manager moves up the newsroom ladder, the job becomes more conceptual (ideas and planning) and less technical (hands on). The theory of supervision means that, for full accountability for the performance of staff, the manager must be able to control the following:

- hiring and firing
- work assignments
- performance assessments

- performance rewards
- assignment of resources
- decision making.

National papers have a night editor, who is in overall charge of the paper production once the main decisions about content have been taken (usually at the daily news conferences). Assistant editors occupy the area between the deputy and the various department heads, such as the news editor and the features editor. They usually have complete responsibility for specific areas of the newspaper, with titles such as assistant editor (news); assistant editor (features); assistant editor (special projects or future projects). Their job is not to run the administration, but to initiate new ideas with individual reporters and co-ordinate stories.

There are also other titles, such as city editor, political editor, foreign editor, sports editor, business editor, leisure and lifestyle editor.

Newspapers are built on autocracy and democracy. Newspapers work on delegation from the editor. Daily editorial planning and decisions about the contents and plan of the paper occur at a twice-daily news conference, usually held in the morning and afternoon. Subjects are discussed and decisions taken about the news and future features. The editor is solely responsible for the policy of the newspaper, and it is the editor's responsibility and duty to make policy announcements and to discuss the previous paper, mentioning good and bad points and how the next issue can be better. At the conference, the various editors present their story ideas (which the reporters have already given them) and the balance of the newspaper is discussed. An important function of the news conference is for everyone to find out what the others are doing. This provides the all-important interdepartmental communication, and communication between editors and reporters.

News managers manage and communicate by involving themselves in various roles. They are leaders, figureheads, liaison. They have to represent the organization internally and externally. They have an important informational role, communicating up and down the workforce and with other management levels. They also have a public relations role, sometimes making personal appearances, giving speeches or writing editorials for the paper. They have a vital decision-making role within the newsroom and the whole organization, and are the main initiators of change within the organization. Planning for change means decision making. Editors and newspaper executives decide how much time, money and equipment can be committed to a project, and there are many projects all going at the same time. There are also daily personnel decisions to be made, sometimes in consultation with others and sometimes alone.

Good editors spend a proportion of their time making the judgements of Solomon between competing and sometimes warring staff and higher management, deciding in areas of employee competition and conflict. In the news media business there's lots of staff rivalry, friction and infighting because of the creative, competitive nature of the business. The editor or deputy is called on to mediate in disputes of all kinds. They will have to decide who is at fault, and then make critical decisions that might involve disciplinary action or termination.

The modern editor is also a negotiator combining the technical and creative operations. These negotiating duties can be formal or informal: with trade unions, staff associations, with manufacturers over the cost of new equipment. Media managers must be skilled negotiators.

Successful news media managers have to have basic technical, human and conceptual skills. Technical skills are needed because the media is built on a foundation of technical operations. This knowledge of how technology operates allows proper managerial decisions about new equipment, operations and innovation. Managers in the media need interpersonal skills to lead and motivate the creative and often competitive and difficult individuals who make up the media workforce. In general, media managers have extrovert, gregarious, charismatic personalities. They also need conceptual skills: intellectual, analytical and judgemental abilities to make difficult decisions extremely quickly. Their tasks include: planning (this is vital since the industry is always in crisis and in the midst of some change or other); organizing (vital since media facilities are characterized by internal structuralization, departmentalization and the need to delegate); staffing (constant turnover through staff burnout, competition – there is usually great turnover in media industries); and controlling (using preset objectives to assess corporate and employee performance appraisals). Managers communicate internal successes and failures to staff, make changes and revise or restate corporate and departmental goals. They also need to have new ideas (developing new and better ways to conduct a news media business). This is a particularly important management function, since the industry is always at the front of new technologies and managers must decide which new products and services are worth buying or developing.

Managers lead their staff and company and serve as liaison between the organization and outside groups and institutions. They monitor external conditions and obtain, synthesize and present information to their staff. They keep them informed about what's happening. They allocate resources, adjudicate differences, supervise negotiations and make the hard choices facing management in a dynamic, constantly changing industry. And, of course, they are where the buck always stops.

Motivation in the newsroom

News managers need to know how to motivate themselves and their staff. Old-style media management was 'by the seat of the pants'; managers could do everything their staff could do and better – write stories, lay out ads, set type. However, increased competition, new technology and reader expectations have changed all that. Now, personality and motivation are as vital to management as the ability to perform set tasks.

Bad managers will try not to let go of the skills they have grown up with (and possibly the reason they have been promoted). They feel comfortable with them. They must learn the new skills of management. Managers must be motivated to **lead** others. Managers must **lead, direct, delegate, train**. What they do not do is the jobs their employees should be doing. Bad managers create low production, low morale and other serious problems. An efficient and effective management team matches jobs to people, and this in turns improves production and motivation.

The trick for a manager is to get staff to believe they can do the job. A manager has got to get staff to believe that their talent is equal to or above the demands of their current positions, and that specific career goals and hard work, confidence, freedom and creativity will lead them to their goals.

Efficient managers motivate their staff by getting them to believe in themselves; in their ability to do the job; and that if they work harder and better they will have a better performance and achieve their goals of more money and promotion. To understand the motivational factors driving staff, managers must first acknowledge that staff are individuals who are all different. They also have to achieve a happy workplace. Happy journalists are productive, creative journalists. For journalists, who are usually highly motivated and dedicated people, there is also a desire to do the best they can, without fear or favour. Satisfaction comes from doing the job itself.

A US research study found that the portrait of the journalist at work showed that public service, helping people, was the most important aspect of a newspaper journalist's life. Second was autonomy; third was freedom from supervision. Then came job security, followed by pay and fringe benefits. Most journalists are achievement-motivated. They need to excel or reach challenging goals, and demonstrate the following characteristics.

Journalists tend to be high achievers, and managers need to take this into account. Telling a high achiever to do something in a particular way may achieve the opposite, and they may decide not to do it. If a manager defines the tasks and the means of performing the tasks, and journalists feel restrained by tradition, they won't be satisfied. Co-operation is needed from copy editors, specialists in reporting, freelance writers, photographers and artists. The journalist high achievers tend to move quickly into senior management positions and become senior news executives. The challenge for the editorial manager is to fit the needs of the high achiever (feedback, for example, and independence) into the framework of an efficient news operation.

Journalists are very conservative, and usually don't like change. Editors are agents of change, and have to use good management and persuasion to make subordinates realize that change is good. They also have to help initiate change. The editor's approach to managing change can vary, depending on the individual management style and personality. Some editors use trust – in other words, they foster trust from their reporters and, as a result, the reporters allow change to occur. For change to succeed, managers and editors must be committed themselves to the change and show staff that it is a good thing. They also have to learn how to integrate new ideas and change into the existing system or environment. It is never a question of changing everything. Change should be introduced in small doses, otherwise staff see it as threatening. Some changes alter routines, others mean more work or different ways of working and changes of responsibility (more or less). The editor's main role in this situation of engineering change is to strengthen individual staff skills and knowledge and improve the way they work. Changes in individual behaviour are sometimes necessary. Because this is so personal, it can sometimes be very difficult. Change of this kind can involve emotions, attitudes, experiences, customs and traditions that have developed over many years.

To succeed in having change adopted willingly, staff in the newsroom must be aware of a problem that needs sorting out. They must be made to understand that what is happening is an integration of old knowledge, equipment or ways of working with the new. The best of old practices will be kept, and integrated with new ideas. Staff have to be coaxed to accept the change, and actually adopt it. There is no point in introducing change if no one works to the new system. Change must always be seen as positive not negative for each individual, rather than solely for the organization. There can only be change if the staff member realizes there is a need for it. Show staff how beneficial a new work practice can be for them, otherwise there will always be suspicion that change is only for the good of the company, and to the detriment of the staff. Managers have to change that way of thinking by assuring staff that the changes are for the benefit of everyone. The editor must then get staff members to accept that change is necessary, and also to accept responsibility for the change. Changes will work if staff think the change is a result of their own decision, or if it will satisfy a need and is for the best. Nothing is secret for very long in a newsroom, and news of an impending change won't remain confidential in a news organization; gossip about it will be everywhere. So don't withhold information. This creates anxiety and starts rumours. Providing only partial information is bad. Inform peer group leaders, and get them on side before the full announcement. Involve the informal leaders in the planning for change.

Technological change is becoming very important as new technology is being implemented all the time. Staff will want to know whether new technology means fewer jobs and redundancy for those who can't master the new equipment. There must be cultural change if there is to be an organizational change; for example, staff on an afternoon paper must be prepared to change to a morning newspaper; from a news to a business paper. Staff are sensitive to a new lifestyle that represents a change in both their personal and professional lives.

There also has to be personal change for people changing roles within the organization. Here, the emphasis is on assisting staff members to adapt to new roles within their own newspaper. Orientation programmes acquaint new management with their responsibilities as supervisors, as well as helping them examine the value of finding and working with a mentor, building a network for peer group support, and understanding the dynamics of the new newspaper organization.

REPORTERS

Newsrooms consist basically of editors and reporters. The roles and organization differ from newspaper to newspaper. Editors edit and manage; reporters research, find the news, write it and then give it to the editors for final approval before printing. Reporters do hard news (the 'beats' of crime, politics, etc.) and/or features ('Focus' etc.), which take longer and involve investigation and lots of deep background reading and knowledge.

Newspapers look to the reporters for their main news content. Staff reporters provide a specific flavour to a specific newspaper – they give the newspaper the best control over news coverage and news gathering and allow individual newspapers to get exclusives, that is, stories before any other newspaper.

The reporter's job

The following are the basic qualities that reporters should have, whatever medium they are working in:

- credibility
- curiosity
- confidence
- courage

- the skill to understand complex detail and present it simply and clearly
- interest in many different subjects, all at the same time sometimes
- impartiality (hang your opinions up with your coat when you enter the newsroom)
- a healthy scepticism (check and recheck: *If your mother says she loves you, check it out*)
- wide general knowledge
- sources and contacts.

One editor once described reporters as *people who get what they are sent to do* (when I was young, I was told: *don't come back without the story*). Other editors define reporters as people who can meet deadlines, write well, are able to gather information fast and accurately and generate story ideas. Reporters need to be self-critical, and not worry about being criticized. In fact, they must expect to be criticized; it's all part of the job. Reporters are people who know how to dig out information, whatever the source, and no matter how hidden or obscure. They should be skilled at:

- seeing and hearing
- taking notes
- finding information
- asking questions
- checking and verifying information
- analysing and interpreting information
- writing well.

Young reporters often feel uncertain and angry when they first join a newsroom. They are ignored; they aren't given any work to do. Everyone else is given stories, but they are not. They begin to feel they are not liked; or that others are more favoured. There is favouritism in every newsroom, but it's favouritism based only on how well you do the job, not on other things. Work hard, do a good job, find good stories, and you will sooner or later be rewarded with the best assignments. In the meantime, reporters have to earn the trust and confidence of the editors. They are not going to give the most difficult stories to the most inexperienced reporters. New reporters have constantly to prove that they are good enough to do the top stories in the top way. In the meantime, the new reporter will be expected to have the following skills and abilities.

Checklist of necessary reporter skills

- Works fast and enthusiastically on a story
- Aggressively follows-through on stories
- Gathers facts carefully and accurately
- Seeks a variety of sources in covering a story, and effectively develops sources of continuing stories
- Uses documents effectively
- Handles a variety of stories and writing approaches
- Writes clear, well-focused and well-organized stories
- Writes effective appropriate leads
- Writes with authority based on clear understanding of the topic or beat
- Produces stories that are fair and balanced
- Self-edits for crisper, cleaner copy before giving to editors
- Works well under pressure and meets deadlines
- Maintains a steady flow of ideas and stories.

Checklist of professional approaches to work

- Can use library and computer systems
- Understands the newsroom and can work effectively within it
- Is a good team player and can work with other reporters, photographers, artists and editors
- Takes direction, suggestions, criticism
- Lets people know about schedules, work in progress, problems, changes
- Is co-operative
- Reads newspapers and watches TV news every day
- Can work on more than one story at a time when necessary
- Comes to staff meetings and meets story deadlines on time
- Maintains good staff communications and relationships
- Helps less experienced reporters.

Checklist for doing the job

- Is willing to perform routine but necessary duties, such as the calls
- Consistently suggests ideas for stories, photographs and graphics
- Produces new stories and story ideas without being told

- Tries fresh ideas and approaches in writing and reporting
- Stays ahead of stories by anticipating or uncovering new developments.

Types of reporter

Reporters are either generalists or specialists. Most are general reporters, and can be assigned to cover any sort of story, either individually or as part of a larger reporting team (a disaster or deep investigative story normally requires a team effort). Reporters must be trained to assess news value in various situations so they can be relied on to identify it for their readers as they do their assignment. Such news might come from something completely new: disclosure about pollution on farms in the country, or rumours of an outbreak of disease in pig farms. It might mean expanding on a known news story (doing a follow up); for example, a chat to the wife of a newly appointed member of parliament or the family of a policeman who has just won an award. Reporters are in charge of the facts once they have been briefed by the news editor or specialist editor (political editor, finance editor, sports editor).

By the story deadline, the reporter must have checked the facts, talked to the people concerned, and written it in interesting, accurate, readable form for the editors finally to assess. It is essential for every reporter to check the facts of every story they do. Editors must be able to trust the accuracy of the reporters, and the reporters must take this as a primary responsibility to check and sometimes re-check the facts of the story, and to get the quotes absolutely right. This includes the spelling of names and places, the style and titles of people in the news, geographical information, the business and literary backgrounds of people, and information arising from references in previous news stories (context). Reporters should check the cuttings files in the newsroom or library before leaving to cover a story, and use reference books when writing the story. If they need a particular fact while in the field, they can always ring the office and ask them to check. Reporters doing the story must verify the important facts while they cover the story by making sure they take careful notes of interviews with the people concerned, or of the evidence in court cases.

Reporters must ask the people who are competent to give the right information. If there are two sides to be considered, both must be allowed to offer views. Good relations with important people and those such as the police, hospital staff and people in public life are most important. Every reporter needs to cultivate contacts. One of the basic jobs is to make the calls: to visit or telephone contacts in local life, such as the police, the hospitals, local councils and public services. This is where news is found firsthand. Other areas, such as airlines and transport companies, also help. Such contacts can provide valuable names for future reference, and should all go into a personal contact book.

As well as hard news, young reporters also get involved in other parts of the newspaper: writing entertainment pieces, shopping guides, helping out with sports coverage. This is how the reporter learns; by doing these easy things.

Survival tips for young reporters

1 Keep in touch with the editors when covering a story. Telephone or let them know any new developments or change of angle, or that copy might be late or different. It helps the editors to plan the pages.
2 Immediately discuss with the editors any point that might be a legal problem.
3 Keep a copy of the story and check it with the final version that is going into the paper. This is a valuable learning experience; it also enables reporters to let the editors know if there are any problems of accuracy from changes, or if there is any disagreement over the changes. This is particularly important if the story carries the reporter's byline. A byline on the story means that the story really is yours.

The broadcast reporter

Broadcast reporters are the 'foot-in-the-door' people, actually getting the news, the facts and the eye-witness accounts, either for writing up themselves or for others to write in the newsroom, or for a direct contribution to a news or current affairs programme. They are particularly important on local stations, because it is they who reflect the goings-on of the local community. Local radio and TV stations, in whatever country or locality, are first and foremost for the community they serve. And it is in the news service of a local station that this service to the community is mainly manifested. Newsrooms should, as much as staff and resources allow, be self-originating in their news output. It is the reporters who make this self-sufficiency possible. Their job is very similar to that of a detective. Their ear must always be near the ground for news and possible news.

Reporters should build up their own set of local contacts and make their own set of calls regularly. Some, like police, ambulance and fire stations, should be rung or visited at least twice a day, as close to major bulletin times as possible. Then there are calls which should be made at regular but more infrequent intervals; local council and civil service contacts, local business leaders and professional people. If, for example, there's some big construction job in the neighbourhood, it is always a good idea to keep regular contact with the various firms connected with the project: consulting engineers, architects, builders etc. It's amazing the snippets of information that can be picked up from such sources. Local travel agents and airline offices are also useful contacts. There's sometimes a VIP on a local visit, which is said to be private but might turn out to be very important. Reporters need to make it their business to know everything that's going on, newsworthy and seemingly unnewsworthy. Something apparently insignificant can often assume importance later.

Whatever other reporters a station has, there are two at least that are specialist jobs and vital to local news and information: crime and local government. Crime news needs a reporter who can become known and trusted by the local police. Sometimes this reporter might even be asked to help the police, and it is here that a local station can score, both locally and nationally. Local government, the other vital beat for a local station, should also have a specialist reporter who can become known and trusted by local councillors and members of local government committees. Local radio and TV is community broadcasting. The community needs to know everything about its government.

When a story breaks, the reporter sent to cover it should contact the station as soon as possible, either from a radio car or telephone, and provide a report that can be broadcast live into a programme and recorded for further use until it can be replaced by an updated version. These voice reports are the staple bread and butter of broadcast reporting.

The reporter's next job is to record on-the-spot interviews with eyewitnesses and officials, together with actual sounds of what is happening: gunfire, for instance, or the crash of a collapsing roof. 'Actuality', the jargon for this kind of material, always adds that extra bit of flavour and colour to the station's reporting. Sound is essential for radio; pictures for television.

Before returning to the station, the reporter should send material back from the scene, live for each news bulletin, and should also dictate copy stories for someone else to read in bulletins; record a wrap-up piece for broadcast later. This enables the newsroom to alternate and ring the changes so that, while the reporter is on the way back to the studio, the story still sounds fresh and live. Often, when the reporter is back at the station before the next bulletin, there will be time to prepare a longer package, wrapping up the whole event with inserts of interviews, sound effects and scripted reports. The producer of a local magazine programme may well also want a piece or longer interview for later. Reporters must always remember that there are a number of outlets for any one story, and should provide appropriate material for as many as possible.

Reporters and pictures

Reporters have a responsibility for getting the best pictures to go with their story. Sometimes they take the picture themselves; sometimes they go out with a photographer and tell them what to shoot; sometimes the photographer will go out separately after being told the general outline of the story and what kind of picture is wanted. Pictures are vital to any news story. Reporters should take a pride in getting the best possible picture to illustrate graphically what they are trying to tell the reader. Pictures give information such as how a person or a place in a news story looks, or what actually happened, more effectively than words in many cases, and they thus add and extend the text. They can of course also be news in their own right. Every story should have pictures. Normally, however good a picture is, it cannot stand alone without some relevant explanatory text. Reporters should get used to thinking of a suitable piece of text to go with the story (a caption) to create an emotive effect in the reader's mind.

THE EDITORS

Editors were once reporters, and they have individual editorial management styles. Some hate reporters. They rewrite everything they get their hands on; they focus attention always on the news writing and feature writing style. Other editors leave this to their staff. They are production people, and have probably been promoted from the 'back bench', the executives who control the putting together or production of the paper. They are mainly concerned with the look of the paper – with the pictures, headlines, etc. They see editing as a job of good presentation. They are fussy over the wording and fit of headlines; the amount of white space between items on a page; the way a picture is likely to print and the visual balance between the top of one page and another as the paper is opened. The editor (or chief editor) is the person physically responsible for what goes into the paper, how it is edited, how it is presented to the public, and for getting the paper out on time. If there is a serious problem – legal or otherwise – it is the editor who is responsible and who will go to gaol. The editor is always presumed to have seen everything and to have authorized everything (unless they are out of the country and uncontactable at the time). Newspapers always have a deputy editor. The deputy will do what the editor isn't doing; if the editor is a writing editor, the deputy will probably be responsible for the production style of the newspaper. In general, the deputy editors take the weight of administrative duties.

The editor as manager

The job develops the editorial mission of the newspaper, including the organization of the staff, the news policy, major operational practices and performance standards. The editor:

1 Plans the budget, changes in news or feature content
2 Organizes resources based on the budget plan
3 Selects and develops newsroom staff

4 Directs the work of the staff

5 Controls performance through feedback, appraisal, rewards.

The editor manages by forming a unified news staff out of a group of individual journalists and creating a newspaper out of a whole selection of different news stories, photographs and illustrations. The editor is the conductor of the newspaper. Editors, like conductors, maximize individual strengths and minimize weaknesses. The editor, like the conductor, has to balance interests: journalistic standards and economic goals. Satisfying one at the expense of the other can cause trouble. The editor has to balance the long-term goals of the newspaper with the short-term daily decisions on coverage and staffing.

Good editors are planners. This involves thinking, looking ahead, anticipating the future, setting goals, generating ideas for improving the newspaper and making appropriate decisions. Planning establishes the foundation for organizing, staffing, directing and controlling.

Editorial planning involves the 5 Ws:

1 What – the goal
2 When – timing
3 Where – the place where the plan will reach conclusion
4 Who – the people involved in performing the tasks
5 Why – the justification.

It also involves the how – the steps to take to achieve the goal, including cost.

There are two kinds of editorial and managerial planning: strategic and tactical. Strategic planning involves the whole news operation, and requires co-operation of individuals at all levels. It needs thought, analysis, imagination and judgement. Tactical planning involves the goal; the plan must be pursued in a systematic, well-organized manner that converts a plan into action. The tactical plan follows from the strategic plan (which means the editor gives the overall strategic plan to a lower level team to implement).

Many editors don't like planning. They prefer to react to situations (crisis management) rather than plan ahead. Their plans should:

- be realistic (not just wishful thinking)
- be specific (details should be clear about what is to happen, how, how much it will cost, how long to achieve)

- have a deadline (this is a control mechanism for the editor and gives everyone a target).

Others on the staff should also participate in the planning.

The relationship between planning and organizing is close. Organization has four activities:

1 Determining what work is to be done to achieve the objectives
2 Classifying the type of work and the groups of workers into manageable units
3 Delegating appropriate authority and assigning work to individuals
4 Designing a hierarchy of decision-making relationships.

Newsrooms are organized both functionally (with separate operations for reporting, editing, photography etc.) and as a production line (the product of a particular desk, such as sport, is different from the product of the politics desk, but they all come together to form the final news content of the paper). Authority flows from editor to each news area through the principle of unity of direction. There is one authority figure for each major task. This makes for a proper decision-making structure. This then allows an effective flow of information and decisions up and down the chain of command.

People are the most important part of a newsroom; journalists the greatest resource. This means the editorial manager has to be closely involved in the people activities, such as recruitment, selection, orientation (integrating a new employee into the staff), training and development, performance appraisals and employment decisions (which flow from appraisal: pay, transfers, promotions, termination).

Delegation

In all these matters, editorial managers have to delegate. Other members of management have to have the ability to make decisions. There are two types of delegation:

1 The regular task (the daily news meeting)
2 The special situation (the morning routine meeting with the managing director. If the editor is away this has to be delegated once-only to someone else).

However, when editorial managers delegate, the 'Buck still stops with them'.

Managers need time to manage, to think, to plan. The best manager can leave the office and not be called to sort out a crisis. An effective delegator has more time to think. Many don't delegate out of fear – the subordinate might do the job better.

Guidelines for delegating

- Specify the expectation
- Explain why you are delegating
- Give necessary authority
- Let others know about the delegation
- Display confidence in your subordinate
- Delegate important tasks; not just small ones
- Set high standards
- Invite participation
- Audit the work thoughtfully, but don't check up all the time – delegation means trust
- Give credit for results.

The editor monitors the other functions of management, and establishes standards to measure performance; measures performance against the standards and takes action to correct performance that falls short of the standards.

The news editor

All newspapers have a news editor. The news editor's main job is to organize the news gathering and news writing activity of the day by assessing information at hand, briefing reporters and local correspondents, planning the coverage of stories in the light of the day's news schedule, and checking the finished work before it is passed to the subeditors. Stories are mostly in the diary beforehand, so that it is easy to tell what is coming up and who is covering what. The news editor prepares a daily news schedule from the diary for the information of the editor and senior colleagues. This shows the stories that are being covered and by whom. The news editor must also authorize any money spent by reporters, such as transport costs.

On morning papers the newsroom works a long day, usually from about 1000 hrs until after the last edition has been printed at about 0300 hrs the next morning. The duties of the news editor and deputies and of the reporters are divided into shifts, with some on early shift, a few on the night shift, and the bulk of shifts overlapping to give maximum coverage for the main part of the day. Reporters should have a good idea well beforehand of likely stories that are coming up. Reporters can and should therefore have story ideas well in advance, and be assigned to cover them for later editions of the newspaper. Not all news works day-to-day. Some works months in advance. Reporters should learn to think well ahead, and so, of course, should editors.

Picture editing

This is important, and should be discussed by the relevant editor and the reporter whose story is involved. Imagination and experience is needed to look at a photograph and decide whether this will make the right picture that will print well and enhance the page. Factors about the choice will include the relevance to a story and the position of the figures in the picture in relation to the space available on the page. For instance, figures should not look away from the story that the photograph illustrates.

The photograph may have been chosen from a large number of the same person or incident. Once it has been chosen, and the final decision must always be the picture editor's, it is then actually edited by the reporter or artist involved. Decisions about photographs include how much to use – in other words, which parts to exclude, such as people or detail not essential to the story – so as to give the best picture. This is cropping.

The features editor

There is a features editor whose function is similar to that of the news editor although the news editor thinks today and the features editor thinks well ahead. Staff reporters might be moved to in-depth investigations that tie them down for weeks and involve much detailed assessment of a situation which might have a 'news peg,' but is a news feature rather than a report. Non-news editorial content is usually called features. There can be news features or timeless features.

Reporters need to be able to do all kinds of reporting. A reporter writing features needs to think differently from the news reporter. The reporter writing a feature assembles a number of facts (some current, some old) and some figures, quotations and descriptions and writes them into a pattern of argument in order to come to a conclusion. The conclusion can be the explanation that lies behind a news story, behind some government policy or current economic problem or simply behind someone's success.

The feature reporter must have facts and quotations from people, though it is not the newness that is important. The feature reporter is concerned with what people say or do, but for more selective purposes. The feature uses facts, quotes, background and new statistics to illustrate a point of view. The feature reporter is looking for argument and conclusion that is important, not the 'happening now news event'. Feature reporters explain, deduce, and have the material pinned specifically to their name. It is their point of view.

Features editing

The process of news and features editing follows the same basic procedures. Some newspaper features relate very closely to the news of the day and are in effect extensions of them on another page. Others are quite separate and topical. However, features have a different type of editing to news stories.

Features should not be rewritten very much at all. Features are ordered from a reporter who will be expected to become an expert very quickly in the subject, and they will often be to a specified length and pre-planned for a specific page. The editing of features should therefore be much gentler than for a news story. Features should be edited for accuracy, grammar and legal safety. Any rewriting should normally be checked with the reporter first (or the reporter asked to rewrite, expand etc.). Such rewriting must always be within the style of the original reporter. Some writers actually forbid any changes or cutting, but editors can and should still edit features to fit the page etc.

The sub-editors

All newspapers have sub-editors (sometimes in American newspapers simply called editors). They carry out the detailed editing, usually working under a chief sub-editor. Their job is to:

- check the story facts, names and places in a story
- check and put right grammatical errors and spelling mistakes
- cut the text if necessary to fit a given space on the page
- combine material from different sources to make a composite story of the required length
- reword all or part of the material, if need be, to attain the required balance, length and house style
- check the story is legally safe
- key in the appropriate command instructions so that the story is set in the right type size and measure, with correct header instructions indicating catch line, page, column and edition number
- revise the story as needed for editions in the light of later information or edition requirements
- provide any captions for pictures
- write a headline for the story in the required type to fit the space available
- make sure the procedures are carried out so that the story is ready on time for its page and edition. In other words, to make sure the reporters give in their stories to deadline.

In the newspaper world, it is the editor who is finally responsible for accuracy. Sub-editors should be always suspicious of everything, especially the spelling of names and places. They should check with the reporter. Sometimes the sub-editor might find in the checking that the reporter's story is old, or the particular angle is. There should then be discussion between them about how to fix the story and give it a new angle or drop it. Sub-editors should always be checking and talking to the reporters. There might be vital facts that the reporter has forgotten to put in the story, or there might be very good reason why the reporter has left out a certain fact. This requires constant communication.

Rewriting

Sub-editors might do some basic, but not too much, rewriting. They might also decide that a story is so poorly written, with the facts in the wrong sequence, or the wrong lead, that the reporter needs to rewrite. This is normal, and communication between the two will solve any problems. Some newspapers – particularly in the US – have rewrite subs, whose sole job is to do this.

Caption writing

The job of the caption is to explain the subject of a picture, and there are two sorts:

1 Self-contained stories built around the subject of the picture and often carrying a small headline
2 Simple line captions to explain the pictures used to illustrate the story.

Caption writing is a skilled job, and is usually given to a specialist sub-editor. Writing captions gives lots of scope for imagination because it often has to establish a justification for using a picture which in itself may look good but may not be newsworthy.

Getting on with the editors

This is an always problem. Reporters and editors don't get on very well professionally because reporters want the story to be used in their way and editors always want to change it for some reason or other. The secret of success is not to take things personally. Editors are busy people, who only have their mind on one thing: getting out the newspaper. Reporters should also have their minds on one thing only: getting the story, first, and accurately. Get used to it: that's life.

When the editor receives copy there are some basic questions and decisions to be made:

- Is information missing?
- Does the story need to be developed?
- Does it need more background?
- Are there enough/too many quotes?
- Are the quotes good enough to use?
- Does the lead need to be polished?
- Has the reporter chosen the right lead or should another angle be emphasized?

● Is it worth publishing at all?
● How long is it worth?

The editor will then discuss these points with the reporter and sometimes ask for changes, further information that is needed etc. After the changes are made, the story is re-submitted to the editor, who will look at it more closely this time. If the editor is happy (unusual), the reporter's job is finished; if the editor isn't happy (usual), the job continues with another rewrite. In some newspapers and news magazines there is another level through which each story goes: the fact checker. This is always a frustrating experience for all reporters. Reporters are egotists, who think they know what makes the story and how it should be written. They don't like editors, who are also egotists and think they know how the story should be done, telling them to make changes. This can be discouraging, but generally the story is improved (although not always).

FURTHER READING

Albarran, A. (1997). *Management of Electronic Media*. Wadsworth.

Breen, M. (ed.) (1998). *Journalism Theory and Practice*. MacLeay Press.

Crissell, A. (1998). *An Introductory History of British Broadcasting*. Routledge.

Crook, T. (1998). *International Radio Journalism*. Routledge.

Czech-Beckman, F. (1991). *Managing Electronic Media*. Focal Press.

Gage, L. (1999). *A Guide to Commercial Radio Journalism*. Focal Press.

Giles, R. (1995). *Newsroom Management*. Media Management Books.

Hodgson, F. W. (1993). *Modern Newspaper Practice*. Focal Press.

Holland, P. (1998). *The Television Handbook*. Routledge.

Keeble, R. (1998). *The Newspaper Handbook*. Routledge.

Keene, M. (1995). *Practical Photojournalism*. Focal Press.

Kobre, K. (1996). *Photojournalism*. Focal Press.

Mayer, M. (1993). *Making News*. Doubleday.

McNair, B. (1994). *News and Journalism in the UK*. Routledge.

McNair, B. (1998). *The Sociology of Journalism*. Arnold.

Smith, A. (1974). *The Shadow in the Cave*. Allen and Unwin.

Smith, A. (1980). *Goodbye Gutenberg: The Newspaper Revolution of the 1980s*. OUP.

4 The purpose and meaning of news

Events, dear boy, events

Harold Macmillan

quoted in Hayward, A. (1997). *Politics*. Macmillan. p. 387.

News values, news judgement, can only be exercised if and when news is collected. Potential news is everywhere. It is lying waiting to be reported. To collect this information, reporters need to know what is going on, and where.

Tunstall (1971) says that news flow (by which he means news collection) is similar to the flow of other sorts of communication, such as telephones or transportation. This is true, for example, of North America and Western Europe, where there is both particularly heavy news collection and telephone traffic. Of course today this is where the heaviest Internet and computer traffic also originates. Facts provide a major source of hard news: scores, dates, numbers killed, votes counted, sums of money spent or robbed, results. Another source of factual news comes from 'the newsmakers', the people in the news. They provide the quotes. So the fact provides story one; the quote about the fact provides story two.

Anthony Smith (1979) says it is no coincidence that journalists speak of 'news values'; the value of something is decided in a market place among buyers and sellers, some of whom are richer than others. He says:

The 'values' of the journalist are established under constant pressures within the society he serves; there is a tension between his existence as a free or creative craftsman and the nexus within which he works. He has a certain autonomy; the constraints, however, are the subject of permanent and unavoidable contest.

Over the years, but particularly since the 1950s, there have been a number of concepts of the press, journalism and the meaning of news. These various ideas have been developed to try to understand journalism and to locate it within various ideologies, both western and non-western. Existing models tend to mix prescriptive with descriptive concepts (another way of describing this is normative/reflective). The underlying idea of most theories of the press and of news reflects the political system of the society in which it is located. Theories also tend to be developed by academics rather than practitioner professionals in the area, so they are therefore critiques of the press and journalism rather than theories that can be translated into practical applications for journalists to improve their work practices. They are therefore studies *of* journalism and the media, rather than studies *in* journalism or the media.

The basic theory began in the United States with the publication of the work of Siebert, Peterson and Schramm, with their 1956 book, *Four Theories of the Press*. Their theory stated that the press always takes on the form and coloration of the social political structures within which it operates. The view that the different media systems are based on political differences was also part of Hatchen's five concepts of the press (Hatchen, 1981). Merrill (1995) added that the press not only reflects the ideology of the system in which it functions, but supports it and cannot exceed the system's limits. As a result, the main category for systematization has been the different societies' political perspective on government–press relations, and this has often resulted in confusion between 'the actual working principles of a given media system; the theoretical ideals of the system; and the dominant ideology of the society (capitalist, socialist, revolutionary, developmental or whatever)'. However, the relationship with political systems is not enough to discover a modern theory of practical journalism and the press. The categorization of media systems in the digital age must also take account of economic criteria. In fact, the underlying dimension of descriptive press concepts is economic. In contrast, the underlying dimension of prescriptive journalism concepts concerning news and the way they operate is philosophical. Ralph Lowenstein (1971) was one of the first to add an economic criterion to the various classifications of journalism and the press. To the standard of government–press relations he added the category of press sponsorship. Lowenstein's model distinguished between various levels of economic development and different types of media ownership. His argument for a constant transition of media philosophies depended on changes of ownership, media consumerism and technologies and also recognized the various stages of transition in the press in society. This transitional element was expanded by John Merrill. His 'development triangle' model emphasized the progression of normative concepts in a press system, flowing from one to the other. This model had the press moving from authoritarian to libertarian. Merrill further developed this theory in his 'political–press–circle' model, which presented a continuing evolution and transition of the press and the world societies. Robert Picard (1985) revised these various press concepts and believed that a major premise of Anglo-American libertarianism has been that press subservience to government ended with the transition from state market control to commercial market control. The end result was an increased freedom. But, he continues, 'economic developments in the press during the twentieth century have made it clear that the press can become subservient to market forces which also restrict freedom'.

Picard's revision included a democratic concept referring to western libertarian systems with a state ownership of broadcast media. Picard proposed three types of media systems: libertarian-tending, which may be either libertarian or socially responsible or democratic socialist; duo-directional, which may be developmental or revolutionary; and authoritarian-tending, which may be authoritarian or communist.

J. Herbert Altschull (1984) used the economies of the media as criteria for describing the world press systems. Economics was the basis for his world press model, and he expanded the idea of the economic dependence of the press in a capitalist society to a concept of universal economic restrictions on the press. He believed that press freedom is always restricted by the dependence of the media on capital. As Altschull believed, economics is a more inclusive and comprehensive criterion than that of social and political control, while still including the nature of government–press relations. He says that media in the communist societies were controlled through economic means as well as in the western media. In the former communist countries the press was politically restricted because it was economically dependent on the government, even when it was not the immediate publisher. Not only does the government in such countries allocate resources for the media, but it also takes their profits.

As early as 1969, Raymond Williams took a different classification view. In his model the classifications were authoritarian, paternal, commercial and democratic. All of these, he found, operated within the British press system. It is obvious in considering news and the process of the media that every model operates within various degrees of freedom and control. This is certainly the case in many non-western press models.

As well as these definitions and attempts at a coherent press theory to match various societies in which journalism operates throughout the world, there are also innumerable definitions of news, news values and news judgement. It is perhaps relevant to begin our travelling through the maze of journalism with the following BBC definition:

News is new and honestly and accurately reported information which is about current events of any kind anywhere in the world set against a background of other honestly and accurately reported information previously gathered as news; selected fairly but without artificial balancing and without political motive or editorial colouring by trained journalists; included in a bulletin because it is interesting, significant or relevant to the bulletin's audience in the eyes of the journalists; and presented fearlessly and objectively but with respect for the law and the BBC's own rules concerning taste and editorial standards. (The Task of Broadcasting News, 1975, p. 9)

The purpose of news then in a democracy is to satisfy the rights of people to know what is going on around them. And nothing more quickly destroys the credibility of a journalist than the deliberate manipulation of news to serve other ends than information. Journalists are often accused of depressing the nation by deliberately playing up the bad news. People and politicians say: *Why can't news give us good information rather than disasters all the time?*

The answer is simple. Encouraging the nation will only work if everyone does it, which they won't, and if people were more gullible than they are. One of the most depressing aspects of all the suggestions and manipulation theories is the low view that they take of the viewer's and reader's intelligence. Another is that it is not realized that the theories would have a more harmful effect on democracy than the ills they are intended to cure.

NEWS VALUES

Typical news coverage tends to overlook ordinary people. Gans (1980) points out that when the news media do treat the nation or society as a unit, they tend to treat it as a person. For example, the nation is said to be in mourning if a great statesman or Head of State dies. Gans also believes that the news value of conflict often leads to the media giving the impression of a society in conflict. Sometimes, of course, society is in conflict; sometimes it is merely an impression caused by taking a small snapshot of a particular event.

Traditional news values tend to focus on those with power in society as sources of news. Those who are at lower levels of social hierarchies often have to resort to disruption to be noticed by the news media. In deciding news, the sources are frequently chosen on the basis of availability. Eager sources eventually become regular ones, appearing in the news over and over again. Many journalists believe that news values are immediately recognized and intuitively sensed by the 'real' reporter. They don't believe that it is possible to train someone to have proper news values; to spot the 'news angle'. There is some truth in that. If there is no instinct there at all, it is unlikely the person will make a success of the journalist profession. What is news to one journalist or editor is not news to another. Thus news is subjective, yet true and fair for all that. The meaning of news not only involves the subjectivity of the reporters, editors and copy-tasters; it also involves in integral fashion such criteria as target readership, reader interests, likes and dislikes and cultural tradition. It also depends on what the editor considers important, since what is worth reporting to one editor may be of no interest to another. One simple definition of the practical aspect of news is: what the editor and reporters think is worth reporting to interest and inform the target audience.

News depends on other factors, such as geography and the unexpected. The closer an event is to the audience geographically, the more interesting and newsworthy it is. Proximity to the reader, or viewer, together with dramatic happenings, go together to form the newsworthy happening. The unexpected is also newsworthy; although the marriage of two people who have been engaged for 15 years is hardly unexpected, the newsworthy event could be that they waited so long. It is newsworthy because it has actually happened.

So news is first and foremost a happening event. Old happenings are history; something happening now is news. News can be either a surprise (unexpected) or expected. Unexpected news satisfies the audience love of the shock of surprise. Expected news satisfies curiosity about a happening of which they already either know or have some suspicion. Frequency can also destroy the element of surprise and therefore news value. However, what is frequent and well-known to a reporter or news editor may never have been heard of by the audience.

News is a *fact* that is *new* and *happening*. It is interesting to a large number of the target audience, and it has relevance or importance to a large readership.

News selection, though, is a group activity. No one person actually exercises inordinate control over the news, because all the way back along the news chain the checks and balances of those involved work very successfully. One of the most successful ways in which these checks and balances operate in relation to news selection and collection is by argument between reporters and news decision-makers within the newsroom. If a news editor leaves out something or restyles or rearranges something in a way the reporter does not like, then the reporter is usually forceful in the condemnation of the editorial action. The links in the news communication chain are complicated and rely on interactions between different members of the news staff. For example, one of the great checks of fairness in reporting is the daily creative argument that goes on constantly between editors and reporters. Out of this constant stream of argument comes a finished product that is in no sense the wishes of an individual. Each news event is very much a collective operation of the news or programme team, and that is perhaps the best safeguard of all against one-sidedness and dishonest reporting of events.

OBJECTIVITY AND IMPARTIALITY

The problem of impartiality has a language dimension. As language users, all journalists are constrained in ways most other speakers are not. The conventions of news writing, specifically the code of objectivity, prohibits journalists from expressing opinions or personal interpretations as part of their normal reporting. Unlike most speakers, objective journalists are expected to stick to the facts and report only material that is factual. However, the language is not simply objective. It can be understood on many levels, and the verbal description is closely linked with interpretation of the words used and their meaning. Journalists, in reporting on the world, therefore also inevitably interpret it (Bell, 1991).

Broadcast journalism is the equivalent of producing hourly newspapers as they are ready. Newspapers have time to check, to read proofs and to ponder before the finished, carefully designed product finally hits the streets. Broadcasters, on the other hand, because their news is live and so often broadcast as it happens, don't have these benefits. As their news is broadcast, it is instantly received by the listener or viewer. Broadcasters never know exactly how their programmes will turn out until they've been broadcast, and by then it's too late. Mistakes or injudicious words and phrases, which so often lead to charges of bias, are often by-products of news freedom and instantaneous reporting.

News is reported by people (who think subjectively) and is listened to by people (who listen subjectively). News is, therefore, subjectively selected and subjectively listened to. The training of the reporter or editor ensures that there is fairness, even-handedness and honesty in news collection and selection. Language and subjective selection means there can be no such idea as objectivity in news reporting, even though it is often held up as a goal. Objectivity is used by news organizations as a strategy for appealing to listeners and viewers. Objectivity is about maintaining a neutral perspective, detached from politician partisanship and ideology. Some scholars describe the notion of journalistic objectivity as 'strategic ritual'.

Objectivity emphasizes what is good and fair, and has as a goal news reporting that is fair and impartial. Such an idea of news reporting that is fair and impartial (rather than objective) is crucial in a society that views journalistic independence as a cornerstone of democracy. This perhaps helps explain the difference in attitudes to independence in reporting and notions of objectivity between Western and Eastern democracies. For example, the ideas of independent impartial reporting practised in North America, Europe, Britain and Australia are very different from ideas prevalent and underpinning journalism in other developed countries such as Singapore, Malaysia, Indonesia and, of course, China.

What is necessary for journalists is not objectivity or even a lack of bias, but rather a *perception* on the part of the viewer or listener of lack of bias.

In other words, impartiality. This even-handed approach to reporting can cause problems, particularly in market-driven media organizations, where advertising pays the bills. Non-public service broadcasting organizations and newspapers are economic institutions. Profit is maximized by maximizing audiences. Neutrality and an unbiased centrist approach targets the average listener and viewer. Mainstream commercial media have to maximize their audience by appealing to the largest number of viewers, listeners or readers. The danger is that news organizations can appeal to the largest number by taking the middle-of-the-road position in news coverage. For whatever reason, the end result is that objectivity and the deliberate detachment of a reporter's personal and political beliefs from the stories covered and reported has become a traditional part of Western democratic journalism. Although absolute objectivity is impossible, the quest for factual accuracy, balance and fairness remains the goal of every professional reporter, whether in broadcasting or print. This is a core professional value. Philosophically, impartiality is an empirical method of collecting and presenting evidence (facts) without bias, truthfully and accurately. Tuchman (1978) argues that objectivity is a defensive mechanism for journalists to be efficient in their work and, ultimately, successful. She believes that every story presents dangers to journalists and news institutions as a whole. Stories must be written in an efficient manner by taking an impartial position, presenting correct information, and citing credible sources. This in turn helps meet deadlines.

Impartiality, even-handedness and fairness are possible, attainable and necessary. The stress is on impartiality. In the past, the concept of impartiality tended to mean balance within programmes. Broadcasters thought that to be impartial meant to be internally balanced within a controversial programme; however, there is nothing worse than an analysis programme in which all opposing opinions cancel each other out. Sometimes one has to use that method but, in general, it makes for greater liveliness and impact if the balance can be achieved over a period, perhaps within a series of related programmes.

The concept of impartiality is simple; it is all about fairness to all sides. However, even the doctrine of fairness in journalism does not imply some kind of godlike neutrality or detachment from those basic moral and constitutional judgements and beliefs on which our society is founded. No journalism organization dealing as it does with attempts to get to the truth of an event can be impartial between, for example, truth and untruth.

Reporters are always searching for the truth of the event. So news is based necessarily on moral codes such as truth, justice, freedom, compassion, racial tolerance and the law. To that extent, news is never impartial. Impartiality, fairness and balance sometimes have to be set aside because of the demonstrated law of the land or professional ethics. Impartiality can be objective; news selection can only be subjective.

Newspapers have a long tradition of partiality in reporting a particular party or owner's line; broadcasting by tradition is very different. There are many who feel that (leaving aside the worst excesses of popular jingoism) the newspapers try to reflect accurately the mood of the people. Broadcasting is not able to do that; its role is to be the steadying influence, the medium that can really be trusted to tell as much of the truth as it can. People expect something altogether more perfect from their broadcasters. Newspapers are allowed considerable latitude, and are often considered as pure entertainment. Radio and television are allowed no quarter by either the politicians or the viewers. It is this which makes the work of the broadcast journalist so difficult.

There is no free media if, when the going gets tough, the principles of freedom are jeopardized. The purpose of news, at least in a democracy, is to satisfy the right of people to know what is going on around them. Nothing more quickly destroys the credibility of a news organization than a deliberate manipulation of news to serve other ends than information. It may seem harmless to instruct news editors to help cheer people up; it can be very dangerous indeed, for the only place where news bulletins offer a regular and exclusive diet of such news is in totalitarian countries where there is no news freedom. The difficulty with being a reporter at times of crisis is that people, particularly politicians, try to see journalism as a press agent for the government, and anyone who tries to step outside that view of journalism is immediately treated as a traitor.

Right from the initial stage in a news decision-making process the event is subject to individual interpretation, and that in itself means it is subject to a personal value judgement. News judgement is largely subjective, and the results are all too often in the mind of the beholder. Facts to one person are often lies to another. This is why it is so difficult to discuss and synthesize such concepts as news balance and impartiality; what is important is the preservation of accuracy. However, news values cannot be as subjective as all that, since there is often a great similarity between rival news bulletins. Professional judgement exercised by professionals seeks the same end: truth, fairness and honesty in reporting. The traditional editors of the past didn't want thought; they wanted their readers and viewers to be thrilled by the latest dramatic news. Sensationalism is still the word used to condemn any undue emphasis on the drama of events at the expense of understanding. Journalists are also sometimes accused of being interested only in conflict on the principle that this is more dramatic than a hundred disputes peacefully settled; that grief provides better pictures; that political life and the political story is boring unless everyone is attacking everyone else. They are also condemned for looking for the picture and the soundbite rather than the issues.

It is easy to recognize the definitive information in the statement that 'sixty people have been killed in an earthquake', with accompanying pictures. For the reporter, it is not easy to establish on the ground what the figure may be. The more complicated and imprecise the situation to be reported, the greater are the difficulties of the journalist in finding out the facts and reporting them with sufficient accuracy, qualifications and explanation to make the report understandable and properly limited in its scope. Thus, a political report about the movement of opinion on a given subject within a parliamentary party will be inevitably speculative, but may still be worth making because it is reasonably accurate and will enable the reader or the viewer to make a sensible judgement about the event. Journalists have to make up their minds about what has been investigated thoroughly enough to be reported, and with what degree of qualification. Having reported the facts, there is then the problem of explanation, and speculation. Information can include explanation, but should exclude the interpretation or selection of material so as to point the listener or reader towards a particular opinion about the facts reported. However, all selection implies some interpretation.

TYPES OF NEWS

News can be divided into two basic types: hard and soft. Hard news is news that happens itself, and cries out to be reported. Soft news is not so hard and factual, but is rather news of a more manufactured kind: news that is not so active or exciting, but is nonetheless significant for all that. Soft news can also often be described as current affairs news, less factual, more analytical or speculative. Of course this can also itself on occasion make hard news, but it tends to be interviews on topical questions, newsy pieces and general magazine items or feature news. It is often the discussion that follows the hard factual news. For example, after a rail crash (the hard factual news) there will inevitably be follow-on stories in various programmes throughout the day in radio and television on issues connected with the rail crash, such as the need for a new signalling system or signalmen training, or the inexperience of rescue crews etc. The same applies to additional material as sidebars or features in the following newspaper editions, either the same or following days. It is as important as hard news, because it so often gives understanding to the bald facts of the hard news presentation.

The first editor of Hearst's *San Francisco Examiner* had his own definition of news: *News is anything that makes a reader say "gee whiz"*. This definition is an interesting one, because it emphasizes the difference between the impact of a news event on the reporter and the event itself. It also shows the distinction between news gatherers, news makers and news processors. Reporters are news gatherers; those they interview are news makers; editors are processors. There must be this journalistic interaction for a news event to become news. News is only news when it is reported. Walter Gieber describes it this way:

News does not have an independent existence; news is a product of people who are members of a news-gathering (or news-originating) bureaucracy but until we understand better the social forces which bear on the reporting of news, we will never understand what news is (Gieber and Johnson, 1961).

HUMAN INTEREST

However news is defined, and the definition isn't that important, there is one certain thing: people are interested in people. News must have human interest. People want to hear about other people because this is really hearing about themselves. Human interest is eternal to all news gathering. Human interest should be present in some degree in all news: news should at least be angled towards people, rather than hard cold facts. All news, all facts, should be aimed at people, by translating the facts of a news event whenever possible into human terms. Golding and Elliot (1979) see human interest not so much as an ingredient of all news, but rather as a news event in its own right. This of course can be true to an extent, since there is a type of news story usually referred to as human interest. They define this kind of story as 'those quirky stories about children, animals, or simply the odd and bizarre'.

Reporters always have to be economical with their stories and their thinking. There is usually more than one angle. A factory closes, so there will be job losses. The factory's been in the town for a hundred years, and closure means redundancies. Other stories about this could include a look at what the redundancies mean individually and personally to whole families losing their jobs after years of work in the factory. There could be comments from redundant workers; from older residents who remember the factory's history and who possibly worked there when they were young; from local politicians on what it's going to mean for the town's school leavers about unemployment. The story angles multiply with a bit of creative journalistic thinking.

There is also a clear subdivision within the classification of what makes human interest in a news story. There is the lighter, quirkier, more humorous story, repeatedly used as a final item in a broadcast news bulletin, or on one of the lighter news pages. The Glasgow Media Group call this type of story the 'joke human interest story'. The entertainment value of such stories is higher than their news value. These are important to try to lighten the look of the page or the sound of the bulletin.

NEWS SELECTION

Upbringing, interest, education and general knowledge: they all have a part to play in what journalists will see as newsworthy; in other words, how they value news events. There are some obvious news judgements: political importance, good or bad social effects, novelty, incongruity, humour, pathos, public interest. The ability to judge which of these factors are attached to a factual event, and to what degree, is what journalists mean by news sense or news values.

David Manning White (1950) first suggested that journalists act as gatekeepers of messages, and Warren Breed (1960) studied the socialization of journalists. News, and the content of news bulletins, is a study in its own right, often done by professional media sociologists and seldom by journalists themselves. Gans (1980) and Gitlin (1985) suggested the following categories of news content:

1 The 'mirror' approach which predicts that the mass media are mere channels for conveying the exact picture of reality to the listeners, viewers and readers. Anthony Smith referred to news as 'the mirror of society'. News content reflects reality, mirrors reality and is a balancing act between those who give information to the media and those who select it.
2 The 'routines' approach, which holds that the way in which journalists do their jobs affects the nature of the news covered.
3 News collection that is 'journalist-centred'. In other words, factors intrinsic to journalists affect the way news is gathered and reported. This approach states that the role of journalists in society leads them to project a false view of reality, with consensus as the norm and deviation as a minority phenomenon.
4 News collection that is 'externally-affected'. In other words, journalists are affected in their collection of news by external factors such as economic forces, culture, and the audience. This 'market' approach locates influences on media content in the journalists' desire to give audiences either what they need or what they want. This is the 'mass manipulative' approach, which predicts that media content is influenced by the powerful members of society.

Then there is J. Herbert Altschull's basic assertion (1984) that the overriding determiner of media content is the ideology of those who finance it. Altschull outlines four basic relationships between the ideology of media financiers and news content. Different countries' mass media systems will show these types of relationships to varying degrees at different levels of the system. In the *official* pattern, the content of the newspaper, magazine, or broadcasting outlet is determined by rules, regulations and decrees. Some news media may be themselves state enterprises, some may be directed through government regulations, and some may be controlled under a network of licensing arrangements. No nation is free of official controls; the variations come in the degree of autonomy that is permitted. In the *commercial* pattern, the content reflects the views of advertisers and their commercial allies, who are usually found among the owners and publishers. Even under planned economies, some commercial influences can be detected, although these are exerted only indirectly. In the *interest* pattern, the content of the medium echoes the concerns of the financing enterprise; a political party perhaps, or a religious organization. In the *informal* pattern, media content mirrors the goals of relatives, friends or acquaintances, who supply money directly or who exercise their influence to ensure that the tunes of the piper are heard.

Whatever the theory, news must fulfil certain criteria. Newsworthiness is often used by journalists to denote the important criteria that they use to judge whether a story should be covered, and whether it is news. These indicators include: conflict or controversy; prominence; novelty; oddity; the unusual; sensationalism; importance; impact or consequences; interest; timeliness; and proximity. Johan Galtung and Mari Holmboe Ruge (1965) produced their own hypothesis of news selection judgements in their study. They isolated a series of prerequisites that must be met before an event is selected as 'news':

1 *Immediacy.* The meaning of an event must be immediately obvious. A murder, for example, is an obvious piece of immediate news. On the other hand, economic, social or cultural trends take very much longer to unfold and to be meaningful. They need to be angled to something, such as the release of a report or statistics (the latest unemployment figures for example).

2 *Size.* The bigger the event, the more dramatic the event, the more likely it is to be reported. However, the closer to the audience the event is, the smaller it can be. Two people killed in a train accident in India is not important to a British audience, and would probably not be reported. Two people killed in a London train accident would be a big story in the UK.

3 *Clarity.* The more unambiguous the meaning of an event, the more obviously newsworthy and reportable the event will be.

4 *Relationship to audience.* Events that happen in the same cultural background as that of the readership will be considered extremely meaningful. Events in far-off cultures will be considered newsworthy in direct relation to how they react on the reporter's or target audience culture. Countries and cities that have some cultural tie with the target audience will also be considered newsworthy. For example, Leicester in the UK, with a high Asian population is very interested in news from East Asia.

5 *Unexpectedness.* The more unexpected, unpredictable or rare an event is, the more newsworthy it will be seen to be. This will tend to be bad news, which means that reporters have a duty also to look for unexpected news that is perceived to be good.

6 *Running story.* If an event is covered once, for whatever reason (it might be a quiet news day with little happening, so a relatively minor event gets reported), it will continue to be covered until it is either forced out of the bulletin by a more important story or by more pressing minor news. The danger with running stories is that if a major story gets covered, it continues to be covered often long after its real intrinsic news value has ended. Habit tends to set in.

NEWS AND SOCIETY

News is also about society. Hartley (1982) says that, although news is supposed to be about new, unexpected things, it is quite easy to outline its main preoccupations. He groups them within six major topics:

1 Politics: can be defined as government (local and national) and the decision-making processes
2 The economy: the financial life of a country, its performance, figures and management; trade figures, imports, exports, employment, wages, inflation, prices, etc.
3 Foreign affairs: the relationship between governments; reports on war, military coups, earthquakes etc.
4 Domestic
5 Occasional: 'one-off', topical talking points
6 Sport: football in winter, cricket in summer; other local and foreign sport.

FURTHER READING

Crissell, A. (1994). *Understanding Radio*. Routledge.

Crook, T. (1998). *International Radio Journalism*. Routledge.

Gaines, W. (1994). *Investigative Reporting for Print and Broadcast*. Nelson-Hall.

Gage, L. (1999). *A Guide to Commercial Radio Journalism*. Focal Press.

Gans, H. (1980). *Deciding what's News*. Vintage.

Hartley, J. (1982). *Understanding News*. Methuen.

McQuail, D. (1992). *Media Performance*. Sage.

5 Ethics, law and free speech

If news instinct as born were turned loose in any newspaper office without the control of sound judgement bred by experience and training, the results would be much more pleasing to the lawyers than the editor

Joseph Pulitzer
North American Review, 1904

In an ideal world journalists would work out of motivation and idealism for the truth, and journalism ethics would be about aspirations and goals rather than minimum standards. Such green-light ethics are seen by some as encouraging journalists to view the decision-making process as a moral obligation to create an informed readership with honest, ethical news and information. The difficulty is that ethical journalists first need to be moral journalists; and to be moral journalists they must first believe in some kind of overriding morality of conduct and belief. And yet providing journalists with this ethical morality also means that their selection of news angles could be biased in a certain moral direction, which is precisely *not* what ethical journalism is about. Unless there is this underpinning of personal journalistic morality, there needs to be a written code of conduct that underpins the development of the journalist's moral decision-making process. These lists of commandments are useful when there are no other personal frames of reference for journalists forced to make instantaneous decisions about complex moral or professional problems, not least of which is when this morality is overridden by the ultimate need to expose the truth. Codes of conduct exist in journalist associations and trade unions throughout the world, as they do in most professional organizations. However, as the journalistic workforce increases in intellectual ability and moves on from the apprentice training approach to something much more intellectual, the aim should be to move as far as possible, and as quickly as possible, from the simplistic 'Thou shalt not' approach to reliance on moral reasoning and decision making and professional processes learnt during a proper journalism education. Such a development would draw on the idealism of many young journalists, most of whom are dedicated to serving society and its various truths. Ethics should not be a series of minimum standard actions; journalists of the digital age must see further than the principle that if it is not banned it must be acceptable. Journalism professional ethics should make all aware of the need for aspirations and principles rather than rules. By emphasizing the importance of personal integrity and collective concern for serving the public's right to know, the result will be a cohort of journalists who will actively seek the best possible journalism. A clear and unequivocal emphasis on duty, responsibility and the vital role played by the media in a democratic society should make it abundantly clear to all journalists what sort of behaviour is expected of them. Such an approach will overcome the big dilemma of when ethics makes a journalist self-censor. Self-censorship operates at various levels, and confronts journalists many times in their working lives. Motivations differ for what is sometimes also called self-discipline. Sometimes there are private issues that journalists – editors, columnists and reporters alike – must face when deciding whether or not to exercise a pragmatic self-control of events. Will work that is perceived to be unfavourable to or critical of the government, management or advertisers have severe personal repercussions? What might the degree of these repercussions be? There is greater pressure to conform: the possible loss of job, harassment by the government, or threats of prosecution for subversion or theft of so-called state secrets. In some countries these problems are already acute, with journalists aware of considerable government influence over the media, at times by subtle persuasion and coercion, at others by blunt threats and harassment.

There are other pressures on journalists: from family, peers and from the hierarchy of authority within their own organizations. The climate of self-censorship is often set not by governments but by senior editors, publishers and proprietors. Their position on these matters becomes the tacitly accepted benchmark by which to judge what stories will be covered, and how they are covered. In turn this leads to another problem: the posture that media owners and senior editors themselves take towards political and commercial pressures. Journalists and editors can often find themselves being wooed by authority and business by being offered favours and benefits, with some editors and reporters favoured by politicians because of their self-restraint. The importance of journalism ethics is to highlight the fact that good journalism is journalism which, in the appropriate circumstances, asks the hard questions and refuses to be diverted by attempts at media and political manipulation.

Basic ethical principles transcend media forms and issues. The end result is that every journalist will be able to make a responsible decision alone. The primary objective of every professional journalist is finding and reporting the truth. This demands more of journalists than simply not telling lies. Journalism ethics should always demand honesty, fairness and courage in gathering, reporting, and interpreting accurate information. As a report by the American Society of Professional Journalists points out, journalists should

conscientiously gather as much information as possible so they in turn can inform, engage, and educate the public in clear and compelling ways on significant issues. This goal includes giving voice to the voiceless and holding the powerful accountable.

Acting independently, the second goal of the ethical professional journalist, requires that all journalists try to 'vigorously guard the essential stewardship role that a free press plays in an open society', seeking as many opposing views as possible and placing the public interest above pressure from those in power or position. It also requires journalists to remain free of associations and activities that might compromise journalistic integrity or damage credibility.

Cynics say that ethics and journalism can't exist together. Of course some journalists don't always meet the expected standards of their profession; but that doesn't mean there can't be attempts to give the professional journalist an ethical way of working, which at the same time allows for maximum freedom of expression. The problem with journalism and ethics is that the ethical consideration can often be used as a self-censoring device. The basic beliefs of the professional journalist are not whether it is right to publish such-and-such a piece of information or picture. The basic philosophy should be concerned with truth, freedom of expression, objectivity, honesty of reporting, belief in fairness and the rule of privacy. Even democracy is an ethical, moral term, since it is concerned with the right or the best form of social and political organization. Ethics is inseparable from journalism, as long as journalists understand the meaning of ethics and morality in reporting practices. The problem with ethics as a governor of the profession is that it can be used for control. All governments try to censor and control journalism. Owners use journalism as a means of satisfying their own lust for power and wealth. Even consumers often try to censor the watchdogs of democracy and freedom by their complaints or pressures. The discussions about journalism ethics are centred on serious matters: inaccuracy, lies, distortions, bias, propaganda, favouritism, sensationalism, lapses of taste, vulgarity, sleaze, sexism, racism, homophobia, personal unjustified attacks, deception, betrayal of confidences and invasions of privacy. These are all matters of reprehensible unethical and unacceptable conduct. They all detract from the primary purpose of news gathering and news reporting: the truth.

It must always be remembered that freedom is about choice, and choice is about making a 'right' or a 'wrong' decision. In other words, the freedom of the press is precisely about the freedom to make a mistake. The best way to show the importance of ethics in the profession is to adhere to a set of guidelines or code of conduct. The difficulty is that the greatest good is always freedom of expression. Take honesty, for example. Everyone believes in honesty, of course, and everyone agrees that every journalist should be honest in investigating and reporting. But suppose some public corruption can be investigated only under cover, with the journalist pretending to be someone ready to make a corrupt deal? Or take privacy. A journalist might have the highest regard for the right to privacy, but claim that some information about a politician doesn't qualify for this protection. The question then arises: does the end (in this case the greater public good) justify the means? A code of conduct, with regulations and guidelines by the journalists themselves, is probably the solution. Many countries now have codes for journalists, formulated by the journalists themselves rather than by the countries (which would be the worst solution). Under repressive regimes, a code may be a way of giving moral support to journalists who have been victimized, and of encouraging solidarity within the profession. Under more liberal regimes, codes of conduct place greater emphasis on protecting members of the public rather than the journalists themselves.

Proprietors invariably seem to safeguard their position through the appointment of an editor who shares or accepts their opinions on general policy. The same applies in the relationships between newspapers and the state. The task of a good editor is to allow journalists to write without any conflict with their own principles or knowledge of the facts. This is editorial independence, and it sometimes means independence of complaint. There is never a good reason for not reporting a story simply because of reader or viewer complaint. However, as the battle for circulation increases and money gets tighter, pressures on editors increase to erode journalistic standards on matters of truth, accuracy and ethical acceptability. Commercial decisions on marketing, the publisher's responsibility, easily overlap with editorial requirements.

The ethics of the modern journalist can be summed up in one word: truth. Having said that, there are a number of important ethical considerations and ways of acting that should guide all journalists everywhere. Below are 10 rules of thumb that could apply to journalists everywhere. Journalists should:

1 Be honest, accurate, fair and disclose all essential facts. Never suppress facts or distort them. Always keep editorial control of stories and don't show them to interviewees before publication.
2 Be fair and honest in gathering information. Don't misrepresent and don't use concealed equipment or surveillance devices.
3 Be true and accurate with pictures and sound. Don't manipulate digitally or re-enact without saying so.
4 Always attribute fairly and accurately. Never make up quotes; only quote directly what is actually said. Otherwise paraphrase. Don't let interviewees change quotes afterwards.
5 Disclose any payment made for interviews, pictures or information.
6 Never allow personal beliefs or commitments to change the story.
7 Not use their position for personal gain.
8 Not abuse anyone's right of privacy. Relatives or friends of those in the public eye have a right of individual privacy.
9 Be sensitive and discreet at times of grief and trauma.
10 Always disclose they are a journalist and for whom they work, unless there is an overriding reason for the public good.

Professional journalist associations throughout the world have their own individual codes of conduct, as do publishing organizations and journalist unions. Check them on the Internet.

FREEDOM OF INFORMATION

In countries such as the USA, Sweden, Canada, Norway, Greece, Holland, Australia, New Zealand, Ireland and France, there is freedom of information legislation. In these countries there is a presumption that the public has a 'right to know', and government files are open for inspection (subject to a few clearly prescribed exceptions such as national security etc.). Freedom of information legislation has yet to be enacted in the United Kingdom, and probably won't be fully in force until about 2004. However, a first step was taken when the British government published a draft freedom of information bill in May 1999. The new bill won't come into force for several years, but will replace an existing code on access to government information that came into force in 1994. The new Freedom of Information Act will allow journalists a right of access to records held by public bodies and some private bodies carrying out public functions or contracts. The rights will be enforced by an information commissioner with the power to order disclosures. However, authorities wanting to withhold information when requested will only have to show that release would prejudice various interests, allowing Britain still to be a country where much information can be concealed. The new legal right to know as it presently stands will have 21 separate exemptions where the public will not be allowed to get information that could prejudice government unless the departments decide to release it under discretionary powers. The 21 exemptions include a series of catch-all areas covering the security services and information that could be prejudicial to national security or the economy. The police are covered by the bill, but any information that might prejudice prevention or detection of crime or the administration of justice is exempt. They will also have up to 40 days to provide information. This makes it the slowest information act anywhere in the world.

Even more worrying for journalists are the exemptions with no test of prejudice or harm at all. The police and law enforcement bodies will be allowed to withhold any information obtained during an investigation, even if there is no risk to an investigation or prosecution. Information obtained by safety agencies investigating accidents will be dealt with in the same manner, and journalists will not be able to access information about the cause of accidents. The same applies to information about government policy formulation, which will be secret. The Act differs markedly from those in some other countries, such as Australia, for example, which allows internal discussions to be disclosed if it is in the public interest. Information can be concealed if, in the reasonable opinion of a minister or other person, it would 'prejudice the effective conduct of public affairs'.

The new plans will also double the time public authorities have to reply to people seeking information under the present code – from the present 20 working days to 40 working days. The American Freedom of Information Act (FOIA), for example, has a time limit for disclosure of 20 days maximum. There are other differences between the British proposal and the American Act. In the US, it is used as a major tool for investigating government. It is a federal act, which requires federal agencies to provide certain information. State and local governments have adopted similar laws. The FOIA requires that a letter be written to the agency (which can be done by accessing the website) from the person wanting access. Disclosure laws are not discriminatory, so it doesn't matter who asks for the information. Indeed, British journalists regularly make use of the American Freedom of Information Act to find out information relevant to Britain and the British government. Whether the information is released is determined by its content and whether the law requires its release. A public agency has a certain amount of time to respond to a request (as in Britain). The Federal Act allows 10 days, during which time the agency must determine whether it will release the information. If it decides the request needs an interpretation of law, the agency can extend the deadline by another 10 days. Requests can be turned down, particularly if they are for:

- classified information that must be kept secret because of national defence or foreign policy
- information required of a corporation in an application for a public contract, but which involves trade secrets
- information that is considered to invade privacy of an individual (such as medical records, for example)
- information that would reveal details of an ongoing investigation, such as the names of suspects before an investigation is complete.

FREEDOM OF EXPRESSION AND THE LAW

Freedom of expression is a fundamental human right. It is guaranteed in many constitutions around the world, and it is safeguarded by journalists. For example, the US Constitution prohibits US Congress from making any law that would infringe freedom of speech or of the press.

The European Convention on Human Rights provides that:

1 Everyone has the right to freedom of expression, including freedom to hold opinions and to receive and impart information and ideas without interference by public authority and regardless of frontiers
2 The exercise of these freedoms, since it carries duties and responsibilities, may be subject to such conditions, restrictions and penalties as are prescribed by law and are necessary in a democratic society, in the interests of national security, territorial integrity or public safety, for the prevention of disorder or crime, for the protection of health and morals, for the protection of the reputation or rights of others, for preventing the disclosure of information received in confidence, or of maintaining the authority and impartiality of the judiciary.

Although freedom of expression is fundamental, the freedom of journalists to report is not as universal as it could or should be. Throughout the world the struggle continues to maintain a free press in print, radio and broadcasting. With freedom comes responsibility. Journalists must not abuse either, but must always uphold the freedom of the press and the law. However, freedom of the press and ability to report is not as wide as first thought. Press reporting is always constrained by the relevant laws of the land. In other words, journalists have freedom to report, but only up to a point! Their terms are the ethical considerations already discussed. In addition, there are fundamental legal constraints. These are basically defamation and contempt of court.

These are universal restraints, but each country has individual interpretations of them all; some more stringent than others. Journalists in each country have their own specific requirements, and these will be contained in relevant media law books. It is essential therefore for any journalist working in a country not their own to be aware of these individual laws and ethical constraints.

DEFAMATION

The law is there to protect the reputation of the individual (both moral and professional reputation) from unjustified attack. The law of defamation tries to strike a balance between the individual's right to have his or her reputation protected, and freedom of speech, which implies the freedom to expose wrongdoing and thus to damage reputations. Defamation applies to statements that affect a person's reputation and those that affect a person's business or calling.

The details may differ from country to country, but in general any statement that disparages a person in business, trade, office or profession is defamatory. For example, it is defamatory to write incorrectly that a particular solicitor has been suspended by the Law Society, that a particular doctor is a quack or that a particular bricklayer doesn't know how to lay bricks properly. It is not defamatory to report incorrectly that a doctor has ceased to practise or a tradesman has ceased to carry on business, even though such reports may result in substantial loss of earnings. There is no misconduct implied. That's the important consideration. The law provides certain defences for the person who makes a defamatory statement about another for an acceptable reason. If a statement seems likely to bring a threat of libel, take professional advice first. However, always remember: it is only advice. The journalist and editor may still decide to go ahead and publish, particularly if the disclosure is in the public interest. Lord Justice Lawton put it this way:

It is one of the professional tasks of newspapers to unmask the fraudulent and the scandalous. It is in the public interest to do it. It is a job which newspapers have done time and time again in their long history.

In the USA, there are four rules of thumb often used to help jurors decide in libel cases if someone's reputation has been damaged through hatred, ridicule or contempt:

1 Accusing a person of a crime
2 Damaging a person in their public office, profession or occupation
3 Accusing a person of serious immorality (such as a woman of being unchaste); there are still many states in the USA which allow a claim for libel in such a case
4 Accusing someone of having a loathsome disease.

Types of defamation

A statement will usually be held to be defamatory if, because of it, a person is:

- exposed to hatred, ridicule or contempt
- shunned or avoided
- lowered in the estimation of right-thinking members of society generally
- disparaged in his or her office, profession or trade.

To succeed, an action for defamation must prove that a statement:

- is defamatory
- has been reasonably understood to refer to a person
- has been published to a third person.

The standard in most countries is that of the 'reasonable person'. The test is whether, if the statement were published, reasonable people would be likely to understand it in a defamatory sense. There is, however, a very important part to the test to do with understanding. A statement may be defamatory not in the obvious use of the words, but by a more hidden meaning. Such a hidden meaning can be in the text, or in the way the text relates to some other story or picture not connected with the libellous statement. A statement about someone may seem all right on the surface, but be defamatory to those with special knowledge. Such a hidden meaning is referred to as innuendo. Three examples of innuendo follow:

1 Cassidy v. *Daily Mirror*.
 In 1929, the London *Mirror* published a photo of a Mr Cassidy and a young woman with a caption that they were about to marry. Unfortunately Mr Cassidy was already married; a costly mistake, because the wife sued on the basis of innuendo that her friends might think she was not already married to Cassidy.
2 Hsiang Hsi-kung v. *Singtao*.
 Hsiang Hsi-kung lived in the USA but held a high post in the Chinese Nationalist Government. He brought an action against Singtao, the Chinese newspaper in Hong Kong, alleging that certain articles were expressly defamatory of him and, further, that they contained various hidden defamatory meaning (that he was corrupt) that would be understood only by Chinese language readers. He won his case and had no need to prove the meaning of the innuendoes.

3 Mycroft v. Sleight.

Sleight was a trade unionist, and it was reported that he had tried to work during a strike. This is defamatory because it would be so regarded not just by his fellow trade unionists but by 'ordinary, just and reasonable people' generally.

Mistakes over marriages or marriage dates can be libellous (for example, to say a woman was married a month before her child was born).

To imply that someone is unfit to hold office can also be defamation by imputation. For example, to allege that a doctor's lack of care caused a patient's death could be defamatory.

Unprofessionalism can be a cause for defamation. For example, to write or allege that a journalist is not careful about the truth, or that a university lecturer didn't come to classes, could both be defamatory because of an implied allegation of unprofessionalism.

The words must refer to the plaintiff, who need not necessarily be named. For example, where a person was described as having 'one eye and a name like that of a certain sailor', the words were held to refer to the plaintiff. Another example: 'an Australian', if there is only one Australian in the group specifically referred to. A reference to a person by name only, with no other identifying particulars, may be taken to refer to a namesake and this namesake can sue. There is a classic case in English law: Artemus Jones. A journalist introduced a fictitious character into a descriptive account of a factual event in order to provide additional atmosphere. Unfortunately, the name he chose was that of a real person, a barrister. The real Artemus Jones sued on the basis that his friends associated him with the report. He won and was awarded substantial damages (for a full account, see Welsh and Greenwood (1999), *McNae's Essential Law for Journalists*, p. 182).

It's difficult to libel a group: 'all lawyers are thieves'. No particular lawyer could sue unless there was something to point to that particular individual. However, when a magazine referred to Old Bailey journalists as 'beer sodden hacks', individual journalists successfully sued for libel. It isn't enough not to name the person about whom the defamatory statement is being made, although it may be a defence when it comes to trial.

For the case of defamation to succeed, the plaintiff needs only to satisfy the jury that a reasonable person would take the word complained of to refer to them. Indeed, it's often worse not to identify. For example, a paper quoted a report criticizing the deputy manager of a particular department, without naming him. Unfortunately, between the time of publication of the report and the newspaper piece this person changed, so the new deputy manager sued and won.

There is no safety in generalizations. Indeed, the dangers can be increased. For example, 'I know of at least one member of the local council who has had kickbacks' is clearly defamatory of someone. Many reading it will know who is referred to, and if there are some members of the council who have legitimately had contracts from the council they can sue and will probably win.

Publication

The plaintiff must also prove the statement has been published. Every repetition of a libel is a fresh publication and creates a fresh cause of action. Anyone who repeats the libel is also responsible. So simply quoting someone as saying something libellous is no help; the fact that a reporter is simply repeating the libellous statement in a published form is still a defamatory statement as far as the newspaper is concerned.

Damages for libel can be large. Journalists have to be careful because it could be argued that the balance of law favours the plaintiff, and large awards have been made to those bringing successful actions – particularly in London, described as the libel capital of the world. An offer to make amends by publishing a full apology can be a defence against unintentional libel. Libellous reports about a democratically elected governmental body can be safe in many countries, including the UK. The House of Lords has held that 'it was of the highest public importance that a democratically elected governmental body should be open to uninhibited public criticism. The threat of a civil action for defamation must inevitably have an inhibiting effect on freedom of speech'. The importance of this judgement is that the Law Lords unanimously declared that 'free speech is a fundamental part of common law'. It also means that the press is now free to carry out as much investigative journalism as it wishes into the ways and workings of government without fear of harassment, restraint or penalties.

Investigative journalism

Investigative journalists all over the world have to be aware of the legal problems they may encounter. Not only must the facts be right, but they must be able to be proved in court. If, for example, a journalist is relying on witnesses to back up the case, only the witness can give an account of the incident. Everything else is hearsay and will normally not be admissible. If a journalist is working on an investigative story that could be challenged in court, witnesses should provide a signed statement at the time the story is written. Journalists should also tape all tricky telephone calls whenever possible, and keep them.

It is wise to have originals of documents rather than photocopies. Sometimes a court will allow copies if it can be satisfactorily explained that the original is no longer available but the copy is authentic. Courts also attach considerable weight (as they do with police officers) to a properly kept shorthand note accurately dated as evidence. The difficulty is that much of what is published in newspapers is taken on trust from other people, and it is often impossible to check everything because of deadlines. Because of the possibility that claimants can apply to the court for access to a journalist's notes and anything that might reveal a source, it is very important not to reveal any sources in the way notes are written or to make any personal remarks about contacts that might undermine the credibility of the source, just in case the court grants the claimant access to the source material (see also Chapter 15).

International variations of libel

Australia

Australia has a libel system very similar to that of England and Wales. The definitions are almost identical to those there, although there are some differences. These libel laws can also differ from state to state. There is, however, in Australia a constitutional protection for political discussion. Australian journalists (particularly broadcast journalists) have qualified privilege for discussion about the conduct, policies and fitness for office of political parties, public officers and public bodies. However, it must be remembered that there are significant differences between the states as to what is defamatory and how it is treated. The variations are considerable, but the broad proposition of the Australian defamation laws is the same in all states and territories: a person who publishes a statement of fact or comment that injures or could injure the reputation of someone else is guilty of libel, and would be liable to damages unless he or she can positively justify the publication in the particular circumstances of the case. This was part of the judgement given in the Australian High Court by Judge Deane in the benchmark case of Theophanus v. *The Herald* and *Weekly Times Ltd* in 1994 (see Pearson (1997) for further details).

The United States

The Americans have the First Amendment:

Congress shall make no law respecting an establishment of religion, or prohibiting the free exercise thereof; or abridging the freedom of speech or of the press; or the right of the people peaceably to assemble, and to petition the government for a redress of grievances.

The US Supreme Court, in the 1964 case *New York Times* v. Sullivan, held that: 'debate on public issues should be uninhibited, robust, and wide open and it may well include vehement, caustic and sometimes unpleasantly sharp attacks on government and public officials'. The court also declared that: 'neither factual error nor defamatory contempt suffices to remove the constitutional shield from criticism of official conduct'. This means that it has to be shown that the reporter or newspaper acted with actual malice, i.e. a statement of fact either known to be false or made with reckless disregard as to its probable falsity. Unlike in most other countries, it is not the 'reasonable person' test, but the subjective state of mind of the journalist. The libel plaintiff has to prove the statement is false rather than, as is more widely the case, the defendant proving the truth of the defamatory statement. However, American libel laws are quite liberal when compared with those operating in countries more closely associated with British law.

As in Australia, individual American states can have their own libel variations. While the Federal law makes it necessary for all libel plaintiffs to prove fault, individual states have their own precedents, statutes and case law. If, for example, a report attacks a public figure or official, there will be no First Amendment protection if the journalist had actual knowledge that the report was untrue, or had a reckless disregard for the truth of the statement. If a report libels a private person in a public interest story, it is safest for journalists also to publish a response and explanation from the private person named or identified. This at least could avoid a charge of negligence in publishing a false statement.

Defences against libel

The defences against libel for journalists in most countries are similar. They include truth, fair and accurate reports of court, legislative hearings, and public records.

The best defence of all to potential libel is a finely-tuned and loud internal warning bell. Journalists can't be legal specialists, and certainly the small excursion into the journalistic legal minefield that is contained in this chapter can't do anything except make suggestions about when that warning bell should ring! Keep a copy of a good up-to-date media law book by you. In the UK, for example, the most famous and widely used is *McNae's Essential Law for Journalists*, by Welsh and Greenwood (1999). Equally good books can be found in most countries, that relate specifically to the local media law.

Journalists should check with the editor and with the lawyers if necessary. In a quick-moving broadcast situation, for example, it is often wise to leave something out if there is any doubt until the possible libel is checked. When in doubt – leave it out.

Having taken as much care as possible, there will still be situations that become libellous for good journalistic reasons. Don't despair. There are defences to libel, and these are the main general ones:

1 Justification. Truth is always a complete justification. In the US, as already mentioned, it is up to the plaintiff to show the words are false; in most other countries it is up to the defendant – the

journalist who has uttered the libel – to show the words are true. This defence applies when the words complained of are a statement of fact; if the words are merely an expression of opinion they may have to be defended by some other defence, such as fair comment, since comment is obviously not fact.

2 Fair comment. If journalists accurately report what some public person has done and then say: *such conduct is disgraceful*, that is merely an expression of opinion, a comment on the person's conduct.

3 Privilege. The law recognizes that there are occasions when the public interest demands that there be complete freedom of speech without any risk of proceedings for defamation. It may be safe under absolute privilege or under qualified privilege. Absolute privilege is a complete defence, and it does not matter whether the words used are true or false. They are protected by absolute privilege. This refers to words used during the proceedings of parliament. However, the defamatory words, privileged when used in parliament, are privileged only in a qualified way when used in print. Court reporting is also privileged if the report is fair, accurate and contemporaneously reported.

4 Accord and satisfaction. This applies when you publish a correction and apology that has been accepted by the plaintiff in settlement of the complaint.

Summary

Libel is about protecting a person's reputation. If someone believes a story has damaged him or her by a false statement, then legal action may be taken. Libel actions can be very expensive, both in damages and costs. If the damaging statement published is true, the newspaper generally has a complete defence. However, the newspaper has to prove the truth of the statement; the libelled person does not have to prove it is untrue. The newspaper also has to prove that any hidden meaning (innuendo) that the plaintiff says the words contain is also true. Reporters writing a story that contains damaging material must therefore make sure they get it right. In particular, reporters must make sure they get all sides to the story so that there is a better chance of presenting a story that is balanced. This will help mitigate, although not necessarily eliminate, any liability.

If reporters can't check the accuracy of the story, they should tell the news editor immediately. There are several other possible defences against libel: fair comment when the statement is opinion not fact and is honestly held by the writer, and if it is based on true facts or privileged information. The law in England and Wales, and in many other countries, recognizes that damaging statements will be made on some occasions when it is in the public interest that these be reported. Reports of these occasions enjoy a protection called privilege. Matter protected in this way includes reports of court hearings, council meetings and public meetings, and official statements made by police and local authorities. (They have to be official statements, not simply a police officer giving an opinion that someone has committed the crime.) Again, the report must be fair, accurate and balanced, giving due weight to both sides of the story; for example, if defamatory statements are reported, denials should also be reported.

Reporters must always take care not to say that unproved allegations are facts. All such remarks must be attributed to the person who made them, preferably by using direct quotes and qualifying them as 'allegations'.

It is not a defence to say that a damaging report does not name the person about whom the statement is made. The person can successfully sue if he or she can convince a jury that acquaintances believe the story refers to that person. It is not a defence to say that the reporter was merely repeating a damaging statement made by someone else. The law says everyone who repeats a libel is responsible for it. It is important for journalists to make sure they have as much evidence as possible; eyewitnesses and admissible documentation (originals), both written and taped. Notes and documentation should be kept so that reasonable care can be shown if the need arises.

COURT REPORTING

There's no big mystery about court reporting. All the rules of normal reporting apply, and a court story is a story just like anything else. However, there are additional responsibilities that every reporter working on a court story needs to be aware of.

The job of reporters and journalists in reporting court cases is to make sure that justice is not only done but seen to be done. That's their role, as well as reporting news and what is in the public interest for readers to know. It is vital that newspapers publish nothing that might prejudice a fair trial. Journalists have a right to observe and report what happens in court, but it is a right that has certain restrictions attached to it. Court reporting must be a fair and accurate report of legal proceedings in open court, published contemporaneously and in good faith. Points to remember include:

1 An article is considered to be published contemporaneously if it is published as soon as practicable after the events in court. It is then treated by law as having been published or broadcast contemporaneously with the committal proceedings (next day is acceptable for a newspaper).
2 Always check the indictment or the charge sheet.
3 Remember, report only what has happened in open court. Extra background details from court clerks or lawyers not in open court may destroy the privilege under which journalists report.
4 A statement from someone concerned with a trial made outside the court must be clearly stated to be happening outside court.

Pre-trial stories

Reporters can find themselves in contempt of court once an arrest has been made, or once police have started questioning the suspect. Although the crime can still be reported, the story must be carefully worded lest it suggest that those in police hands are the same people responsible for the crime. Thus a robbery can be reported, and a later report can say that *a* man was arrested, but not *the* man (i.e. the person who did it) was arrested. It would also be contempt to describe the appearance of three men who raided a bank as being tall, or dark-haired or bearded, lest those arrested answered to that description. To publish that would be to deny the defence the possibility of contesting identity. Once a person has been charged with an offence, specific details about the case cannot be mentioned (such as the person's name and what happened) until the person appears in court.

Reporting restrictions

There are some specific reporting restrictions, which differ in different countries, e.g. reporting reasons for bail applications or objections to bail. In many countries, if a story reported reasons which, if revealed, would prejudice a fair trial, this could be contempt. Likewise, if a case is heard in a lower court first before being sent for trial to a superior court, there are likely to be restrictions on what can be published about the initial court hearing in case there is any prejudice of the later trial. Again, check in a local media law book for precise details. There are some areas of the law where there will almost certainly be specific reporting restrictions. Areas such as reporting juvenile court cases and sexual offences such as rape all need to be looked at closely before attempting to write even the simplest story. In most countries there will be strict laws about not identifying juveniles (and each country will have its own definition of the age under which someone is a juvenile) and not identifying the victim of a sexual offence. Often, because of the strictness of the non-identification rule, no identification will be allowed of anyone connected with the case because of the possibility of accidental identification of a victim.

There may be occasions when the court allows identification of the victim, but these are strictly governed and are always for very specific purposes, such as if the judge is asked and agrees in order to induce possible witnesses to come forward. Reporters must listen to the proceedings with great care to make sure they know what they can and can't report.

As well as the specific restrictions mentioned above, there can often be others. Sometimes reporters are allowed into court, but are not free to report what happens. It is vital always to be aware of whether the court proceedings are open or closed, so that it is apparent what can and can't be reported. Unless reporting restrictions are lifted, and this must be quite specifically by order of the presiding judge, journalists can·only report very specific facts. These usually refer only to such things as:

- the names, addresses, ages and occupations of parties involved and the witnesses (unless there is some reason, e.g. prohibition by the judge or the nature of the offence, for not publishing the names or anything that might identify them)

- the charge
- the names of counsel and solicitors
- the decision
- the charges on which each defendant is committed
- the date and place to which the hearing was adjourned
- arrangements for bail.

Lifting the restrictions

The press can usually apply for the lifting of restrictions on the grounds that the ban imposes a substantial and unreasonable restriction on reporting. Sometimes a defendant has the right to ask for the restrictions to be lifted. This restriction is sometimes applied by judges for questionable reasons, and reporters should not back away from making formal requests or appeals against such decisions since they mean the open justice system is in danger. In fact it has been held by the European Convention on Human Rights that if there is no mechanism for an appeal by newspapers, a judge's secrecy order is a potential breach of human rights (Crook, 1998).

Protection for court reports

Court reporting is fully protected from libel, whatever is said in court, so long as the conditions concerning all court reporting are followed. Fair reporting means that, when publishing details of the commencement of the proceedings, journalists should at least also publish the result. Reporters can have qualified privilege in reporting if what they report is fair and accurate but not necessarily contemporaneous with the court proceedings (it is therefore possible to write a later 'think piece' or a book).

Pictures

Publication of a photograph can in general be contempt just as much as an accompanying story. The rule is that publication of the photograph of a defendant is not likely to be contempt provided there is no question of his or her identity being at stake. However, if the case is about the witnesses identifying the defendant in court or at an identity parade, using a picture would be clear contempt.

Journalists' sources

Reporters never reveal their sources. The law does not, however, recognize any special protection for journalists when asked questions about this in court, and some journalists have been fined or jailed for refusing to answer questions about sources. However, a judge of the British appeal court held that:

while a journalist had no privilege entitling him as of right to refuse to disclose the source of his information, so the interrogator had no absolute right to require such disclosure. In the first place the question has to be relevant to be admissible at all; in the second place it ought to be one the answer to which will serve a useful purpose in relation to the proceedings in hand. Both these are matters for the consideration and, if need be, the decision of the judge, and there may be in addition other considerations which may lead a judge to conclude that more harm than good would result from compelling a disclosure or punishing a refusal to answer. The judge should always keep the ultimate discretion; and this would apply not only in the case of journalists but in other cases when information is given and received under the seal of confidence.

Criticizing the courts or judges

One of the most important judgements for journalists came with the following words from Lord Justice Atkin in 1936:

justice is not a cloistered virtue: she must be allowed to suffer the scrutiny and respectful, even though outspoken, comments of ordinary men ... provided that members of the public abstain from imputing improper motives to those taking part in the administration of justice, and are genuinely exercising a right of criticism and not acting in malice or attempting to impair the administration of justice, they are immune.

However, if a reporter says the judge is biased or even may be biased, it will be contempt. Write something about a court case and the judge and, so long as it is done in good faith and without imputing improper motives to those taking part in the administration of justice, it will not be a contempt. Journalists now have much greater scope for criticizing the judiciary than in past times. There are now regular criticisms of sentencing by judges, and of decisions by judges and the courts. For example, if a story said that a particular case would not get a fair hearing from a particular, named judge, this would be contempt of court. But if a newspaper criticized a decision of the court, it might not be contempt if the story had been written in good faith and did not imply improper motives.

CONTEMPT OF COURT

In general, the laws of contempt are aimed at protecting the administration of justice and ensuring that every person charged is given a fair trial. However, the law is not always simple. In most legal systems there are problems that can result in contempt of court. It is a continuing source of conflict. Journalists can be in contempt because of disobedience to a court order. This could involve journalists whose actions bring them into conflict with the court, or it could come about because they interfere with the course of justice. Publication of matter that could interfere with the administration of justice remains the greatest danger, since judges take a serious view of anything that is published and that might hinder a fair trial. Punishment can be severe.

It's contempt if there has been a serious risk of interference with the course of justice. Anything written or reported before and during a trial must never imply (or say) that the accused is guilty. That's what the court case is all about and, in British-based law, there is always a presumption of innocence. The law takes the view that if there is a real risk, as opposed to a remote possibility, that publication of a statement or photograph would prejudice a fair trial, then publication should not occur. The danger in criminal cases is usually that a potential juror might read an article and be prejudiced. This would mean that a defendant might not have a fair trial, something on which the law is very clear. The legal fiction applies, however, that judges are not capable of being prejudiced in this way.

For contempt, a useful test that can be applied in most countries is that of a substantial risk that the course of justice in particular proceedings will be seriously impeded or prejudiced by something that is published.

Again, there are different interpretations of contempt in various countries, mainly between Australia, the UK and the USA.

In the United States, all criminal court proceedings are open to the public and reporters cannot be denied access. The Supreme Court relies on the common law traditions of England and Wales to justify the absolute nature of the open justice principle. However, it should be noted that, in the UK, courts are moving towards a rather arbitrary practice of closed proceedings from which the press and public are excluded. All UK bail applications at crown court level are heard in secret, as are applications by the police to seize reporters' notebooks, tape and video recordings of events to help them investigate a crime.

In the United States, judges are required to hold a hearing when deciding to exclude the media or public.

In Australia, there are similar restrictions to those in the UK but there are also differences. There are, for example, strict rules preventing the media from identifying the parties in a family case, but the courts are open to media scrutiny.

The identification of children who appear in children's courts as well as adult courts is prohibited in Australia, as it is in the UK. The law also applies to children who are witnesses or victims, and the age at the time of the offence is taken into account rather than that at the time of the trial. The age is normally 17 years and under. In Scotland, youngsters can be identified over the age of 16 years. In Australia, in some states – Victoria, Tasmania and Queensland – a child has to be under the age of 17 years at the time of the offence. In all other Australian states the age is 18 years. In Britain, journalists have a legal right to attend youth courts even though members of the public are excluded. In Australia, journalists can attend children's courts in South Australia, Queensland, the Australian Capital Territory, Northern Territory, Tasmania and Victoria. In New South Wales, however, the magistrate has to give permission. In Tasmania publication of the result of a children's court case is forbidden by state law.

The other type of restriction common to Australia and the UK is prohibition of identification of the victims of sexual offences, and any information such as their address, school, place of employment and other details that may lead to identification. In Britain, the anonymity is from the moment someone complains of a sexual offence and remains forever unless the victim provides written consent or a court has been persuaded to lift the restrictions for a serious reason.

In federal systems such as in Australia and the United States, journalists need to be aware of particular state laws. The open justice principle, which is fundamental to freedom of reporting, is coming under considerable attack in many parts of the world. This open justice principle still remains intact in the United States. A diminution of the open justice principle can result in censorship and an erosion of the public right to know. After several cases in Australia in recent years, the federal government asserted the principle of openness and set up an appeal machinery to enable journalists to challenge reporting bans by individual courts or judges. In the UK, there is a growing problem with journalists involved in court reporting who are being subjected increasingly to censorship and interference by judges and lawyers. This is certainly not the situation in the United States. The First Amendment and a more liberal culture of media rights means that American journalists have considerably more freedom. There are no statutory controls on the identification of sexual offence complainants, children and other participants in court cases. American journalists tend to believe that open reporting helps underline the nature of the offence, and often helps to provide other witnesses.

In Australia, the *sub judice* rules come into force when a warrant for arrest or a summons has been issued, and in civil actions when the writ has been issued. Australia also allows for a public interest discussion defence. The principles of contempt in Australia are more or less identical to those in the UK. This means that journalists cannot prejudge the case; should avoid publishing previous criminal convictions of an accused person; should avoid publishing anything that is prejudicial before or during the trial; should not publish photographs of defendants where there is likely to be an issue of identification; and should never publish evidence prior to it being given before a jury or do anything that might look as though pressure is being applied to a witness or another participant. In Australia, judges and magistrates sometimes stop a lawyer's questions being answered by a witness. In these circumstances the court considers the question never asked, and any reporting of the question is probably contempt.

Summary

The law of contempt of court is about not hindering the administration of justice. The greatest risk is when a reporter writes a story that might create a substantial risk of serious prejudice of a trial. After a crime has been committed and the criminal is on the run, the newspaper is, in general, free to give full details of the offence (being careful of libel). After a person is arrested or a warrant is issued, a reporter must not include any material that would seriously harm the defence or prosecution. In particular, there must be no link between the accused person and the crime. Neither should any mention be made of anything that would imply that the person arrested is capable of committing the crime.

Newspapers cannot publish a photo of an accused if identification might be an issue at the trial. When reporting trials, reporters cannot include anything the jury has not been allowed to hear, e.g. any discussions about the admissibility of evidence or guilty pleas to charges that the jury are not trying. Courts may ask that reporters delay publication of a report to avoid a substantial risk of prejudice. Courts may also order that a name be withheld and not reported in public.

Remember: Reports in open court will normally be safe to report, but be alert for any specifically imposed court restrictions. Warning bells should ring when the cases concern children (as defendants and witnesses), family proceedings, sexual assaults and rape cases.

COPYRIGHT

In Britain and the rest of Europe copyright lasts 70 years after the author's death, or 70 years after the first publication if that takes place after death. Copyright on photographs lasts for 70 years after first publication. The Copyright Act protects creative work from being used by others without permission. In Australia the time limit is 50 years; in the USA it is usually 75 years.

Fair dealing

This is a defence against copyright infringement for newspapers and periodicals when reproducing extracts from copyright works. Fair dealing is satisfied when the newspaper reproduces extracts from a literary, dramatic, musical or artistic work for the purpose of criticism or review or for reporting current events. However, it has to be accompanied by sufficient acknowledgement identifying the work and its author. It is therefore permissible to quote from books, plays, films, etc. when writing a criticism of them as a story or feature. However, there cannot be fair dealing (i.e. copyright *is* infringed) if there is a substantial part of the piece reproduced. The UK Copyright Act says: *Any extract may be published if its publication is genuinely intended to enable the reviewer to make his comments and not to enable the reader of the review to enjoy the work concerned without buying it. It should not be an important part of the work, such as that in which the author conveys the main idea of the piece.*

FURTHER READING

Armstrong, M. (1995). *Media Law in Australia*. OUP.

Belsey, A. and Chadwick, R. (1992). *Ethical Issues in Journalism and the Media*. Routledge.

Braithwaite, N. (ed.) (1995). *The International Libel Handbook*. Butterworth-Heinemann.

Carey, P. (1998). *Media Law*. Sweet and Maxwell.

Crone, T. (1995). *Law and the Media*. Focal Press.

Crook, T. (1998). *International Radio Journalism*. Routledge.

Gage, L. (1999). *A Guide to Commercial Radio Journalism*. Focal Press.

Mckain, B., Bonnington, A. and Watts, G. A. (1995). *Scots Law for Journalists*. Sweet and Maxwell.

Pearson, M. (1997). *The Journalist's Guide to Media Law*. Allen and Unwin.

Robertson, G. and Nicol, A. (1992). *Media Law*. Penguin.

Welsh, T. and Greenwood, W. (1999). *McNae's Essential Law for Journalists*. Butterworth.

6 Journalism language

*'Two thousand words from Boot,' said Mr. Salter. 'Any good?'
asked the general editor. 'Look at it.' The general editor looked.
He saw 'Russian plot . . . coup d'état . . . overthrow constitutional
government . . . real dictatorship . . . goat butts head of police . . .
imprisoned blonde . . . vital British interest jeopardised'. It was
enough; it was news.*

Evelyn Waugh
Scoop, 1938

Language has evolved throughout civilization according to the way the
message has been transmitted. Language changed when ancient
civilizations learnt to write their spoken thoughts, and again when the
written word was printed. As will be seen later in this chapter, it
changed further when the printed word was transmitted to vast
numbers of people by means of broadcasting and it is changing again
as computer-speak takes over the digital revolution. The earliest
writing conveyed messages with pictures. Only a small part of the
population had the skill to draw these pictograms, but with the
invention of the Phoenician alphabet writing became widespread and
non-specialist in its skills. The coming of writing brought knowledge
and information to parts of society that had not been trained to
evaluate and understand such things. Socrates saw this, and it worried
him:

*Once a thing is put in writing, the composition, whatever it may be,
drifts all over the place, getting into the hands not only of those who
understand it, but equally of those who have no business with it.*

As spoken language was transferred more and more to the written
form, the style and formality changed. When printing became
widespread in the fifteenth century, language was involved in another
set of alterations. As Anthony Smith (1980) points out: *Printing*

evolved from a series of divisions of labour that had been introduced in an effort to speed up the task of manuscript copying. Europe began to enjoy not only the relative wealth of until now unavailable old texts and manuscripts, but also new texts and information of all kinds. Out of this new need for information and facts emerged the newspaper and, with it, a new kind of language, the language of journalism. Newspapers were first developed as small news sheets in Holland, Great Britain and France, to carry news about foreign events and commercial or economic issues. At the start of the printed newspaper, the important person was the printer. Printers had the know-how and the skills to produce the end product that people wanted to read. As newspapers prospered and became more complicated, the language used required a different kind of person to be in charge of collecting and writing the newspaper information. The printer yielded centre stage to the editor, and then to the publisher-owner. With the growth of the newspaper, a new profession arose; that of the reporter, who specialized in using the best kind of language to entice more readers and in gathering and writing the news. Reporters were the key to the whole editorial process, as they are today. The quality of the performance of reporters, with their freedom of access to essential sources of information and freedom to write and publish the truth, determined the quality of the information given to the reader. Accuracy was the first requirement; the second, the ability to use the printed word to the best advantage to excite, interest and inform the reader in the most elegant way possible. At the start of newspaper journalism, language was long-winded, discursive and florid. The arrival of the telegraph changed all that. When Morse's invention came into widespread use for the transmission of information, the costs involved were considerable. Style and wordiness came under fire from editors, who saw their news budget costs escalating alarmingly, so the style of language changed again.

Some of these changes were for reasons other than cost. The much greater speed at which news could be transmitted and received gave an immediacy that had not been available before. When news from far away places was written by hand and sent by mail, reporters had plenty of time to contemplate before writing the story. Speed was not important. With a good story to tell, reporters could go to great lengths to produce a story of literary classic proportions. Reporters would make every effort to refine the language they used and to include as much florid description as they could, as well as comment on how they saw the events. With telegraph transmission costs, this kind of writing became a luxury that newspapers could no longer afford. Brevity became important as a matter of economy. Plain facts took precedence over much-considered and well-honed thought and impeccable, formal language. The shorter the report, the more quickly it could be transmitted; the clearer the facts, the better the reader would be informed; this made it more likely that the whole report would be read, not just the first few sentences. To do this, a new journalistic style was invented using the language of the people for reporting news. It changed the look of the stories as well. Telegraphed stories now used leading paragraphs which presented the essential facts, often in one sentence. The whole story was shortened, often to only three paragraphs. Language had to cope with this new brevity and with a new way of ordering the facts. Reader interest was heightened with a more interesting lead, and facts and detail were presented in order of diminishing importance. This made it possible for an editor to cut the story from the bottom. A new type of lead to the story emerged, the summary lead, containing all the basic elements that a reader would want to know in one sentence: the *what, where, when, who* and *why*, and *how*. The five 'Ws' and the 'H' are still in use, although, as will be shown later, the need today is for brevity and simplicity of a different kind. This way of telling a story in simple, familiar language replaced the old discursive style of writing in which the bigger and more unusual the word, the better the writing. Editors wanted stories that told the story with point, interest and clarity, so that the reader would understand the story quickly and without a dictionary. Editors and readers liked this new approach to the language of journalism because it meant better and more accurate writing, and allowed more space for more stories.

In a newspaper, everything other than advertising is called 'editorial'. Most editorial content is called written 'copy'. Some is visual (photographs, graphs and other visual elements), and the rest is print. Unlike, for example, letter writing, print journalism is a language that is usually a combination of many efforts. Journalists, printers, editors and subeditors all contribute. The international news magazine, *Time*, has at least five layers of editing interfaces between reporter and reader. However, all journalism starts with information, gathered by someone, the reporter, and written at least in draft by the reporter. The language of print journalism is forever changing. The original is changed by editors; that in turn can be rewritten, shortened or expanded by others as more information is gathered about the story, or other stories take the place of the original. Just as it is the role of the print journalist to write the news, it is the role of editors to cut and modify the original written language. This is one of the big differences between print and broadcasting. In broadcasting, such editing is unusual because of the technology used and the time constraints. In print journalism, it is much easier for this to occur. Print therefore has a greater tradition of editing than does broadcast journalism, where reports are usually in the own words of the reporter. Severe editing can result in a story that is unrecognizable as the original. Each different editing process in the news assembly line produces a different version of the original. The final version of course does not show this multiple editing process; that would be bad editing. Editors edit a story to read well in a coherent style, and good newspaper editing should improve the language and the story flow. It should make it clearer and simpler, and make the maximum news point possible. It also standardizes the language and ensures that it is 'house style'.

The first pre-language problem in writing any journalism story is the news focus, which is most often shown in the lead to the story. A story in a newspaper attracts or puts off a reader with its first sentence, the lead. Readers want simplicity; they want a simple language of journalism. Some researchers over the years have developed what they called readability formulas; mathematical equations that give numerical values to various criteria of style. The main criteria are the average sentence length in number of words and the complexity of words in the sentence. The resulting readability formula then yields a rough determination of the story's ease of reading. Readability formulas were generally created by critics of the boring, long-winded print journalism language of the early part of this century. In the digital age, it is time to make journalism language as readable and interesting as possible. In fact, readability formulas never quite caught on in the journalism profession because, by and large, they look only at individual word complexity and word count, not at the broader syntax and semantics of the language of journalism. However, they do appear to prove what all good journalists and editors know instinctively; that terseness and simplicity make the story easy to read. The Gunning Fog Index, for example, emphasizes simple words and short sentences. Then came

Rudolf Flesch, who worked with the American international newsagency, Associated Press, in the late 1940s. He created the most widely used readability formula in the United States, and this reaffirmed the importance of sentence length as a key element of good readable journalism language. Flesch believed that crisp newspaper language was the key to good readership. He told journalists to keep their average sentence length *at not more than 19 words*. More than 20 words, he thought, was past the danger line (Gunning, 1968).

A series of studies in the United States found that a story's average sentence length of about eight words was the most readable and understandable to readers. At 15 words a sentence, comprehension dropped to 90 per cent; at 20 words, it dropped to 75 per cent; at 25 words, it became 62 per cent. So starting a story with a long sentence is usually a bad idea. It creates a barrier to reader interest. A long lead sentence is usually due to the particular form of writing used and the amount of detail. Simplicity in the use of the language of journalism not only makes the information and stories more instantly accessible, it gives the readers what they want. And that means they buy the newspaper in preference to those of the competitors.

This simplicity and clarity is not just restricted to the lead of a news or feature story. It applies to all the writing techniques that should embody the language use of all journalists. No matter what the delivery method of modern and future journalism is, there will always be a need for good writing as the fundamental element of the information revolution of the digital age. The primary skill needed in the modern journalist is the ability to use and write language well to tell the story in the most accurate, interesting way. Lack of good writing is perhaps the major criticism by industry professionals of university educated journalism students. They do not know how to write and tell a story well. A good piece of print journalism almost always reflects the personality of the writer, as well as being an accurate reflection of a news fact or event. The inverted pyramid newswriting formula is much used, and occasionally abused, by journalists. However, it provides a useful starting point for discussing the language and structure of news and feature stories in journalism. Under this formula, the story begins with a strong lead identifying the main news point, and precise attribution of sources to give authority. However, newspapers are more and more using a more flexible formula for constructing a story to give added interest and more of a story-telling feel to the news report; in its place is a more conversational style of literature and language.

In traditional print language, the basic unit is the paragraph. This, of course, is not necessarily the case in broadcast journalism, where the look on the page is not important. The paragraph in print language provides new information (this can be the lead) or contains several types of supporting material, such as quotations, examples, anecdotes, paraphrasing and interpretation. Direct quotes usually support a proposition, and new information is frequently introduced by a statement from the journalist, or through paraphrased comments. Traditionally the inverted pyramid story begins with all the main facts and relegates less important details to the apex of the pyramid, and can therefore be cut from the bottom. What print language in journalism is doing is taking part in the general current trend of convergence. Print is converging with broadcasting in the use of language. It is becoming simpler, clearer, shorter and more graphic, conversational and informal. All of these qualities it draws from good broadcast writing and language. Clear, informative, informal journalistic writing, performed with integrity and an understanding of social and political contexts, is the journalism of the digital age. Creativity, style and a deep concern for critical reflection will define good print journalism language. The journalists of tomorrow will write more as they talk, and this will be the style learnt from broadcasting as it is practised now.

However, there is a general distrust by reporters and editors of formulas for making news writing and reporting better. There is an apt story in Dodge and Viner's (1965) *The Practice of Journalism*:

The rule at Northcliffe's Daily Mail *when it had the world's biggest morning sale was to give the kernel of the story in the first sentence which had to start, for preference, with a verb of action but never with 'the' or any word beginning with 'th . . .'. When this instruction was pinned up on the notice board, an editorial joker added what he called a 'specimen introduction': 'Banging men's bowler hats over their eyes and yelling "strike a blow for dress reform," a sandy-haired youth wearing a vivid green jacket and spats scattered monkey-nuts among MPs arriving at the House of Commons yesterday'.*

Higher executives were angry – Northcliffe amused. He joined in the fun by banning inverted sentences.

LANGUAGE AND BROADCASTING

Good broadcast language is divided roughly into two types: narration and actuality. Narration is the words spoken by the newscaster working from a script. Actuality is non-scripted or unplanned spoken language used by the broadcasters or those being interviewed by the journalists. Actuality is the electronic equivalent of print quotations; in radio news they are the audio equivalent of newspaper pictures or television illustrations. However, in broadcast language actuality takes on additional functions: soundbites call attention to non-verbal aspects of the story and are used so that the audience can hear or see the speaker's emotional reaction to the words being spoken more than to the language used itself. It also refers to the sound of the story, and this forms a part of the overall broadcast language used by journalists.

Broadcasters are a unique creation of our times, but at the same time are closely related to the pre-literate storytellers. The difference is in the audience. The storytellers of old knew precisely who their audience was. They could see them and change their language or message to fit the audience reactions. Broadcasters cannot see their audience, and have to guess at their reactions. What they say and how they say it has to take account of whether listeners are on the move (a Walkman™ for a jogger; a car radio for the car traveller; a small transistor in the kitchen, office or hotel room; or the most modern type of expensive stereo system fixed in the home). Account must also be taken of the various types of radio sets within the home; from the kitchen with a small transistor where quality is not good and certain voices can be misheard, to the lounge room hi fi set where every breath is noticeable (requiring therefore in all broadcast journalists the ability for example to speak without a breathy sound). Then there are distractions; the breakfast rush needs a very specific kind of broadcast language (short sentences, simple construction, short pieces of information). The early storytellers had no such problem. They knew when their listeners were being distracted and were able to change their language accordingly. The broadcaster can never know, and so must always try to overcome any possible listener distractions or inattention by a careful use of the language.

After the storytellers came the early religious missionaries, who knew exactly how to speak with impact directly to their audiences. They developed their own technique of imposing presence, booming voice and a simple, direct language style that ensured they were understood and remembered. When the British Broadcasting Corporation began, announcers could only learn the techniques of these successful pre-broadcast public speakers and, with experience, adapt and improve them. It is perhaps no accident that John Reith, the founder of the BBC, was a Scottish Presbyterian of very firm and sincere religious beliefs. He became, knowingly or not, a missionary. The early BBC reflected this approach and attitude. It became, in effect, a missionary organization, which preached its beliefs about broadcasting and the need to educate, entertain and inform throughout the British and non-British world. The last 70 years have provided a record of broadcasters relearning the earlier art of intimacy, informality and conversational communication, which was lost during the time of the travelling public speakers.

The search for a modern conversational intimacy which at the same time provides speaker credibility induces in both broadcaster and listener a kind of schizophrenia: on the one hand there is a definite need for a set of rules to which broadcasters must adhere (rules governing presentation, style of speech, pace); and on the other there is the need for a *laissez-faire* approach to allow for the most informal, conversational, intimate sound so the speakers can be themselves. The paradox in broadcasting is that rules are necessary to allow freedom of expression.

Out of radio speech developed a particular style of radio writing that was informal, intimate, simple and immediately understandable. Early broadcasters were told to use the kind of language they would use to their friends or to 'Aunt Maud ironing in the corner of the room'. They were asked to imagine an individual listener, and the language evolved to become an electronic form of the pre-literate storyteller idiom. Broadcasting was becoming a personal language of its own.

Broadcasting reminded people that speech, not print, is the basis of language. The printing press had provided only a one-dimensional language. Print showed words, but not the full range of spoken language features; the rhythm, the stress, the accent, the quality of the voice, which can do so much to a cold piece of prose. Then came radio, which gave a two-dimensional language of information; the use of sound and spoken language. With television came three-dimensional language, which used speech, sound and pictures to transmit many ideas to people who would otherwise never be exposed to them. Pronunciation, intonation, the structure and composition of the language were all affected. The problem was that broadcasting, the ultimate weapon of popular information, entertainment and education, took its role so seriously that it became an elite: the few talking to the many and giving them what was good for them. The missionaries took over the church, and everyone had to be converted.

Herein lies the basic dilemma of broadcast journalists. Somehow, they must respect the storytelling tradition so that listeners and viewers will care about the news they are being told, and yet do so without pandering or descending into sleaze. Broadcast journalists must be sceptical towards those in power, and yet not degenerate into the cynical detachment of ironic knowingness. They must be fair, and yet not succumb to some kind of moral neutrality that leads to paralysis in the face of injustice. Radio and television are the most popular storytelling media in this country. They are representing to the listeners and the viewers, as well as to the broadcast journalists themselves, a new cultural form. Both radio and television, but particularly TV, are particularly suited to a dramatic rather than an analytic scientific model of news. As such they are especially vulnerable to the pressure to appeal to the lowest common denominator, to serve up reconstituted tales of sensation and fluff that meet the dramatic requirements of the medium and yet rarely fulfil the requirements of quality journalism. Fiske (1987) believes that rather than increasing 'its objectivity, its depth or its authority, television news instead should aim to increase its openness, its contradictions and multiplicity of its voices and points of view' to become more, rather than less, popular. Today, the majority of the population receives its first news of an event from either radio or television. Newspapers come third in the primacy of information. The language and format of broadcast news is therefore of great importance to the would-be broadcast journalist.

Reith (1924) wanted a type of broadcast English language for the BBC that would offend as few people as possible. According to Reith:

the language, the speech and pronunciation . . . that the announcers were taught to speak . . . was the very best thing we could do. What I tried to get was a style or quality of English which would not be laughed at in any part of the country. I was as vehemently opposed to what variously has been called the Oxford accent or the south-eastern accent.

In 1932 one of the first BBC broadcasters, Hilda Matheson, said:

A generation accustomed to relate much of its thought to spoken English may question whether even our words need remodelling as well as our spelling, if they are to be adequate for new purposes and ideas.

In Britain, announcers became an elite priest caste of their own. They were about as untypical of the normal English speaker as it is possible to get; the norm was southern received English from the major public schools and Oxford and Cambridge.

Unlike Reith's broadcasters, the modern BBC uses a wide range of accents, depending on the type of station and target audience. Over the last few years there has been a rapid surge in the use of educated Scottish and Irish on BBC networks to decentralize the London-based received pronunciation (RP) speech. The serious public service networks such as BBC Radio 3, the classical music network in the United Kingdom, and Radio 4, the national talk station, for example, now use accents comprising received pronunciation and educated varieties of Scottish, Irish and Welsh. The classical commercial equivalent in Britain, Classic FM, uses a variety of British accents: Cornish, Welsh, London, Northern, educated Scottish and Irish, New York American as well as RP. Regional and local stations use regional British accents. Local stations tend to foster the very local accents of the community and county. The trend is away from elitist speech on all British broadcasting networks and local stations and towards an increased cherishing of the riches of local speech accents and dialects. The dinner jacket is being replaced by jeans.

These changes have not been universally welcomed. Many criticisms of broadcast language relate to the basis on which listeners have developed their English language style and grammar. In older listeners the basis on which their judgement is made occurred long ago, often more than 40 years, during their essay writing school life. Most expressions of concern about the state of broadcast language come from people with the best of intentions, but who are unaware that more grievous or fundamental changes to the language have occurred at various periods since it was first recorded in written form in the eighth century. Examples of such fundamental changes include the loss of grammatical gender in the late Old English and early Middle English periods; the absorption of large numbers of foreign words at all periods since the days of Edward the Confessor and earlier; and the great vowel shift at the beginning of the fifteenth century, when nearly every long vowel in the standard language radically changed its nature. For example *goose*, which before 1400 was pronounced in the manner of modern English *close*, as in *a close thing*, gained its modern pronunciation when the great vowel shift occurred, as did *house*, which before 1400 was pronounced with the main vowel sound of modern English *moose*. Other changes that have occurred include the severance of the home varieties of English into many overseas varieties, especially in North America and Australia; and during the twentieth century, the adoption of English in varying degrees of adequacy as a common language in many of the countries throughout the world. Changes continue to occur in the English language, as they have done for 1200 years; broadcasting is merely making them more obvious and more quickly assimilated.

Some of the widespread complaints about the use of English in broadcasting concern the stresses on words, with emphasis on unimportant words, and fractured speech rhythm. The indefinite articles *a* and *the* are often unnaturally stressed; the auxiliary verbs (such as *can*, *could*, *has*, *is*, *may*, *might*) are often pronounced with too much emphasis rather than neutrally; prepositions are unnaturally stressed: (*The Prime Minister went TO the palace*); verbs are unnaturally stressed (*The temperature yesterday WAS 26 degrees*).

In modern broadcasting the elegance of well-written prose may well be slipping; but then, broadcast language is not prose but speech. Broadcasting has created a cultural shift away from an elite form of language to the speech and writing patterns of the common man and woman. Broadcast language has made English more colloquial, simpler, clearer and immediately understandable, with simple construction, familiar words, and short sentences. Broadcasting is not destroying language but changing the language. Some people do not like some of the changes, but the resulting extensive language revolution caused by broadcasters has given the ordinary person a national and international voice as never before. Broadcast language is the first to show the changes of style in conversational usage, and is often ahead of the grammarians and therefore a cause of complaint by those who wish to keep the standards they grew up with.

Broadcasting has also developed its own grammar. For example, verbless sentences like

This report from . . . and *And so for the main points of the news* are characteristic of broadcast English. Similarly, the present tense often replaces the future tense: *The programme is on the air tomorrow at this time*; *President Clinton goes to Europe tomorrow*. There is other language usage in broadcasting that is resisted by listeners but is permissible in informal speech. For example, prepositions at the ends of sentences are common in speech, and in broadcast language. The rule for broadcasters should follow that of Fowler: *It was once a cherished superstition that prepositions must be kept true to their name and placed before the word they govern in spite of the incurable English instinct for putting them late. . . . If the final preposition that has naturally presented itself sounds comfortable, keep it.*

Similarly, split infinitives also cause some rage among listeners and viewers. However, infinitives have been split in English since at least the fourteenth century, and are commonly split in ordinary conversational language. Fowler (1978) divides English speakers into:

1 Those who neither know nor care what a split infinitive is
2 Those who do not know, but care very much
3 Those who know and condemn
4 Those who know and approve
5 Those who know and distinguish.

Some listeners have perceived such things as 'faults'. They are not, and are perceived as faults only by those who judge these things by the standards of written English. Listener attitudes to broadcasting techniques and what are thought of as *suitable* voices have changed considerably over the years. The old-style RP is less and less the voice of the international BBC. Regional accents, once considered unsuitable, are now common. However, other international broadcasters, and some local broadcasters in countries with a British colonial past, still cling to the old style BBC English. Even on the BBC World Service there is the sound of change; first in that women are being used extensively, and secondly in that the male voice stereotypes have changed to a lighter, more natural voice quality. This gives in all a younger, more neutral accent and sound. There are also different accents: Welsh, Scottish, Northern Irish, Indian subcontinent.

The BBC, by choosing RP as its form of speech, gave it a seal of approval that made it the national norm. Radio became the accepted social norm of authoritative speech. These British accent hierarchies spread, via the World Service of the BBC, across the English speaking world.

However, that too is changing as American broadcasting becomes more widespread through cable and satellite global transmissions. In Hong Kong, for example, where since the start of broadcasting the BBC model has been the norm, new American role models are being used. It is now no longer usual for British English Chinese speakers to be heard as reporters and news readers in Hong Kong; the management-required accents are American, and usually very strong regional American accents that would only be heard on local stations in the United States, never on the networks.

AMERICAN BROADCAST LANGUAGE

The English language has always been one of the battle grounds of Anglo-American rivalry, a fascinating window onto the tensions of the special relationship. Divided by a common language, each generation has made the discovery that the English of England is different from the English of America. As early as 1735, the settlers were being attacked for what was described as 'barbarous English' (McCrum, 1986). As pioneers, the Americans had to make up a lot of new words: *lengthy*, which dates back to 1689; *calculate*, *seaboard*. These words entered what was fast becoming a new American dialect, which Samuel Johnson referred to in his famous complaint about *the American dialect, a tract of corruption to which every language widely diffused must always be exposed*. Among Americans, there was exasperation at the superior airs of their British cousins. The statesman John Hay, having witnessed his ambassador in London, exclaimed:

How our Ambassador does go it when he gets a roomful of bovine Britons in front of him . . . I never so clearly appreciated the power of the unhesitating orotundity of the Yankee speech, as in listening – after an hour or two of hum-ha of tongue-tied British men – to the long wash of our Ambassador's sonority.

In 1776, the spoken language in both countries was essentially the same. A contemporary diarist reported that the Americans in general *speak better English than the English do. No country or colonial dialect is to be distinguished here.* Now, however, no one who listened to a conversation between the British Prime Minister and the American President could possibly be in any doubt that there were two distinct sounds of language. Language nationalism grew from the beginning in the United States as part of its badge of independence; a language, it felt, of the future. Language nationalism inspired the recommendation made by the American Continental Congress in 1778 that when the French minister visited the new Republic and its legislature, *all replies and answers* to him should be put *in the language of the United States* (not in French, or British English). In 1790, when the first census was taken in the United States, four million Americans were counted and 90 per cent were descendants of English colonists. Their English, though, was already different; hardly the English of the old oppressor, *the turgid style of Johnson, the purple glare of Gibbon.*

The uniformity began with Noah Webster, the most famous of all American dictionary-makers and a great champion of American English in speech and writing. Between 1783 and 1785, while still in his twenties, Webster published three elementary books on English; a speller, a grammar and a reader, to which he gave the title *A Grammatical Institute of the English Language.* The Speller was a great best-seller, selling over 80 million copies in his lifetime. His intention was 'to introduce uniformity and accuracy of pronunciation into common schools'. *The American Speller* was put to wide use in all the schools; as one newspaper proprietor explained:

It was the custom for all such pupils (those sufficiently advanced to pronounce distinctly words of more than one syllable) to stand together as one class, and with one voice to read a column or two of the tables for spelling. The master gave the signal to begin and all united to read, letter by letter, pronouncing each syllable by itself, and adding to it the preceding one till the word was complete. This model of reading was exceedingly exciting, and in my humble opinion, exceedingly useful; as it required and taught deliberate and distinct articulation...

Webster now devoted himself to championing the cause of the American language, its spelling, grammar and pronunciation. In 1789, Webster published his *Dissertations on the English Language*:

Several circumstances render a future separation of the American tongue from the English necessary and unavoidable . . . numerous local causes, such as a new country, new associations of people, new combinations of ideas in arts and science, and some intercourse with tribes wholly unknown in Europe, will introduce new words into the American tongue. These causes will produce, in course of time, a language in North America, as different from the future language of England, as the modern Dutch, Danish and Swedish are from the German or from one another.

In retrospect, Webster's influence on American spelling, and therefore on American speech, was enormous. The distinctive pattern of American speech, the due emphasis given to each syllable in a word can, in part, be attributed to the influence of Webster's spelling bees and to his saying:

A good articulation consists in giving every letter in a syllable its due proportion of sound, according to the most approved custom of pronouncing it; and in making such a distinction, between syllables, of which words are composed, that the ear shall without difficulty acknowledge their number.

Hence, American English says *sec-ret-ary* instead of the British *secret'ry.*

The precise degree of Webster's influence on American speech rhythms will always remain controversial. However, probably largely because of his influence there is a remarkable uniformity in much of North American speech, nothing like the patchwork of local variation in Britain. The actress Fanny Kemble, professionally trained to listen to the spoken word, observed during her tour of the eastern United States that: *The southern, western and eastern states of America have each their strong peculiarities of enunciation, which render them easy of recognition.* The speech of the north-east was usually clipped and tended to elide the *r*. New Englanders are recorded from an early time as saying *r'ally* for *really*. In the south, according to novelist Thomas

Low Nichols, *speech is clipped, softened and broadened by the Negro admixture.* Southerners tended to retain the traditional English *a-doing*, dropping the final *g.* They are also recorded as saying *wunst* for *once*, *hoss* for *horse* and *aks* for *ask*. Towards and beyond the Mississippi, American speech grew richer and stronger. *It is certain that men open their mouths and broaden their speech as they go West*, said Nichols. He described how the westerner *walks the water, out-hollers the thunder, drinks the Mississippi, calculates that he is the genuine article, and that those he don't like ain't worth shucks.* These vast speech regions in which almost all people were broadly intelligible to each other contrasted sharply with the regional varieties of English. In 1828, the novelist James Fenimore Cooper wrote:

In America, while there are provincial and state peculiarities, in tone, and even in the pronunciation and use of certain words, there is no patois. An American may distinguish between the Georgian and the New-Englander, but you [his British audience] cannot.

He continued:

The distinctions in speech between New England and New York or Pennsylvania or any other State, were far greater twenty years ago than they are now. Immigration alone would produce a large proportion of this change.

Many nineteenth century travellers to the United States also commented on the nasal quality and drawl of the American voice, characteristics about which some Americans feel defensive to this day. The Victorian novelist, Captain Marryat, travelled widely in the United States, and noticed that: *The Americans dwell on their words when they speak, a custom arising, I presume, from their cautious, calculating habits; and they have always more or less of a nasal twang.*

In *The Philosophy of the Human Voice*, the American James Rush (1852) gave a physiological foundation and explanation of vocal theory that put an entirely new emphasis on the study of speech. He divided vocal sound into quality, force, time, abruptness and pitch. On the subject of voice quality:

The thirty-five elements of speech may be heard under four different kinds of voice; the natural, the falsetto, the whispering, and that improved quality, to be presently described under the name of Orotund.

He then goes on to describe these qualities:

The natural voice is said to be produced by the vibration of the glottis. This has been inferred, from a supposed analogy between the action of the human organ, and that of the dog, in which the vibration has been observed and on exposing the glottis during the cries of the animal; and from the vibration of the chords, by blowing through the human larynx, when removed from the body. The conclusion is therefore probable but until it is seen in the living function of the part, or until there is sufficient approximation to this proof by other means, it cannot be admitted as a portion of exact physiological science.

Later, another American writer on the subject, Stuart Flexner (1976), made the following prediction:

We Americans are still moving and communicating from one part of the country to another. As easterners and midwesterners continue to move to the sun belt, the local Florida and Texas speech patterns will be diluted as people continue to leave large cities for small ones and for rural areas, pockets of local dialects will tend to weaken or disappear. Perhaps someday in the future regional dialects will be no more. Then we may have only two dialects, that of educated, urban Americans and that of rural and poor Americans.

American broadcasting had in its early days a similar approach to the importance of broadcast speech, developing an accent known as Network Standard, the accent of the newscasters in which the regional characteristics of Southern or Texan or Brooklyn speech were modified in the interests of clarity, intelligibility and neutrality. For example, an NBC training pamphlet had this to say about those becoming announcers with them: *An announcer in NBC is expected to average well in the following: a good voice, clear enunciation; and pronunciation free of dialect or local peculiarities; ability to read well.* Not everyone agrees that there is a Network Standard speech for American broadcasters. The *Oxford Companion to the English Language*, for example, says in its entry about American Broadcast

English: 'The efforts of some networks, such as NBC, to provide their announcers with authoritative guidance on pronunciation have not been widely influential or successful'. However, broadcasters hoping to work on the networks or on large metropolitan stations do modify their speech by eliminating pronunciations likely to be associated with a particular area or social group. Dan Rather, one of the most watched American newscasters is a case in point. He grew up in Texas, with a Texan accent, but on air he worked hard to avoid peculiarities of pronunciation and even went to a speech teacher to improve his elocution: *I worked on my own for a while trying to say 'e' as in 'ten' correctly. Texans, including me, tend to say 'tin'. I also tried to stop dropping 'gs'. It never seemed to be a problem except sometimes when I was tired, I tended to say 'nothin' instead of 'nothing'.*

However, unlike in Britain, the Americans did not foster a broadcast elite, a priest caste from Oxbridge that provided a role model for the ordinary people. The Americans used journalists to read the bulletins; something not mirrored in Britain or other British-led broadcasting organizations in Commonwealth countries such as Australia, Canada, New Zealand and elsewhere.

The first American network, NBC, began in 1926, and promised 'quality programming and good journalism'. NBC hoped it would be possible to broadcast every event of national importance widely through the United States.

CBS started 2 years later, and both of them covered the 1928 election on radio for the first time. However, American radio journalism was a haphazard affair, with stories pasted on sheets of paper for an announcer to read. Unlike at this stage in Britain where announcers read the bulletins, the Americans at least had journalists. The first daily network newscaster was Floyd Gibbons, a newspaper correspondent who covered World War I for newspapers. He started as a newscaster with NBC in 1929 and his programme, which started as a weekly and soon moved to 6 nights a week, was *The Headline Hunter*. CBS followed with their own brand of newscaster shortly afterwards. He was Lowell Thomas, a professional lecturer and newsman of 20 years standing. The Americans too believed in auditions. He was given two auditions, with prospective sponsors listening to see whether they liked it enough to buy him. After the first audition, it was decided that he should try a newscast for the second audition. No one had ever done such a thing before, so there was much discussion about what to try. They couldn't work out what kind of newscast to do so, after much discussion, they bought all the late editions of the afternoon papers, 'rewrote the news we liked and did the broadcast'. The significant thing about these early newscasters and reporters in the United States was their journalistic training. This understanding of the importance of a journalistic edge to radio reporting was well put in 1934 by Theodore F. Koop, a CBS vice president:

Because it was evident even in those experimental days that an announcer could not impart the understanding and authority of a reporter, [David Lawrence] offered one of his own reporters, H. R. Baukhage, to read the news on air. Here was the exact combination NBC was seeking: Baukhage had been an actor before he progressed to reporter. He went on the show, and 'Baukhage talking' became a familiar self-introduction year after year.

Again unlike in the United Kingdom, women were also in evidence in the early days of American broadcast journalism; Mary Marvin Breckinridge and Betty Wason for CBS, Margaret Rupli and Helen Hiett for NBC and Sigrid Schultz for Mutual. Of the five, only Schultz was an experienced foreign correspondent. In September 1939, when Germany invaded Poland, Breckinridge provided a radio report in what was later described as a 'natural radio voice and a gift for reporting'. Bliss (1991) quotes her as saying: *Before the broadcast Murrow gave me just one instruction: 'keep your voice low'* . And he also added: *Remember you're American and speak like an American.* Betty Wason had worked on stations in the midwest, and covered the Munich crisis for the news service Transradio. She made her first broadcast for CBS on April 12, 1940, after Hitler invaded Norway. Network officials complained about her voice: 'too young and feminine for war news', though no fault was found with her reporting. Hosley says that Wason's voice was not so low-pitched as Breckinridge's: *She sometimes ran out of breath and stumbled more often.* Margaret Rupli was NBC's first woman correspondent. She recalls Murrow reminding the two recruits of the strengths in language that is restrained: *When you report the invasion of Holland, or I report the invasion of England, understate the situation. Don't say the streets are rivers of blood. Say the little policeman I usually say hello to every morning is not there today.*

The news bulletin, the 5-minute news summary on the hour, had been a fixture in radio. During the war and for a while afterwards, most of these summaries were read by staff announcers. With the arrival of television, radio executives saw news as an area in which they could remain competitive. To make the hourlies more attractive, says Bliss, it was decided that they should be aired by experienced reporters with names listeners recognised. 'Anchor' was first used as a term at political conventions. The two TV anchors were Douglas Edwards for CBS and John Cameron Swayze for NBC. At that time there was no such word as anchor. The president of CBS news is usually credited with inventing the word because he needed a term for Walter Cronkite at the 1952 conventions. Sig Mickelson says:

I visualized the 'anchorman' as the best-informed person at the convention. All our communications lines would terminate with him. Reporters on the floor, in the wings, or in downtown hotels would transmit to a desk that would screen information to be relayed to him. The studio where we stationed him would be the heart and brain of our coverage.

The term stuck.

Today, as well as broadcast journalists on air, there is a growing band of specialists who are hired not so much for their ability to communicate news but rather to specialize: doctors, lawyers, farming experts, economists, weather people, gardeners. Increasingly reporters of specialist news are from relevant professions: reporters on legal matters are lawyers; space reporters are science graduates (while Walter Cronkite, who pioneered space reporting, had no expert knowledge but learnt all he knew from independent study). This development away from the traditional broadcast journalist as reporter and anchor has had other effects, as Ed Bliss says:

Generally speaking news had been something broadcasters did because it was expected of them. Station owners provided it in part to keep their licences, but many did news out of their own sense of duty. The reputation for public service was a medal worn with pride. Then it was discovered that money – lots of money – could be made in news, and so in many instances it became, instead of competition for journalistic achievement, competition for audience. The 'happy talk' school of newscasting was founded. One symptom is the inordinate amount of yukking it up between anchor, sports reporter and whoever is doing the weather. The happy talk format, says critic John Leonard, 'giggles its way to apocalypse'. As part of the format, Edwin Newman sees what now appears to be a competition in wishing the viewers well. They are urged to have a good day, have a good night, have a good weekend, have a good week . . . a local New York anchorman signs off: 'We care about what happens to you'. Newman asks, 'what has this to do with news?' Tom Shales, the Washington Post *critic, once wrote a satire on the trivializing of news. After the 'Cronkite and company' disco theme, the eminent anchor is forced to read: 'this is WAL-ter CRON-kite. Join me and the CBS news team tonight for exclusive coverage of the end of the world, live via satellite. At eleven-thirty eastern, ten-thirty central, right after the latest sports scores on your local station'.*

AUSTRALIAN BROADCAST LANGUAGE

The roots of Antipodean English, New Zealand and Australian, lie in the south and east of England (the counties of Norfolk, Suffolk, Essex, Middlesex, Hertfordshire, parts of Bedfordshire, Cambridgeshire, Northamptonshire, and London). But there are other roots as well. There were also Irish and Scottish speakers. As with the early settlers in the United States, these many voices blended to make the distinctive tones of a new variety of English.

The children of the original immigrants lost their parents' Irish or Midland or Scottish accents within one generation of their arrival. As early as 1820, one writer observed a distinctive, and for him 'euphonious', type of Australian speech: 'The children born in these colonies and now grown up, speak a better language, purer, and more harmonious, than is generally the case in most parts of England. The amalgamation of such various dialects assembled together, seems to improve the mode of articulating the words' (McCrum, 1986).

Another writer, W. S. Ransom (1970) spoke of a 'voice of that mixed accent which distinguishes the offspring of Dublin parents of the lowest class born in one of our great English cities'. The unified nature of Australian speech was emphasized from the beginning by the peculiar social conditions of the colony. Beneath the governor and the overseers, everyone was equal. It was a one-class society united in a mixture of hostility and nostalgia towards 'Mother England' and by the isolation of Australian life.

Charles Darwin, visiting Sydney in 1835, noticed that even the children of Standard English-speaking colonial officials were affected by the convict talk:

There are many serious drawbacks to the comforts of a family [in Australia], the chief of which, perhaps, is being surrounded by convict servants . . . the female servants are, of course, much worse; hence children learn the vilest expressions . . .

Apparently, says McCrum (1986), the Cockney element predominated. He quotes another early visitor to New South Wales as saying that:

The London mode of pronunciation has been duly ingrafted on 'the colloquial dialect' of young Australians. For some observers it was 'more harmonious' but for others it was noticeably different, even inferior: 'Pure English is not, and is not likely to become, the language of the Colony'.

Many Australians, in trying to get a better class of speech, turned their attention to the way announcers spoke on the radio, particularly on the Australian Broadcasting Corporation stations. When broadcasting arrived in Australia, the problems with 'proper' and 'acceptable' speech multiplied. What should the voice of Australia be? The *Sydney Morning Herald* newspaper, in 1932, had doubts: 'If Australians were to develop an accent of their own, there was no legislative power to prevent them, but the American production, as heard over the wireless, should act as a salutary warning'.

Until the Second World War, in fact, Australian actors and broadcasters were trained to play down, if not actually eliminate, all traces of their accent. Broadcasters were certainly trained to sound as British as possible. Then things started to change, in broadcasting at least. In 1945, the appearance of Sidney J. Baker's *The Australian Language* was a milestone in the emergence of a separate Australian Standard speech.

Just as, elsewhere, there are people who believe the 'British standard' is better, there are still Australians who are ashamed of the Australian accent, especially when heard on radio. Linguists estimate that roughly a third of Australians speak what is called 'broad' Australian; about half the country speaks a milder 'general' Australian and about a tenth use 'educated' Australian.

It was this 'educated' Australian speech, often called 'near RP', which was most acceptable on broadcasting stations. There was a basic change in Australian broadcasting in the 1970s, when the British accent gave way to the search for good, clear, pleasant Australian accents on radio and television in news and current affairs programmes, to follow what had already been happening with DJs. At the same time there was an attempt to change the news reporting approach in broadcasting from the old style BBC World Service type (declamatory and authoritative) to the more natural, friendly, pacy American style of newscaster and reporting. The accent that was preferred became a more natural Australian English form of speech regarded as distinctively and respectably Australian, instead of as evidence of colonial decline from the norms of the standard English of England.

Australian broadcast news began with radio people reading newspaper stories over the air. In the 1950s, announcers in commercial radio stations in small Australian towns would use their spare time when records were playing to cut out pieces from the local newspaper, and these were the scripts for their news bulletin. It was part of the excitement of radio in Australian small towns at that time. Newsrooms were what the local newspaper used. At the ABC, however, it was different. They had newsrooms, and journalists. The newsrooms were organized exactly like print ones, the journalists all were newspaper trained, and the listeners regarded this news as instant truth. If the ABC said it, it must be true. This was one reason Australia put so much emphasis on the news from the ABC, even though even it did not then understand that radio was a different medium to print. The question is: what makes the news on the ABC so credible and therefore so important to past, present and future Australia?

In the early days of news on the ABC, the authority of a news bulletin came not from the way the story was written but from the way the announcer read the news, in a declamatory headmasterly style. Often, the newsreader even stood up to read the bulletin. The ABC style was slow, deliberate, declamatory; a spin-off from the way the early broadcasters recognized the news as heard on BBC World Service. The commercial news style, of course, has always been different; faster, with shorter sentences and more familiar words. As radio grew, it became obvious to many broadcasters that there was a particular style of writing that suited the broadcast medium and that best suited the comprehension of the listeners. And just as importantly, listeners recognized there was a particular style of vocal presentation that suited them best. They found the news content, style and delivery more to their taste on commercial radio because it was more entertaining, more lively, and the sentences were shorter and easier to understand. However, at times of emergency listeners switched to the ABC to hear what the real news was. There was clearly something about the way the ABC presented and constructed its news bulletins that gave the listener trust in the truth of what was being said. Country listeners, of course, might have no choice; for them there was only the ABC, sometimes on shortwave.

Broadcasters slowly began to understand that the writing and the presentation of the writing combined to form a credible news message. With this understanding came a new approach, which allowed the new profession of broadcast journalist to transmit not just the message but also the emotion and the credibility of the message. The challenge was to make best use of the broadcast medium to provide truthful news, credibly reported. It wasn't a style related to drama, acting or public speaking, all of which sounded false and non-credible when reading news on radio. The style became personal; one speaker talking to one listener. The construction of the sentences became more colloquial and informal, because that was what listeners understood most easily. News reporters and newsreaders on radio (and later on TV) had to sound believable. They could certainly no longer afford to sound as though they were standing in front of a microphone declaiming the news like a town crier. New techniques had to be developed. The credibility of broadcast journalism also required a search for a special kind of voice, vocal delivery and voice quality that would be most acceptable to the listeners and, subsequently, the viewers of broadcast news and broadcast reporting. It also meant the development of a style of speech that would be acceptable and carry the right information, both in the presentation of news bulletins and the reporting of factual journalism on air. Broadcast journalism combines a specific style of writing and a specific style of speech to allow the listener to believe what is being said.

The news service of the Australian Broadcasting Corporation was the first and only news organization for many years to distribute a national news service. From 1939, when the ABC began collecting its own Australian news, and particularly from 1946 onwards, when it established its own independent news service under the requirements of the Australian Broadcasting Act, great efforts were made to present its news fairly, impartially and fearlessly. Over the years ABC news has been able to retain its essential credibility. Broadcasting began in Australia in 1923, several years before the BBC began in London. However, it was not until 1932 that the Australian Broadcasting Company started, by Act of Parliament. The start in Australia was purely commercial, as distinct from the debate that occurred at this time in the United Kingdom and America about radio's potential for serving purposes of state and society. The press of course, as elsewhere, saw radio as a rival, although at the start there was great excitement in Australia's wide expanse in actually hearing the news as distinct from seeing it in cold print. In Australia journalists were learning how to present the news. Walker (1973) describes how it started:

at 12.59 and a half, the warning voice came on telling all to get their watches ready for correction. Then came the stroke of one and the listeners checked their watches. Spoken slowly, and with emphasis, the news then came through.

Walker continues

on those terms it must have been a sombre and sobering experience. Many stations had arrangements to take what they wanted out of the morning and evening papers provided it did not exceed, say, five minutes. Thus, news up till the middle thirties was mostly just read from items circled by the announcer on duty – and often garbled.

Today things are different in Australia, and so is the sound. Newsreading journalists are now required to study presentation techniques suitable for radio; crisp colour reporting with the emphasis on now. Announcers do not, of course, all speak alike, and in the programmes as a whole there is even greater diversity of speech. In the various magazine programmes large numbers of people are interviewed, speaking a wide variety of local and class dialects. However, what the ABC and comparable broadcast organizations with a national and international influence have done is to make available a wide range of varieties of English for those who wish to study them.

BROADCAST NEWS STYLE

Apart from pronunciation and the peculiarities of voice quality, broadcast journalists, especially in news bulletins, have begun to develop their own particular and definable sound.

If listeners don't like what they hear, they won't listen, or listen only with difficulty for a short time. The object of good broadcast journalism is to get listeners to stay with the news for as long as possible. The language used in broadcast journalism therefore is of primary importance; it provides conversational, intimate one-to-one credibility in the transmission of facts and information. However, the language of broadcast news also provides for an additional aspect of communication that must be taken into account in its preparation: non-verbal as well as verbal language provides information. In broadcasting, news mainly consists of a number of short items of hard news gathered into a bulletin 3–5 minutes in length. Once or twice a day there are longer bulletins, perhaps of 30 minutes or more, to cover the news up to that time. These combine short news items with longer items, giving background to the news, interviews and packages of colour material. On a 24-hour general radio station, for example, only about 10 per cent of airtime will be given over to news bulletins. On television, the proportion is considerably lower. The significance of news on radio and television far exceeds the amount of time given to it; so much so that radio and television are now the major sources of primary news information for people in most western countries. The language of broadcast news is therefore of vital concern; it is important to get it right.

In broadcast journalism there are two distinct types of language used: prepared and *ad lib*. The prepared language is scripted, and can be a talk or a piece of news copy. The *ad lib* is exactly what it implies; a piece of unscripted, unrehearsed (to any great degree) piece of conversational reporting or speaking on radio or television. It can also, of course, be an interview, both questions and answers. The production of broadcast language is therefore a difficult and serious business for all concerned, and requires professionalism far in excess of that required to produce a daily newspaper. Broadcast journalists may have to shift without pause from direct announcing at the microphone to interviewing a newsmaker guest in the studio or 'down-the-line', to talking off-air to a technician in the control room. Of course there is also the problem uniquely associated with broadcasting; the need for broadcast language to be appropriate for individual newscasters to read aloud, trying to manufacture the language style to individual vocal styles and within the tight constraints of difficult pronunciation and familiarity of vocabulary for the audience, who only get one chance to hear and therefore understand the language. There are certain factors in the quality of broadcast news language that are essential to the transmission of the information. It is essential for journalists making the transition from print to broadcasting to be aware of and practise them.

It's the old copy taster's rule: if the first few words grab the attention, the rest will be fine. Miss out on those first few words and the story will never get published (or in old fashioned pre-computer newspeak, it'll be spiked). Clarity, shortness and colour are the three aspects that are needed to grab the attention of the reader and of the listener or viewer. Good broadcast language is made simple and listenable by the use of various formulas: unnecessary or complex information is deleted (details of place, age or time are done away with); generalizations are used whenever possible (a list becomes a category, e.g. *a dog, cat and canary* become *pets*) and lots of concrete verbal actions are used (making it essential that verbs are in the active voice rather than the passive). Rumbelhardt (1986) developed a *story grammar* specifying a set of rules that allowed a story to be generated and understood. He believed a story consists of a setting and an episode. Settings consist of a series of propositions (once upon a time there lived . . .). Episodes consist of an event plus a reaction.

Good broadcast language is full of soundbites, and is also full of sound effects that show the listener particularly that the reporter is 'on the scene'. These sound effects must also be considered part of the language of broadcast news. Without them the action is less memorable, credible or understandable. Good television language is also full of pictures. Pictures in television news are part of the language of explanation. They are part of the text. Television news lives by moving pictures, and both pictures and sound speak to the viewer. Pictures give news the appearance of authenticity, reproducing a version of reality without any filtering process. A news picture creates the illusion, without any words being spoken, that the viewers have seen something with their own eyes. The truthfulness of a text can be doubted; the truth of a picture is seldom questioned, although it should be – pictures can lie as well as a reporter. Pictures in the news do not just represent authenticity; they also communicate actuality. Television and radio news must be live, authentic and at all costs as close to the event as possible. Pictures and sound are additional parts of broadcast language that allow this to happen. The sound and picture language allows broadcasters to give the audience the impression that they are participating in the event. Correspondence of text and pictures enhances the communication of information in television news. Pictures that either exemplify or describe the news text contribute to the retention of the news text.

In contrast to this, standard news pictures (those from the library) that suggest actuality and authenticity but do not directly support the text have no positive effect on audience retention of the facts. Television without pictures is merely radio, and of course radio news allows the listeners to make up their own pictures because of the sound of the event. So pictures aren't as important to the news story as it would often seem, although for television news pictures are vital to differentiate it from radio or other forms of broadcast communication. In fact, the visual element as part of broadcast language, or the sound element as part of radio language, is very important. Sometimes it can be the most important element of a piece of broadcast journalism. In bad news, which forms the predominant basis of broadcast journalism, tragic and otherwise adverse events are considered newsworthy because they tell the viewer or listener about society. Victim reactions and comment are often laden with negative emotion and are an integral part of the television news ethos. The soundbite appears in the package or the news bulletin along with reporter narration and other visual or audio elements. They all combine to provide the language of broadcast news.

The language of soundbites conveys the human drama in ways that a reporter's verbal description cannot. Moreover, soundbites appear to make events seem more credible. They give authority to the report. They also serve to maintain audience interest because of their vividness, and they can add insight about possible causes and the impact of events. However, there are some broadcast journalists who are questioning the importance or need for what they call 'soundbite journalism'. The BBC, for example, has become increasingly uneasy about the use of soundbites in political stories. This unease is probably a spillover from the general concern about politics and political coverage. The soundbite culture has become a way of telling stories on radio or television that doesn't really advance the argument beyond the sound of someone speaking. The broadcasters like soundbites because they are given a ready-made, edited length for broadcast. The soundbites provide them with general statements that can be used across a variety of different outlets, rather than as a specific statement suitable for only one programme. They also give a chance for everyone to have a say in the shortest possible time. Politicians find them useful because they can push out their own easily digestible messages. Soundbites can only be part of broadcasting language when they are used properly and discriminatingly, when they add something vital to the report and advance the argument. Soundbites can be a loss of editorial control unless used carefully. They should basically be an edited extract of a longer interview, rather than just a prepared short statement given by the speaker. Soundbite language can take the policy out of politics; the meaning out of content. When used properly, though, soundbites are simply good quotes, and quotes are what journalism is all about. The language of soundbites is the basis of all reporting; they are the quotes that sum up an argument; the quotes that sum up someone's point of view. The more colourful, the more expressive the quote, the better the person is able to get a point of view across.

Length is an important aspect of soundbite language. Soundbites must be short enough to be attention-grabbing, but long enough to contain something significant. They must never become merely a piece of entertainment rather than a piece of information. They must never become the equivalent of the stained glass window telling the story of the Bible. The length and way soundbites are used in radio and television has changed over the years. In the early days of television, packages by reporters were almost unheard of. Newsreaders would read perhaps 15 seconds of script to wallpaper pictures, which would lead into a minute-and-a-half sound grab. Today the grabs are called soundbites, and are about 7 seconds long. They are considered very long if they are about 10 seconds; an eternity if they are 20 seconds. In 1968, the US Presidential election candidates got an average of 43.1 seconds of air time for each news appearance. In 1988, they got an average of 8.9 seconds and in 1992 it was 9.2 seconds. In the 1992 US Presidential campaign, 29.8 per cent of the total story time devoted to campaign news stories was soundbites. Politicians and other newsmakers were until then getting less and less time to put their case directly in their own words to the audience. Perhaps 8.9 seconds average in 1988 was about as short as anything can get and still be meaningful, which is probably the reason the bites were slightly longer in 1992. News items now have more and more moving pictures, and shorter and shorter sound clips. This is designed to make the news more interesting, the language more instantly identifiable without any thought. Digital technology makes it extremely easy to edit television pictures, and it is now very easy to cut, edit and assemble much more into the conventional news item. New technology has made it possible to use more images and to edit soundbites to a very short duration. The language of image is dangerously close to taking over the language of words, with contemporary communication of journalistic ideas increasingly relying on look and appearance, the careful choice of backdrop and the metaphors used to present ideas without language. Television is very keen on using these pictorial metaphors to illustrate the story without using any language; for example, the stormy sky or the rough sea when there is a stormy political debate. The language of the soundbite must not be allowed to move away from sustained political discussion to image politics.

Soundbites offer the viewer additional non-verbal aspects of broadcast language. They often feature prominent facial displays conveying strong negative emotions. Much of television news content places great emphasis on close-ups during interviews and in reaction shots, especially when the reporter is trying to capture emotional reactions to a newsworthy event. The demonstration of emotion, especially in the facial expression of adverse emotional reactions, may be considered imagery that compels attention and, presumably because it evokes an emotional response, is also remembered. Emotional imagery in a broadcast news package functions as a powerful addition to spoken language, and sometimes imposes a visual memory on the viewer more than speech. Of course, imagery can also occur in the actual spoken language used in broadcast news, and this too can have a heightened effect on the viewer or listener perception of a story.

Novelists and print journalists also use images in their language, as well as other narrative techniques such as plot, characterization and detail. The use of some of these techniques is in part driven by the desire to create a mental image for the reader, listener or viewer. It can be argued that even the shift in newspapers to colourful visual formats is an attempt to close the image gap between print and television. The more concrete the language used in broadcast news, the better the image. Listeners and viewers cannot imagine something abstract; they easily imagine something concrete. They know how big a jumbo jet is; they don't know how much 1200 metres by 50 metres is. So broadcast language needs to be as concrete as possible. This will be discussed at length in other parts of this book. In addition to concrete language, the way verbs are used also has an effect on the comprehension of a news story by the listener or viewer. Action verbs are particularly effective because they make the story more concrete and therefore more easily understood and remembered. Research has shown that concrete nouns in particular in broadcast language are more easily understood and remembered than abstract nouns, *dog* gives an image; *loyalty* does not, except as an expression of that image, for example, the loyalty of a dog. In fact it has been found that recall of concrete sentences has an almost two-to-one edge over abstract sentences.

In broadcasting, the journalist will also go for certain facts to lead with, followed by an explanation of the action of the event, adding perhaps some conflict or criticism, in as short a time span as possible so that attention is not lost. Together with the type of language, there are also other aspects in the construction of broadcast news language: time and place (the *where* and *when*); facts and figures; talking heads; a high rate of use of speech verbs (*say, tell, according to, announce, declare, refuse, threaten, denounce etc.*); direct quotes (which in broadcast language are often actuality speech inserts); and considerable use of modifying words such as *according to, speculation* etc. One of the most striking differences between print and broadcast language is the use of speech verbs. This often occurs in radio and television language by switching to the actual voice of the person being quoted; the link to the soundbite. Written texts often don't have many direct quotes, whereas in radio and television language there are many.

The most common broadcast language speech verbs provide greater variety and emotional content than the equivalent press reports of individual stories. Many broadcast language verbs occur in the present indicative tense. At the same time, they give the impression the story is being told in the participant's own words. In other words, in Goffman's language, broadcast language often gives the impression that authorship, principalship and animation are predominantly those of the participants, and the role of the radio or television reporter in selecting either the contents or the wordings is minimal. Another difference between print and broadcast language is the use of attribution. The difference in the amount of attribution between the two forms of language is striking; broadcast language requires a high degree of attribution, whereas newspaper language does not.

Another example of word use in broadcast journalism is the use of what are called stance adverbs. Adverbs such as *obviously, clearly, apparently, presumably*, convey something about the speaker's attitude towards the facts being reported. They also guide the listener and viewer towards a particular understanding, interpretation and meaning. In other words, they destroy the notion of objectivity. Some scholars attribute the lack of objectivity in news to the practices of language use itself and, more specifically, to the complex interrelationships between language and ideology. Like ordinary conversational speakers or politicians, journalists use various metalinguistic strategies to raise expectations in the minds of the listeners and viewers. Through their choice of vocabulary, syntax and discourse structure, speakers on radio and television make it possible to perceive and interpret objects and events in the world. In so doing they contravene the rules of objectivity, which ask the broadcast reporter to let the facts speak for themselves. Adverbs such as *unfortunately, importantly, happily*, express the speaker's attitude towards a judgement of some claim or event. Adverbs such as *certainly, obviously, clearly*, express the speaker's assessment of truth or reliability of a fact or claim. Journalists should not make value judgements about news content, good or bad. They do of necessity, because of the language used, imply judgements about the reliability of the truth or of a fact. In this way the listeners or viewers also believe, because they have been told it is true. In news, the reliability of claims or facts can be signalled with truth-oriented adverbs such as *obviously, certainly*. Similarly the uncertainty or unreliability of claims can also be signalled with adverbs that convey doubt, such as *presumably, supposedly, allegedly*, and by the use of the verb *claim* itself.

The language of broadcast news is therefore much wider in impact and interpretation than the words used. All news stories on both radio and television require the use of verbal and non-verbal language. This language can also be seen in the way presenters speak, and from their own non-verbal language.

THE LANGUAGE OF THE NEWS PRESENTER

The focal point of any news broadcast, radio or TV, is the presenter, the anchor, the newscaster. Presenters introduce the programme, read or introduce the stories, and are responsible for the smooth running of the show. Since the 1950s, when anchors emerged in their own right, they have become recognized as perhaps the most important ingredient of a successful news programme. They often become celebrities in their own right and command huge salaries on the same scale as showbusiness stars. Television, particularly in the United States, spends vast sums on research to find out if the presenters are right for the job. This is sometimes given more significance than journalistic ability in selecting the news team.

Among the major performer characteristics investigated have been the dress, facial expressions, gaze (eye contact) and sex of the presenter. Audience perceptions can be significantly altered by physical appearance. Eye contact is usually direct, because the presenter uses a teleprompter. One thing is certain: audiences for both radio and television are very unforgiving of presenters who make mistakes in their speech. All of these considerations have to be added to the formal language structure used by broadcast journalists to provide an end product that is clear, simple and immediately understood. The listener cannot turn back the page and reread. Coldevin (1979) reported that, following a period of monitoring news broadcasts in Canada, he had observed a number of different types of errors in news programmes, including slurs in pronunciation, repeated words or phrases, hesitation in responding to an on-camera cue, or looking off to one side of the screen when the shot returns to the studio from a report elsewhere. He subsequently conducted an experiment to examine the effects of mistakes on an audience, and concluded that not only the newsreader but also the programme suffered a severe loss of credibility.

Broadcast journalists now use many varieties of accent. Accent refers only to pronunciation, and can therefore be seen as the phonetic aspect of dialect. For example, expressions and words such as *it gars ye fash*, *ginnel*, *mawther* or *grouts*, though they are English, will not be readily recognizable to all English speakers. The first comes from rural Scotland, and means annoyance with someone or something; the second comes from Yorkshire and means a narrow passage between houses; the third comes from East Anglia and means a big, awkward girl; and the fourth from south-east England meaning 'what is left in a tea cup'. All of these are dialect expressions and are not easily understandable to everyone because they are not part of the dialect called Standard English.

On the other hand, if one of these dialect words (for example *ginnel*) is given national exposure in the voice presentation of a broadcaster, then it becomes part of the standard English knowledge (if not necessarily common usage) of listeners. This indicates the importance of the usage of language on radio and television. It also applies equally to the voice quality and accent of the unseen speaker on radio and television. To a wide enough audience, in the right way, an inherently unpleasant voice quality becomes acceptable and normal. Listeners then tend to forget the kind of voice they are listening to, and accept it as normal. It could be assumed that Standard English has become the most important of any present-day English class dialect. Standard English started as a London-based dialect in the fifteenth and sixteenth centuries, when London became the centre of all major trade and commerce, the Church, administration, literature etc. Quirk (1978) describes it as 'normal English . . . basically an ideal, a mode of expression that we seek when we wish to communicate beyond our immediate community with members of the wider community'. Standard English is used more for communication outside the family, beyond close friends and acquaintances. Dialect, on the other hand, is often kept nowadays for intimate circles.

There is, however, a cross-fertilization between the regional dialects and Standard English. Expressions and terminology used in other dialects have often been influenced by Standard English, so that even though grammatical constructions may be different the sense is still understandable.

For example, *he run*, as still used quite commonly in East Anglia, is not really any different from the Standard *he runs*. Indeed, in the Norfolk radio stations there are local presenters who would use such local phrases and whose voice quality is very different to the voice quality considered acceptable in northern England or London, or nearby Cambridge for that matter. Voice quality acceptability is highly subjective. Although there is a strong similarity of language used to describe the quality of voices played to focus groups, regional, national and international likes and dislikes clearly play an important part.

By contrast, whilst Standard English exists as a dialect separate from regional dialects, this doesn't apply to pronunciation. There is no universally acknowledged Standard accent for English, and in theory it is possible to speak Standard English with any regional or social accent. There is, however, one accent that only occurs with Standard English, the 'English' English accent, received pronunciation (RP). This was the accent required of BBC announcers; hence one of its other descriptions, 'BBC English'. This accent emerged as the closest nationally accepted form of speech as a result of many regional and social influences through England's historical development. In the past, broadcasters considered this accent to apply in Scotland and Wales as well. Now, broadcasting is giving rise to a new phenomenon: Scottish or Welsh RP.

Voice quality is one of the basic ways of attracting an audience, and by which broadcast journalists create the impression of authority and credibility. There are problems about broadcast voice quality and its adaptation of natural voice production to the peculiarities of the radio medium. If listeners don't like what they hear, they won't listen, or will listen only with difficulty for a short time. The object of good broadcast journalism is to get listeners to stay with the news for as long as possible. So what is it that will achieve, for the broadcast journalist, this end of conversational, intimate one-to-one credibility in the transmission of facts and information? There are, of course, stereotypical broadcast voices (for example, the 'laugh-in' announcer with smiling bass voice and hand cupped over ear). In the same way there are stereotypical vocal qualities that typecast other professionals: the 'fire and brimstone' preacher, the 'pedantic' academic, the 'caring' social worker.

One of the first mentions of voice quality seems to be by the sixteenth-century writer Roger Aescham (1570) when he wrote of '. . . a voice not softe, weake, piping, womanish but audible, strong and manlike'. Writers in the seventeenth century, while never approaching even a basic general description of voice quality, often noted small details about voices, such as 'hoarseness'. Wallis, discussing voicing and the larynx, says *the hoarseness which often accompanies catarrh originates in the same place, hindering this vibration of the larynx and trachea.* Kemp (1972) points out that the first three editions of Wallis's *Grammatica Lingua Anglicanae*, written in 1653, were worded slightly differently from the sixth edition, which was the basis of Kemp's translation of Wallis, and that the relevant passage in those three editions made the catarrh itself the factor hindering the vibration of the larynx, not the hoarseness accompanying it.

In his 'Essay on Elocution', Mason (1748) begins with some comments on using conversational voice quality in public speaking and reading aloud (storytelling, the precursor of today's broadcast journalism):

The only rule is to endeavour to speak with the same ease and freedom as you would do on the same subject in private conversation. You hear nobody converse in a Tone; unless they have the Brogue of some other country, or have got into the habit (as some have) of altering the natural key of their voice when they are talking of some serious subject in religion. But I can see no reason in the world that when in common conversation we speak in a natural voice with a proper accent and emphasis yet as soon as we begin to read, or talk of Religion, or speak in publick, we should immediately assume a still, awkward, unnatural Tone.

Brook (1979) says: *The invention of the telephone has introduced a new register to the English language.* When microphone technology was less advanced, broadcasters were taught to be over-precise in their pronunciation and over-projected in the vocal delivery. In any case, untrained broadcasters tend to speak more loudly than necessary, as many people often do on the phone. The characteristics of this kind of register are a raised pitch and increased volume. There is a stereotype speech acceptable in broadcasting programmes; another acceptable in news bulletins and programmes. BBC announcers do not, of course, all speak alike, and in the programmes as a whole there is even greater diversity of speech. In the various magazine programmes, large numbers of people are interviewed speaking a wide variety of local and class dialects. The BBC has made available a wide range of varieties of English for those who wish to study them. Apart from pronunciation and the peculiarities of broadcast voice quality, radio speakers, especially in news bulletins, have begun to develop their own register, which clearly modifies speech to indicate an attitude towards the subject or the listener. Voice quality changes in the radio context take account of the constraints of the medium upon itself and its listeners.

The younger the announcers, the more their speech varies from the accepted RP norm. This variation is the result of changes in language, the accepted norm being based on the speech of older speakers who are reluctant to allow change. Many American presenters, for example, have deeper voices than British ones, and this is very apparent in American broadcasting. There is little doubt that listener response in America to this type of sound is extremely positive. The question then is whether such voices are learned or natural; and by what rule of stereotyping does such a voice have the positive effect it does on American listeners? According to Giles and Powesland (1975), such voices are not due to physiology but to the fact that they have learned to use a lower part of their possible pitch range than have British broadcasters. It is, they say, cultural not physical. There is little doubt that such voices give the American listener a sense of credibility and pleasantness. However, it cannot be assumed that certain voice quality types are universally perceived as pleasant or unpleasant across different cultures and different languages. Indeed, say Giles and Powesland, there is some evidence to the contrary. Nasalization is a component of voice quality commonly associated with many unpleasant Australian accents, but it is also a feature of many pleasant RP speakers.

Modern broadcast journalists need to realize the importance of the way they speak, the way they tell the story. The language of broadcasting is connected with the visual and the vocal, and the three dimensions fit tightly together to express the meaning. Pronunciation therefore affects the message and has to be considered. Over the last four centuries, one type of regional pronunciation has a acquired social prestige. This has been geared to the pronunciation of south-east England, particularly London, and came about from the growth of Standard English due to politics and commerce, but particularly because of the presence in London of the Court. In 1589, Puttenham (in *The Arte of English Poesie*) recommended *the usual speech of the court and that of London and the shires lying about London within 60 miles and not much above . . . Northern men whether they are noblemen or gentlemen or of their best clerks use an English which is not so courtly or so current as our Southern English.* So the speech of the Court acquired an ever-increasing prestige and by the nineteenth century, through extensive use in the established public schools, it was being seen as the speech of the influential classes of society. Over the years it has lost its distinctively London characteristics, thus becoming social rather than regional. To be posh you now have to sound posh. Speech became a marker of social position. This pronunciation and accent was further regularized by the BBC, who considered it the best kind of speaking, a national example to which everyone should aspire. So powerful was the influence of the BBC that this became prevalent in other countries as broadcasting began there. In Australia, New Zealand, the USA, Hong Kong and Singapore there arose an accent called educated speech, which was basic RP with a few local modifications. RP is the result of inadvertent social growth, not a conscious decision or agreement to speak in a certain defined way, but the BBC, by choosing this form of speech, gave it a seal of approval that made it the national norm. Despite this, nowadays RP is not the exclusive property of any particular social level, precisely because in becoming national it also became more widespread. With the levelling of society itself and as a result of broadcasting on television and radio, which exposes everyone to RP, more and more speakers from all regions were influenced by this pronunciation – sometimes for conscious social reasons, but also quite unconsciously because the radio became the accepted social norm of authoritative speech.

Nowadays, local radio is redressing the balance. Local voices are being heard and the same broadcasting organization that tried to nationalize the speech of the country is succeeding in doing the opposite. Radio is now accessible to ordinary people. Some believe that certain accents bestow more prestige than others. Brook (1979) says, *Scottish and Irish dialects enjoy greater prestige in England than do the dialects of the North of England and it may be that the reason for that is that they are national and not merely regional dialects.* Wilkinson (1965) suggests that there are three level of accent prestige in Britain. The first class accents comprise RP, some unnamed foreign accents and forms of old Scottish and Irish. Second class accents, he says, could be the British regional accents, which may also have a hierarchy among themselves. The lowest prestige accents, third class accents, are those from some of the large industrial towns. There have been many empirical studies into the status and values of different accents as perceived by the listeners.

Experience in local broadcasting also suggests that there is a trend towards acceptability of local accents for broadcasting purposes, at least among the younger generations. In a study by Giles and

Powesland (1975) it also seems clear that the status once attached to BBC English has changed as social levels have changed. However, there is still a certain amount of prestige attached to RP in some regions in Britain (and of course overseas as well), even above the local accent of the region. These regions tend to be those relatively untouched by local radio, which still rely in the main on national radio for their broadcast sound.

When is a voice on radio acceptable? What should be looked for in regard to pitch, loudness, quality, speed? For many years it has been assumed that a so-called good voice is a matter of opinion and the judgement is rendered more valid when the opinion is a collective one. As soon as a person speaks, a sound emerges that is unique to the person producing it. The sound produced reflects the size and shape of the vocal tract, the anatomy and physiology of individuals. This creates an individual, distinctive voice quality, which enables listeners to recognize us and determine certain perceptions about us: whether we're tired, happy, sad, bored, drunk, young, old, male, female, sick or healthy. Once a listener tunes to a voice quality, it is simply accepted or rejected. Awareness of the broadcaster's voice quality affects interpretation of what is said.

Accent, pronunciation and the quality of the voice all give information to the listener, in addition to the basic textual message. They affect the way the listener receives and understands the message. The most obvious social information comes from accent. A particular accent often has a special voice quality associated with it, and the voice quality can thereby act as a partial clue to any social characteristics that are typical of speakers of that accent. Voice quality may serve as an index of features of regional origin, social status, social values and attitudes, and profession or occupation where these features characterize speakers of the particular accent in question. It can often happen in broadcasting as well as in other clearly defined social groupings. Everyone is a listener; an expert in using indexical information in voice quality to reach conclusions about physical, psychological and social attributes of speakers. Social status often denotes indexical labels, and the vocal correlate is usually the whole amalgam of the speaker's accent. Indexical labels of this sort include 'upper class', 'middle class', 'working class' and, possibly, such terms as 'superior'. Educational status labels often carry a connotation of social class, when people speak of an 'educated voice' or an 'illiterate voice'; and there is the further possibility that the aspects of vocal behaviour to which implicit reference is made may well be aspects of higher-level dialect choices as well as features of accent. Indexical labels denoting a professional, particularly when used as a disparaging comment on the sound of the speaker's voice, seem often to be concerned with features of voice dynamics and with extrinsic aspects of voice quality. Examples include: a lecturer's voice, a politician's voice, a schoolteacher's voice, a sergeant major's voice, a newsreader's voice, a DJ's voice.

Another category concerns the type of interaction involved between the speaker and listener, but still with the emphasis on the speaker, in labels such as 'the radio or broadcasting or newsreading voice'. There is also the effect a voice has on the listener (annoying, boring, calming, frightening, interesting, persuasive, soothing, soporific). The personality of a broadcaster may be judged by the listener not only on the basis of choices of vocal behaviour but also possibly on physical features over which they have no control. For example, a man with a long vocal tract and large vocal folds, with a correspondingly deep-pitched bass voice, may well have attributed to him personality characteristics of mature authority that have little in common with the actuality of his psychological make-up, purely because of our cultural stereotypes of 'authoritative' voices. This of course has vital implications for the best type of voice quality for the broadcaster; even though he may be only 17 years old and 1.5 metres tall, the unseen voice, the vocal personality, says differently.

The language of the broadcaster therefore gives the listener much additional information on which to base an understanding of the message text. It also tells the listener and viewer a lot about the speaker. As the broadcaster speaks, the story is conveyed with acoustic cues that identify the individual speaker. These cues tell the listener or viewer whether they like this reporter or that one. This appreciation of a particular broadcaster has little to do with the quality of their reporting, but is mainly to do with an impression perceived by the listener that this broadcaster is 'good' or 'not so good'. As they speak, broadcasters also convey their linguistic background. The vocal presentation also conveys the sex of the speaker in radio, or when a TV reporter is speaking off camera. Finally, the speech and language of the reporters also automatically convey their emotional state. There is little doubt that much of the meaning of speech is communicated at these levels. For example, if a reporter is tired, bored, or drunk, these emotional or physical states will be easily and automatically communicated together with the text. Listeners understand emotional cues, and the voice plays a major part in our intelligent appreciation of the language used to express the story.

It is apparent that each member of any audience receives a clear impression of the personality of the speaker. This impression is gained through judgements made as a result of the broadcaster's voice quality. Complex visual perceptions of physical build, posture, clothes and movements, in addition to auditory perceptions derived from speech and voice, make this impression seem accurate and complete. On radio the rich and informative visual pattern is absent; only the voice and speech remain. The resulting judgement is somewhat fragmentary and uncertain. This situation has already received popular recognition in jokes concerning the disillusionment of those who learn to their sorrow that the radio voice with which they fall in love does not reveal accurately either the appearance or the nature of its possessor.

It is clear that there are definite vocal characteristics that create either a positive or negative reaction in the listener. Identification of the characteristics means employers can have specific voices for specific tasks, knowing that they will cause either positive or negative listener reaction. The radio voices that create the most positive listener reaction are those that listeners judge to be lively, clear and resonant. These are the qualities employers should look for in the modern broadcaster; the voice print for radio listener acceptability.

Experimental studies on the effects of delivery rate in spoken informational sequences demonstrate that listeners and viewers need a certain minimum amount of time to understand what is being said. If the word rate increases too much, listeners rapidly stop understanding. Nelson (1948) investigated the difference in comprehension when a newsreader increased presentation rate from 125 to 225 words a minute. There was a reduction in comprehension. However, speed was related to listener interest. Slower rates made listeners lose interest, even though the slower rates made them understand more. Smith and McEwan (1974) compiled two 5-minute radio newscasts of exactly 800 words each. One newscast consisted of a detailed single topic message only, while the other contained 12 different and much briefer news items. A professional newscaster read each message at four presentation rates: 160, 190, 220 and 250 words a minute. Delivery rate was found to have a significant effect on understanding, and the point at which understanding decreased significantly was anything above 190 words a minute. The results indicated that a newscaster could vary rates of delivery from 160–190 words a minute without any loss of interest or understanding by the audience. The implication is that broadcast language consists of words simple and easy enough to say, so that the presenter can say them fast enough to be understood at that speed.

LIMITATIONS OF BROADCAST JOURNALISM LANGUAGE

Broadcasting is a wonderful medium for expressing the immediacy of news, but it has its limitations. Broadcast language can be misheard and misreported, and therefore easily misunderstood. Voice quality and the way broadcasters speak play a big part in solving this problem. The audience also plays a major role. One thing is clear: listeners tend to hear what they want to hear, and interpret what they hear in terms of what they think and believe. Broadcast journalists therefore have two basic problems: *non*-comprehension and *mis*comprehension. Non-comprehension means that an audience either gets no meaning from the news report or could not even remember it. Miscomprehension means that someone derives meanings that the text did not contain. As Jacoby and Hoyer (1987) indicate, it is possible to recall something miscomprehended and miscomprehend something recalled.

Listeners and viewers have a low degree of recall of news information. Findahl and Hoijer (1981) found that listeners recalled only 25 per cent of basic information heard in radio news broadcasts in Sweden. Van Dijk (1983), however, says that only about 20 per cent of pieces of information in a news story were later recalled. Gunter (1987) found that information received through reading the newspaper sticks much better than information received from broadcast news. Robinson and Levy (1986) believed that only a third of viewers in both the United Kingdom and United States understood the main point of the main stories in evening television news bulletins. Research indicates that recall of broadcast news can be as low as 5 per cent of the information, and rarely exceeds 30 per cent on immediate questioning. Listeners recall more stories when they are written clearly according to the *who*, *what*, *when*, *where*, *why*, *how* technique, and spoken in natural, conversational English. Listeners understand less the longer the sentence and the more clauses contained in the sentence. In other words, simple sentences have the most immediate impact.

What is important in broadcast language is maximum audience accessibility. Attempts to unite communicators and audience have been tried in many countries. The phone-in or talk show is one example. Mody (1986) described an experimental radio station in Jamaica under a United States agricultural aid programme. The station was designed to make the audience the source of the programming they would receive. Researchers were employed to convey local people's needs, and villagers were trained to collect local village news. Instead of scripting standard news bulletins, the station presented its information in an on-air simulation of the casual everyday exchange of news. It also used Creole rather than Standard English, which was the accepted form of broadcast speech. Similar experiments have been tried elsewhere. However, while such attempts may make the audience more accessible, they also reduce the credibility of the news. In any case, newsreading styles throughout the world tend to relate to their audience and respond to it. Otherwise people won't listen; they'll search for a more sympathetic style and approach.

The language of broadcast news must also relate to the target audience and respond to it. The style of news anchor and reporter tends to relate and respond to the perceived audience of the news bulletin. Speakers certainly shift their style to be more like the person they think they are speaking to. If they shift their spoken style but the language used doesn't shift in the same way, there is an immediate lack of coherence between what is said and how it is said. One result will be vocal mistakes. Bell (1991) suggests that communication strategies will sometimes be responsive to the listener or viewer, and sometimes initiative; that is, speakers often respond to their audience in the language they produce, but they sometimes take more initiative and use language to redefine their relationship with their audience.

The broadcast journalist repeats certain information on a regular cycle in the knowledge that radio is rarely the sole object of a listener's attention and that the audience comes and goes. In normal public communication, face-to-face, a speaker gets direct feedback, which provides the speaker with various clues as to how the communication is being received. In extreme cases, failure to interact will make the audience stop listening or go away. In broadcast communication, this is reversed. The audience has the power of choice, and the broadcaster has no real idea of when the listener will exercise that right. It is therefore important in all broadcast speech that the listener be constantly remembered, and wooed. Listening or watching signifies approval of the broadcaster's style and content. If the broadcaster is unsuccessful in keeping the listener, the listener decides what to do. If the style doesn't suit the listener, the listener shifts to a style that does suit. So listeners who aren't pleased leave; those who stay or come will be happy with the speech style. It is of course possible that, as a result of an unfortunate lack of enjoyment of style, the audience accommodates by switching off and the broadcaster finds that there is no audience at all.

Good newsreaders can consistently change style to suit the audience they are talking to. These changes occur most frequently in the speed with which the bulletins are read, the liveliness with which the news is read, and the colour and projection of the voice. Individual newscasters, and reporters need to converge towards a commonly accepted style of speech targeted at their audience. The journalists somehow have to achieve some consensus about what style is suitable for their particular audience. Individual differences are minimized and speakers tend to cluster around the station mean frequency for the variable, giving content to the notion of a station style designed for its audience.

Writing for broadcasting is an act of translation. The printed agency handout material is written for the page. It needs to be understood by the broadcaster and translated into spoken language. Simple rewriting is usually never enough; the language of broadcast news is different. Verbal simplicity is the mark of a truly educated broadcaster. Complexity is not clever. Simplicity of news language that the listener can understand first time is difficult and the mark of a true professional. In order to get the best credibility out of broadcast news language, it is essential first to truly understand, then to put the ideas simply, clearly, informally and conversationally. That provides the intimacy that is essential for conversational broadcast language. The first consideration is the listener. Writing in broadcast language is for saying, not for reading. It therefore needs all the components of good conversational writing and speech:

- clarity
- simplicity
- informality
- logic.

The other difficulty with broadcast language is the look of the words on the page. Broadcast writing should always be punchy, crisp and catchy (memorable on first listening) in both style and meaning. However, what might look punchy and crisp on the page might not sound punchy and crisp to the listener, and might not be said that way by the presenter. Making words look catchy and sound catchy are two very different problems. Language should be concrete rather than abstract. There is no doubt that the best form of language construction for broadcast news is the simple form of direct construction: subject–verb–object. Clauses only confuse, and sentences tend to have a weaker meaning when the verb comes at the end. This allows the listener to follow the train of thought and expressions logically and therefore easily. Additional clauses confuse.

Burchfield (1981) gives a neat example of the difference between spoken and written language, which all broadcasters would do well to take note of. He tells the story of a party of VIPs who were being shown round a new building in Scotland. The VIPs had two guides; the estates officer (who was a professional architect) and the doorman-cum-custodian. On reaching an emergency exit both guides spoke at once. The architect said: *That gives access to the exterior space*; the custodian said: *Yon door gies ootside*.

GRAMMAR OF BROADCAST LANGUAGE

Another problem in broadcast language is what to do about grammar. English grammar is a complicated system never quite mastered even by the best speakers of English. The best writers avoid grammatical solecisms by keeping clear of areas that contain problems that would reveal their own uncertainties about what and how to say something. Many attempts have been made since Anglo-Saxon times to produce an agreed body of rules governing the way English sentences operate. In the eighteenth century this became somewhat of a passion: grammarians analysed sentences into subject and predicate, clauses, moods and so on. The written language has to be considered as different from the spoken, and it is the spoken that forms the basis of broadcast language, and provides us with a language of broadcast news. The situation is further complicated by the fact that the kind of usage acceptable in informal broadcasts, such as unscripted interviews, is different from that desirable in formal broadcasts, especially news bulletins. There is also the problem of verbless sentences. In written English all sentences should have a verb, except perhaps in headline writing – at least that is the common belief. However, verbless sentences do occur in written language and are commonly found in good fiction: *Another sunny day. Still no letters.*

A further difference in the language of broadcast news is the use of the present tense for the future tense. The present tense in broadcast announcements, such as programme trailers, often replaces the future tense: 'at 8.30 we hunt through the archives in search of the odd and interesting'. Exactly the same occurs in broadcast news writing. Such substitutions are perfectly acceptable, both in the spoken and written language.

Another major difference between newspaper and broadcast language is the common use in broadcast news of contracted verbs to denote a more conversational sound: *can't* instead of *cannot*, and *isn't* instead of *is not*. While these verbal contractions are usually not accepted in newspaper writing, they are the norm in broadcast writing (although it is true that many journalists who have spent the formative time of their life in print journalism find it hard to change their style in this and in other aspects of broadcast language). The object of good broadcast language is to be clear, simple, understandable and therefore pleasantly credible. This can be seen in the spoken use of *who* for *whom*. An over-zealous search for correctness sometimes leads speakers to use *whom* in the wrong circumstances. In informal speech *who* sometimes quite naturally replaces *whom*. Thus a sentence like: *Who do they think they are?*, which is grammatically correct, leads to the perfectly acceptable (from the sound point of view) *Who do you think you're talking to?* instead of the very formal, and pedantically correct *To whom do you think you are talking?* One well-known literary example showing the informal substitution of *who* for *whom* occurs in the works of Bernard Shaw: *If it doesn't matter who anybody marries, then it doesn't matter who I marry and it doesn't matter who you marry.*

The language of broadcast news is very different from the language of newspapers. It consists of two aspects; the verbal and the non-verbal. The non-verbal, particularly on television, can incorporate meaning that may differ from the words being spoken. It is also evident that listeners and employers look for a good, fast pace of delivery (about 180 words a minute or slightly more), with an intimate one-to-one approach. The language of broadcast news provides a sound and authority in broadcast journalism that has to be cherished, treasured and preserved. One of the great problems is how technology and the sound will relate to each other in the future. Burton Benjamin had this to say in a speech to the Gannet Centre for Media Studies at the University of Nevada, Reno in 1987:

The good journalist is a treasure, and they won't be able to develop or clone him in a laboratory. The problem that television faces, in my opinion, is for the creativity to keep up with the racing technology. I don't care whether or not a story is coming via satellite, has been written by computer and transmitted by a correspondent with an antenna implanted in his head. If he can't write, he can't write: by satellite or quill pen. If he can't report, he can't report. And all of the technology in the world can't save him. There is so much at stake today that if we simply go with the technology, we are asking to be in trouble. There was never a time when . . . reporters who can write, report, analyse, ask the bright questions were needed more.

Radio and television are tools, and will be no better or worse than those who use them. The vocal tools for broadcast journalists are as important as the literary, journalistic ones. The ability to construct a news story so that its message is spoken with the maximum vocal credibility and conversational intimacy is of paramount importance. It's not a question of elocution or of speaking properly; it's a question of being able to report with the necessary authority. This means the necessary vocal quality and intimacy, linked with the right kind of language. Broadcasting is in the process of creating a language of its own, moving both speaker and listener back to the time of the preliterate storyteller, expert at speaking on a personal basis to each and every member of the audience at the same time. That vocal process of personal communication is now returning via the microphone. It is a question of being able to use the right language for the medium, recognizing that the literary language of print and the spoken language of broadcasting are equally proper; they are just constructed differently. With broadcasting language the wheel has turned full circle, back to the simple, unpretentious, personal intimacy of the storyteller as a means of providing simple and clear broadcast information.

FURTHER READING

Bell, A. (1991). *The Language of the Media*. Blackwell.

Blainey, G. (1982). *The Tyranny of Distance*. Melbourne.

Bliss, E. (1991). *Now the News*. Columbia University Press.

Breen, M. (ed.) (1998). *Journalism Theory and Practice*. MacLeay Press.

Brook, G. L. (1979). *Varieties of English*. Macmillan.

Dixon, F. (1975). *Inside the ABC: A Piece of Australian History*. Hawthorne.

Fang, I. E. (1972). *Television News*. Hastings House.

Fowler, H. W. (1978). *Modern English Usage*. Clarendon.

Giles, H. and Powesland, P. (1975). *Speech Style and Social Evaluation*. Sage.

Gunning, R. (1968). *The Technique of Clear Writing*. McGraw-Hill.

Gunter, B. (1987). *Poor Reception: Misunderstanding and Forgetting Broadcast News*. Erlbaum.

Hyde, S. W. (1991). *TV and Radio Announcing*. Houghton Mifflin.

Petersen, N. (1993). *News not Views: The ABC, the Press and Politics, 1932–1947*. Hale and Ironmonger.

Rush, J. (1852). *The Philosophy of the Human Voice*.

Shingler, M. and Wieringa, C. (1998). *On Air: Methods and Meanings of Radio*. Arnold.

7 The language of print: a style guide

cable fullier oftener promptlier stop your service badly beaten alround lacking human interest colour drama personality humour information romance vitality

Evelyn Waugh
Scoop, 1938

WRITING STYLE

Newspapers use individual house style so that they have their own way of writing and layout. Most newspapers and magazines have their own house style book, which new recruits have to learn. It's therefore difficult for a book such as this to give a prescription of style that will be common to all newspapers. Instead, this chapter aims at making generally acceptable stylistic points. The rest you will learn on the job.

There isn't much space in a newspaper, so the language we use must be:

- clear
- unambiguous
- to the point.

There's no room for too many words. Schoolroom English is not news writing English. The answer is to **write simply**, then what has to be said will be clear. And write it **short**.

1 *Go for shorter words if possible*
Sentences should be full of bricks, beds, houses, cars, cows, men and women.

| Call a spade a spade | not | 'an implement for' . . .; |
| a cat is a cat | not | a 'feline creature'. . . |

Some examples are:

near	not	adjacent to
now	not	at this moment in time, or at the present time
during	not	in the course of
before	not	prior to
because	not	in consequence of
save	not	effect a saving
from	not	as from
watched	not	kept observation . . . or observed
although	not	despite the fact that.

2 *Avoid little used or unusual words*
We should never try to show our readers how clever we are, or baffle them with our knowledge e.g. use 'meeting', not 'rendezvous'.

3 *Try not to use adjectives or adverbs excessively*
An adjective has its uses, when it is employed properly. A sentence with every noun preceded by an adjective is tedious and clumsy and loses its pace. If you want to shorten the number of words, see how many adjectives you can take out without damaging the meaning.

4 *Use shorter rather than longer sentences*
A sentence should be only as long as it takes to make the point, to tell the fact, the *one* fact, that is best per sentence. The longer a sentence is, the more complicated it becomes in structure and punctuation.

5 *Try to write in the active voice rather than the passive.*
'The boy told the truth' is far clearer and better writing than 'The truth was told by the boy'. The sentence is strengthened in the active voice, and the words are fewer.

6 *Keep punctuation simple*
Only use punctuation when the meaning could be in doubt. Punctuation that causes the reader to go back and read a sentence again is bad punctuation. If you find you've written a sentence with a lot of commas and semi-colons, split it into separate sentences.

In general, all your writing should be as informal and as conversational as possible. Conversational writing style does not mean being casual or indifferent about the words you use. The challenge is to convey precise messages using normal, informal language.

Don't use jargon. Government specializes in it; lawyers, doctors, academics, scientists have a language of their own. You have to translate this professional language. For example do not use:

1 'Water scientists will test for parts per million to see if the lead content exceeds government standards.' Use instead: 'The water will be tested to see if it contains too much lead.'

2 'Police apprehended the suspect after he fled the scene on foot.' Use instead: 'The suspect ran away. Police chased and caught him. He was arrested.'

Writing for impact

Sell the story in the intro. This gets attention, tells what the story's about and why it's important.

Tell the story in the body of the story.

End it with a conclusion that is memorable. The ending can do a number of different things. It can tell how to act on the information received, how to get more information; and when readers might expect to get more information.

The intro

The intro (selling the story) should be as universally interesting as possible. It should hook the interest by getting the audience to stop and read/listen/watch. For the intro, include:

- what is *new* about the story
- what is the *most important* fact in the story
- what is the *most interesting* fact in the story
- what part of the story will have the *biggest impact* on the most people, locally
- what does it *mean for me*?

The body

In the body of the story:

- make sure you cover who, what, where, when, why and how
- select which points or facts you will include
- select which points or facts you will leave out
- select which points or facts can be generalized in few words.

Ask:

- Does this fact have any real meaning for the reader?
- Does this fact contain valuable information?
- Does anyone (except me) care about this information?

Put related ideas and facts together. Look for a logical flow of thought and ideas. Make sure the body explains, repeats, amplifies the points made in the intro, and tie the elements of your story together with content-driven connecting or transitional words such as *but*, *still*, *so*, *regardless*, *and*.

However, be careful about using words like *meanwhile* or *meantime*, which are becoming clichés. They have their place in a story to compare the time frame from one event to another, but they are often used mechanically as a crutch rather than creatively as a tool to make transitions from one story to another. Don't do it.

The ending

Look for a logical end that sets the reader up for what might happen next, the follow-up; or possibly restate the ideas and focus of the story. There are various types of ending:

1 The Main Fact: this is a restatement of the main fact of the story, usually the fact you used to sell the story at the start. This should not just be a simple repeat, but should explain and expand the original fact as a result of what has been said in the body of the story.
2 The Additional Fact: adding a fact at the end can put the story in perspective. However, the new fact can't leave unanswered questions. It must be able to stand on its own while bringing the story into focus.
3 The Differing Opinion: when the story is controversial there are always at least two sides to the argument. If one side is making the news in this particular story, the other point of view can appear in the ending – 'Jones's lawyer says there's no way he's guilty.'
4 The What Next: your story concentrates on what happened today, but looking ahead is a natural way to end. What will happen next? What can we expect now? How will the people involved react considering today's developments? – 'Jones was sentenced this morning. His lawyer says: "We'll be appealing".'
5 The Twist: a strange, interesting, ironic or funny twist to the story. The end is a good place to put it – 'An hour later – Jones and the prosecutor were married.'

6 The Reader Information: sometimes it's important to end the story by giving your readers information they can act on – 'If you're interested in finding out more about the subject, call this number'.

Checklist for good storytelling

- What do my readers need to know to understand the story?
- What do they already know or not know?
- What will turn my readers off?
- What is the point of the story?
- Where does it start?
- What happened?
- Am I telling too much?
- What is the *one* thing I want my readers to take away from the story and remember?
- How can I sell this story to the reader?
- How can I stop them doing something else and read the story?

STORY ORGANIZATION

Every story is different, but there are some basic guidelines that will help. Start with a short, hard-hitting lead. Write a brief paragraph as the lead, which gives the major news of the story. Then write a second paragraph that will provide major points of the news event that would not have fitted properly into the first paragraph (you don't want to crowd everything into the first sentence of the story).

Then provide background. The third paragraph of the story, and following paragraphs if necessary, should provide background that will explain things for the reader. Background can come from someone you have interviewed, who might explain something; or from the reporter, to make the story clearer. Even fast breaking news stories need background paragraphs to explain what has happened before. For example, in a story about day one of an accident you might use these paragraphs to give some information about the number of similar accidents there have been at this spot in the last year. If there is more than one major point, use background paragraphs to wrap them all together. Then you can develop them in later paragraphs separately.

Present news in order of descending importance. Continue reporting news of the story using paragraphs in order of descending importance. Inverted pyramids (news point first etc.) are seldom constructed in order of time sequence (chronologically). When you want to write chronologically (from the beginning of the event to the end), you might prefer to use a different writing form (start with the latest news of the story, and then make a transition right back to the beginning of the whole thing – where someone was born, how the story started).

Use quotations. A good time to introduce the first direct quote is after you have given the reader the major news and background information. Get all that out of the way first, then introduce a direct quote. Separate direct quotes by using additional news, background and paraphrases of what was said. Sprinkle quotes throughout the story rather than string them together in a block. That's boring. Remember, quotes are useful because they let the person in the news communicate directly with the audience with a really exciting, interesting saying.

Use transitions. A paraphrase, a background paragraph, a paragraph with additional news or even a direct quote can be used as a transition to move readers smoothly and logically from one paragraph to another. Transition alerts the reader that a shift or change is coming. Transitions can occur in several ways:

- numerically: first, second, third
- by time: at 3 o'clock, by lunch time, 3 hours later
- geographically: in Midlevels, outside the attacker's house, Western residents
- with words: also, but, once, meanwhile, therefore, in other developments, however, and, but.

Do not editorialize. Reporters report the news and are the eyewitnesses to the news. Your job is to tell the reader what you saw and what other people said; what happened. You should not include your own personal opinions. If you think something is wrong, or bad, let someone say it and you can then report it.

Avoid 'the end'. News goes on and then stops. It doesn't have a conclusion, like an essay does. Readers should realize that although the writing might have stopped, the story goes on.

Adding life and power to your stories

Three key ways of improving your stories are:

1 Personalizing (telling the story through people, using their individual stories as examples of a larger concept)
2 Foreshadowing (telling the reader early that there is going to be a problem later in the story)
3 Using sidebars (to add something extra to the story without destroying the main story or idea).

Personalizing

This is not difficult, but means you must think about your story in a different way. Personalizing is using the human element. The story that is humanized jumps out and grabs the reader's attention. Try to humanize, give the 'people-angle' to a story, whenever you can. For example, if you are doing a story about a cutback in welfare money, talk to someone who will be affected, find out what they will have to do to keep living at the standard they are now. This is writing features through experiences; not telling about facts and figures, but using the facts and figures to show how someone will be affected by an event. Showing people's experiences makes the feature come alive. For example:

Jerry stretched out his arm. And closed his eyes and he prays. The white clad figures become a blur as the injection takes effect. The heart by-pass is about to begin.

Foreshadowing

This is giving the reader a warning of something that is to happen later in the story. Good reading gives enjoyment as well as providing information. The best enjoyment comes when there's suspense, so long as it is done properly, with due warning of what is to come. You have to give the reader hints about what is to come in a story. No one wants to read a happy story about someone, only to find in the last sentence that the person has died. The readers need to have some indication that a sad fate awaits the heroine. This keeps them reading. So you have to give some warning clues throughout the story; clues that suggest but don't give away the facts of the ending.

Sidebars

Sometimes you can't include everything you want in the main story because it will make it too long or involved. Not everything that needs to be reported fits comfortably under one lead. You may have a hard news angle and a feature angle. They can't both go in the one story. So you also write a sidebar, a second story that picks up one particular point or explains more fully. The sidebar is a simple device and allows you to break up a story if it is too long or complicated or has too many angles. Write a main story and give the reader an overview, then write separate accounts of other aspects of the story. This breaks the complete story up into manageable proportions.

For example:

- doing a football story: use a sidebar about the coach or one of the players.
- doing a story about pollution in the local river: a couple of sidebars about what kills fish, and about an old man who remembers what it was like before it was polluted.
- covering a speech: the main story might be the news of the speech, with several sidebars about reaction from people to the speech.
- a government meeting story: the main story covers the meeting, and sidebars cover public reaction, the reason behind decisions, history of events that resulted in votes, and public reaction to government decisions etc. The public needs to know the decision, the reasons behind it, and what other people think about it.

NEWS IN THREE PARAGRAPHS

Here is another way of thinking about how to write news stories. Try to do it in three concise paragraphs. Think of the lead sentence as containing two phrases. See each paragraph as three lines, each with a phrase no longer than one-and-a-half lines.

Para 1

The first phrase of the lead contains the most important facts of the story. The second phrase is composed of secondary information (often the attribution). For example, not:

Police Inspector Lee of the Kowloon Police Division said today that two 16-year-olds died of gunshot wounds sustained during a fight in Waterloo Road . . .

but:

Two 16-year-old students from the International School died of gunshot wounds during a fight yesterday in Waterloo Road, according to the police.

Para 2

This would then be important but not essential information to the story. In this paragraph you would give the reader some background information to understand the piece. You might have to explain some aspect of the story. This second paragraph can also be used to give names of sources or victims. The names of the two 16-year-olds, for example, are critical to those who are concerned in the story but not to the general reader, so there's no need to give the names in the first paragraph. If you don't name them in para 1, they have to be named in the first phrase of para 2.

The second phrase of para 2 is reserved for the attribution or background material that is not terribly important, e.g. other names, addresses and so on.

Para 3

Phrase one should in some way elaborate on the first phrase of para 1. If you don't have enough material to write more than one phrase about a story, you probably need to find another lead. The second phrase of para 3 can be used for background material or to identify a source of news more completely.

The first phrase in para 3 often elaborates on the story's first phrase in the lead with a direct quote, for example:

'Taxes must be raised in Hong Kong if quality of life is to be maintained', Legco member Joe Lee said yesterday during a debate on pollution in Hong Kong.

'Taxes have not been raised in the Territory since 1990 and budgeted expenses for next year exceed income by $X million dollars', said Mr Lee, who's been a Legco member for ten years.

'People in Hong Kong can kiss quality of life good-bye if more money isn't found to improve pollution and clean up the city', said Mr Lee who also unsuccessfully called for tax increases last year.

This para can also contain the rest of the story, and some background.

This does not mean, of course, that you can't start a sentence with an attribution when failure to do so would confuse the reader, or that there are only three paragraphs to every story. Para 1 could always be made into several. Third paras could be several if there is a lot of background, or there could be two lead sentences when there is a combination of important lead factors, which together would make one sentence too long. For example:

'Consumers will pay an additional quarter per cent sales tax on all non-food purchases from next year as a result of a new law in Hong Kong. The money will be used for a 5.5 per cent raise for police and fire-fighters', said Legco member, Mr Lee.

This story has essentially two leads: consumers paying more, and police and fire-fighters getting more.

An alternative approach for a major news story with more paragraphs could be as follows:

You should tell the reader:

1 The news and what has happened
2 The historical context (how it fits in with what's gone on before)
3 The contemporary context of the story (how it fits in with what's happening elsewhere, if it does)
4 The impact (how it's going to affect the reader).

Following these paragraphs detailing the facts of the story, more can follow, which readers can read if they are interested in getting the full picture. It works like this:

Parliament yesterday decided not to go ahead with a new anti-pollution Bill. [**the news**]

The unanimous vote was the third time in two weeks that Parliament has blocked a plan by the Prime Minister. He says the plan will go ahead anyway. [**the context**]

If the Bill does not go ahead, this will be the only developed country not to have such a law. [**the scope**]

The proposal would cost a lot of money, but taxpayers would pay only a small proportion of the full cost in implementing the Bill. [**the impact**]

After that you can write the rest of the story at whatever length you like, looking at major themes expressed in these first four paragraphs and developing them as necessary.

NEWS INTROS

There are two types of news intros: hard and soft.

Hard news intros

Summary intro

Everything is hung on it – all the facts. For example:

The Financial Secretary, introduced his last-ever Budget today in Parliament in an attempt to cut taxes and bring inflation under control.

This contains the six basic ingredients: who, what, where, when, why and how. This is a common news intro, but be careful it doesn't get too long and include too many facts.

Instant name intro

This is used when the person you are writing about is so important or so newsworthy that their presence is the main part of the story. For example:

Bill Clinton has just started his final State of the Union Address in Washington.

Delayed name intro

This is used when the person involved is not inherently newsworthy but has become so because of what they have done or said. For example:

A man accused of murder told the District Court yesterday that he had no memory of stabbing to death his lover.

General intro

This is used when the reporter, faced with a number of competing angles none of which seems very important or interesting, and which makes for difficult writing as a single lead, decides on a general angle. For example:

The Governor, John Smith, has presented a revolutionary package of measures to government aimed at getting his old age pension scheme approved.

The second sentence would then support this general intro with a specific fact or quote.

Single fact intro

This contrasts with the summary intro, and is used when one angle is particularly strong and needs highlighting. For example:

The Governor, John Smith, called his new pension package 'a revolutionary idea which must be passed' at yesterday's meeting of the House.

Dash intro

This is used when the main point can be covered very briefly. For example:

Inflation is on the increase – and that's official.

or:

Drinking harbour water can be fatal – so says a leading medical specialist in the Territory.

Personalized intro

Generally in news stories, we try not to use the personal pronoun 'I'. It suggests too much subjectivity (although it's fine in a feature or column). The personalized intro is the exception, and places the 'I' at the centre of the action. The journalist witnessing the event carries its own newsworthiness. For example:

I joined the terrified women and children as they moved back into Kosovo.

This is a feature intro with a byline.

Subjective intro

News often has the appearance of objectivity when, in fact, it is the journalist commenting. For example:

The new Financial Secretary has only been on the job for less than a week – but already he looks just the job to ensure that Hong Kong's finances will stay on track.

This is an opinion reflecting the bias of the paper or the journalist. This is a feature intro, not a news intro.

Punning intro

This is particularly popular in the tabloid papers, particularly in British papers like the *Sun* and the *Mirror*. It provides brightness to the copy. Names of TV programmes, stars or films and well-known conversational phrases are often used. For example:

'Bye bye' to 'Allo 'Allo as the TV comedy finishes.

Story intro

This is used when the unusual aspect can best be conveyed through a brief chronology of events. In this, the intro shows how good the use of 'There is . . . ' can be as an opening, and then moves quickly on to the narrative.

There were red faces among Germany's police yesterday. First they allowed four armed and dangerous criminals to cruise out of their high-security prison, having placed a car at their disposal, as well as DM 2 million in used notes. Then they lost all trace of them.

Soft news intros

Soft news stories have the news element at or near the opening, but the news is treated more colourfully and some of the rules of hard copy reporting are broken to provide a softer feel to the copy.

Direct quote

Starting with a direct quote 'softens' the story, as in this example:

'We might have to fix that before we open – can't have different shades of green there, it'll make everyone seasick!' That's just one of the worries for staff as they put the finishing touches to the new international art exhibit due to open tomorrow. Thousands are expected to come to the exhibition which is being held as part of Scotland's Edinburgh Festival.

Question intro

Beginning with a question mark softens the story, as in this example from the London *Daily Mirror*:

Heard the one about the bank robber who wore his balaclava mask back to front? When he pulled it down he couldn't see to point his

*dummy gun at the cashier and nearly died laughing. But it's no joke –
it really happened yesterday at a branch of Lloyd's bank in Luton,
Beds.*

However, please don't use question intros simply to pose a question:
'have you ever wanted to climb to the top of a mountain at night?'
Readers don't want to have questions thrown at them. They want
answers.

Delayed angle intro

Delaying the main angle is difficult to achieve, and needs to be
handled with caution. It works by arousing the reader's sense of
curiosity and will fail if the reader is not curious to know how it all
ends. It is best kept for when something unusual has happened and the
reader is kept in suspense before being let into the secret. For example:

*John's father never said much. 'Whatever makes you happy' was all he
said when John announced he was going to join the army. So John
joined up as a soldier, at the very bottom of the pile. That was 18
years ago, during that time he's seen the world; fought in many wars;
been married and divorced, and done all the things soldiers do. Today
his life changes forever, he becomes a general.*

Eyewitness human interest

The reporter focuses on a specific person before looking in more detail
at the story. For example:

*A small blonde-haired girl had an expression on her face that said she
could never cause any trouble. Her teacher looked on with quiet
satisfaction. She had helped to turn Gretel's life from misery to happiness
and now she is the star in a training video to help others to do the same.*

Surprise intro

Building up the climax softens the story, for example:

*At 60 mph, all you can hear in this car is the ticking of the clock. But
what else would you expect in the latest Rolls Royce?*

THE INVERTED PYRAMID

This is an old approach to news writing, which traditionally stresses the notion of having the most important elements at the top (all usually in the first sentence) and the least important (often called background) briefly at the bottom. It's a useful notion for stories based in the main on one source. However, for the vast majority it oversimplifies the writing and creative processes. News values operate throughout the whole story and background, and can occur anywhere in a news story. Sometimes when a story is unintelligible without any background information it will be better to put it higher up, even right in the intro. Make your news story a mixture of quotes (direct and indirect), factual details, background information and occasional brief analysis, comment, description. Each of these elements usually comprises separate thematic sections. Within each section news values apply: the most important comes first, the least important last. Instead of a single inverted pyramid it is better to think of a series of inverted pyramids, so a story might turn out like this:

- Lead: summary of story, expansion of the intro
- Second section: new source
- Third section: background
- Fourth section: return to source from intro.

So if you take a news story such as a murder, for example:

- Section 1: the intro with the details of an arrest
- Section 2: the response of the parents of the murdered girl
- Section 3: details of the three men charged with the murder
- Section 4: police reaction.

All hard news stories are built around the conventions:

- Factual details
- Dramatic content
- Quotes
- Reaction/comment/description/analysis.

QUOTATIONS AND SOURCING

Journalists always have to interview people to get information for any story, whether news or feature. The result of the interview is used in the story in one of three ways:

1 As a direct quote
2 As an indirect quote
3 As unattributed background information in your own words

When you interview for a story, you should use a mixture of these three methods of writing the story. Otherwise it will be boring. Direct quotes are useful to a journalist's story: they enable people to speak directly and talk for themselves. Indirect quotes tell what the speaker said without using the exact words.

Beware of pronoun ambiguity: when you use general reference pronouns in a quote (it, this, that) you often water down the quote and make the reader doubt whether the person quoted is actually addressing your point. When you have an effective word to quote, don't use the word in the text before your speaker uses the word. For example:

Flabbergasted doctors made a discovery that may save Joe's life – he has the same cancer. 'I was flabbergasted',
said Dr Smith.

Do not characterize the quote for the reader. Always leave the reader to decide what the quote means. For example:

'He never had a chance', his daughter said. Later, in an interview, she said with dignity, 'A lot of people . . .'

This quote has two problems: 'in an interview' and 'with dignity'. Don't use 'in an interview' unless you feel your reader will not understand that the comments came from the interview. Here, it's obvious, so not necessary. 'She said with dignity' detracts from what is obviously dignified comment from the daughter. Don't intervene to tell the reader how to think.

Where to put quotes

Quotes can be used almost anywhere, but:

- Never in the lead of a news story.
- Almost never in the lead of a feature story (although in a feature lead a quote might work best, but only sometimes). Learn what your editor likes (for example, don't try it without a really very good reason).
- Indirect quotes, of course, can go in the lead, followed in the next sentences by an expansion of a direct quote.

Remember: not everything is worth direct quotation.

Quotes can be:

- direct
- quoted partially (one or a couple of words)
- paraphrased
- used only as background information and put without attribution in your own words.

Direct and indirect quotes

Direct quotes allow people to speak directly. They talk for themselves. When we quote, we reproduce the words that the speaker used. We reproduce – not create – the words.

Indirect quotes tell what the speaker said without using the exact words. You might change the words only a little; the tense may change, and the viewpoint change from first person to second person. Indirect quotes may be:

- paraphrased
- in the writer's own words
- summarized, reduced to the bare essentials.

Direct quotes add a lot to the colour and credibility of a story. By using direct quotes you are telling your readers that you are putting them directly in touch with the person speaking. They are the words of the speaker. Direct quotes tell the readers that something special is coming, and they make the story look better and easier to read by loosening up a clump of dense type. However, the fact that someone says something does not mean it is worth quoting. Most of what you learn gathering the facts and background for the story should be presented as summary in your own words. Only when the direct quote is better than anything you could write, or comes from a source that is so important to the story that it must be quoted, should you use direct quotation.

Direct quotes add impact to a news story. They can bring the reader into direct contact with the action. They can add authenticity and colour to a news story; the firsthand emotion of a participant, the terror a mother felt for her child. When you hear lively, interesting, colourful and appropriate words, you will want to use them in direct quotes.

Indirect quotation can be close to the speaker's words, or a broad paraphrase. It is the substance of what the speaker said put into your words.

Indirect quotes add information, allow the journalist to bring the source of confirmation into the story and give the story authenticity and credibility.

What to quote directly

Crisp, clear, dramatic, meaningful quotes give a story more interest. However, don't have too many. You need some direct quotes, but you also need to have the confidence to recognize what is worth quoting directly. Look for:

1 Unique material. If you can say: 'I've never heard that before,' it'll often make a good quote because your readers probably won't have heard it either. But don't quote it all, or at length. Look for the core of the quote, and use that, not all the rubbish that usually comes with the really interesting quote. There's a famous quote from a movie star. She was asked how she felt about playing the dumb blonde. She said: *I'm not offended at all because I know I'm not dumb. I also know I'm not a blonde.*

2 Important quotes by important people. If I say: *Something must be done about unemployment*, who cares. I'm not important and no one wants to know what I feel about unemployment. But if the Governor says it, then it's news and should be quoted directly. Generally, look for good quotes from public officials or well-known personalities in news stories and features.

3 Accuracy. Accuracy in direct quotes is the main thing. You can only use the exact words in a direct quote. You don't have to use them all, but the words you use must be exact.

Fragmentary quotes

These are partial quotes; a word or phrase of direct quotation dropped into a sentence. Some examples:

The 'element' he was referring to consists of young adults who, he said, 'run around with almost no clothes on' and use 'terrible language.'

Several proposals were discussed last year as a 'minority bill of rights', but never voted on.

Pollution, it was found, was 'highly concentrated' in Mongkok.

If the speaker's words are clear, concise and informative, you can use the full quotation. If not, paraphrase.

Avoid putting quote marks around single words used in their usual and ordinary sense. For example:

Fire officials said they suspect 'arson'.

Parenthetical insertions

Too often journalists use incomplete or vague direct quotes, and try to patch them up by inserting missing words or phrases in parentheses. For example:

'We intend to force them (the laws) through parliament', Smith said.

'They (private donations) are the difference between a good and great hospital', Clarke said.

If direct quotes need to be patched up, like this, they aren't worth using. The parentheses are awkward because they are intrusive. They stop readers in their tracks. The best way is to turn the awkward or incomplete quotation into indirect quotation, and work in the missing material or explain the vague reference. For example:

The law will be forced through parliament, said Smith.

Private donations make the difference between a good and a great hospital, Clarke said.

Remember: direct quotes should be used when the speaker says things in a more forceful, interesting, direct or unusual way than could be achieved by a paraphrase or a summary. If the speaker's words are garbled, unclear or the syntax is awkward, then don't try a direct quote, paraphrase.

Redundancy

In presenting a summary followed by direct quotation, avoid unnecessary repetition or awkward redundancies. It wastes space to tell readers the same thing in only slightly different form in successive paragraphs. For example:

If the firms were to be found guilty at the trial, the door would be open to bring criminal charges against the top executives. 'If the corporation is found guilty, the next logical step may be to prosecute on individual responsibility', the prosecutor said.

Getting rid of the redundancy it would read:

If the firm were to be found guilty at the trial, the door would be open to bring criminal charges against top executives. 'That would be the next logical step', the prosecutor said.

Transitions

Many news stories include only one or two quotes. The quotes are used to add emphasis or to lend support to a summary, and may be attributed or not. It is easy to work the quotes into the story if you begin with an indirect quote and follow with a simple direct quote. The indirect quote is a transitional device that bridges the gap between what went before and the direct quote. For example:

Robert Smith, owner of Bob's Fish Shop, said bad prawns are only a small problem in the fish business. 'Out of a thousand prawns, we might get one that's bad', he said.

Alternatively, the first sentence identifies the speaker and introduces his or her ideas or views. The second sentence gives the speaker's views, specifically and precisely in his or her own words. For example:

According to both parents their son is doing very well since he started going to the new school. 'He's beginning to read and write well,' his mother said.

Or there may be an indirect quote followed by a direct quote, followed by an explanation for the reader. The indirect quote makes it clear who is going to speak about the figures and gives a couple of specific examples. Then the direct quote tells the reader what the figures mean. There is continuity of thought, and the direct quote is introduced smoothly into the story. For example:

The reduction in interest rates is already being felt in the housing market.

After a slow winter, sales are beginning to pick up, according to Henry Lee, director of the Happy Estate Agency.

He quoted statistics compiled by his organization that reflect daily transactions by 39 real estate firms.

Lee said that in the past two weeks, his office has seen from seven to 13 contracts a day compared with three to five earlier this year.

'Right now the housing market in this area is very good', he said, 'sales are about 20 per cent above last year's.'

Mortgage rates peaked at about 8 per cent earlier this year; the current rate is 6.5 per cent.

When you are writing a story in which several speakers are quoted, always use a transitional paragraph of summary or an indirect quotation to introduce a new speaker.

The summary in the writer's words provides the narrative and prepares the reader for the direct quotations. For example:

Mrs Lee chased the men for several blocks, stopped them, and started hitting one of the robbers who had her necklace. 'He really started begging me to stop when he saw my handbag', she said.

Don't just throw direct quotes into the story. Set them up, prepare the reader. Let the reader know who's going to talk, and give some indication of what the speaker will talk about.

Some direct quote examples

1 Quotes that put words together in an unusual way.
2 Quotes that emphasize or highlight a point. For example:

For breakfast, Andy eats a banana, a pear and an apple plus vitamin pills and 'various herbal compounds'. 'It tastes like a mouthful of sand,' he says. Then he swims before going to work. At midday he does more work in the gym. Dinner is steak and a baked potato, 'with only a small bit of sauce', vegetables, and lettuce. And a multi-vitamin pill 'to cover anything I've missed'.

3 Quotes that give a concise, telling story. For example:

The friends of Hong Kong socialite Mrs Williams are still talking about the 'absolutely unique' 35th birthday she gave last month. It was a costume party. Arriving in costume meant that all 38 people invited to the lunch had to dress in outfits costing less than $150.

'Some people thought we should have set the limit at $100 and really made it tough', explained Mrs Williams. 'But I was afraid if I

did that, no one would have taken it seriously. If the limit was $100, a lot of them wouldn't even have tried'. As it turned out, Mrs Williams said, all of her guests were real troupers. 'These are women who spend more than $150 on their hair alone. They just don't have suitable things in their wardrobes, so they went out and shopped at places they'd never shopped at before', she said. 'They were so clever and original.'

When to paraphrase

You can use someone's information without quoting simply by summarizing what the person said or by paraphrasing without quotes.

Attribute information when:

- the person is an expert ('The Treasury Secretary announced')
- the person makes an unusual claim ('Mary Smith saw three cats climbing a tree together')
- the person is identified specifically with an idea ('Einstein's theory')
- someone makes a personal attack or a criminal charge ('Police say they have charged...').

Lazy reporters will quote too much of a person because they haven't checked the story out. You should be selective in the quotes you use. Too many quotes detract from the really good ones.

Always summarize or paraphrase when:

- you can make a statement or clarify a thought better than your interviewee. Explain a theory in simple words.
- you can verify the information from several different sources.
- the speaker talks about generally known information in common language.
- you are writing about statistics or dates (if you read the report, you can say what it says without quoting someone) or if you see something happen (then it happened and you needn't quote).
- what you are quoting is authoritative but unclear (things like government reports, which use difficult jargon as common language); don't quote the jargon, explain and paraphrase.

Speech phrase order

The speech phrase is nothing more than the subject and verb of a normal English sentence: for example, '*She said* she intends to run for office next year'.

Normally it is best to stick to the subject–verb word order in speech phrases just because it is normal word order, as in:

- Smith said
- The Governor said
- The mayor said.

There is generally no real reason to reverse this order. Usual word order helps readers. Unusual word order makes them slow down and sometimes it confuses. There is no reason in this sentence why the speech tag word order is reversed: ' "It was what we wanted and what we expected", said the speaker'. It would be better to simply make it: '. . . the speaker said.'

Sometimes there *is* a good reason for changing this word order. For example:

'Frankly, this looks awkward,' said John Smith, senior manager of the publishing company, 'and I don't like being put into awkward situations.'

Or:

'Frankly, this looks awkward,' John Smith said, 'and I don't like being put into awkward situations'. Smith is senior manager of the publishing company.

Nonsense speech phrases

Avoid nonsensical verbs in speech phrases. No one is able to laugh, cry, chuckle or gasp a coherent statement – ' "I just don't know the answer to that one," he frowned' (frowned????).

Stick to 'said', or perhaps 'replied'. Of course, if a frown is significant, then use it:

Smith paused and frowned. 'I just don't know the answer to that one,' he said.

Speech phrase positions

The speech phrase preceding the quote

These are sentences that follow the normal word order of subject–verb–object. These quotes put the speech tag first and the quotation second. For example:

A Navy spokesman said, 'no one was killed'.

Indirect quotations can also follow this word order:

He said Hong Kong is continuing to grow.
The governor said he does not believe China will do anything difficult.

The word 'that' often appears in these indirect quotations as a connector between the speech tag and quotation, for example: 'The governor said that . . .'. This connector is optional and is frequently omitted when the sentence is clear without it; 'that' is more often omitted than included.

The speech phrase following the quote

In news writing this is the most common form of usage. For example:

'I would hope that passports are sorted out,' said the Prime Minister.

This word order is also often used in indirect quotations:

The low rainfall in February isn't unusual, according to the weather bureau.

Never use the inverted *'said he'*. You can say: *said the Prime Minister*; or *said John*, but never *said he* or *said him*.

The speech phrase placed within the quote

This is also normal and acceptable grammar, and happens when the quote is a complete sentence that can stand by itself. The speech tag is placed at a natural break in the quote, often between the subject and verb:

'But,' he added, 'Our city's too big.'

'My first love,' she whispered, *'is Hong Kong.'*

Again, *never* say 'whispered she' (except maybe in a poem).

The speech phrase inserted immediately after the verb

This can be done in either direct or indirect quotation, for example:

'He did not shoot', he said, *'because there were too many people around.'*

The speech phrase inserted between two sentences

Here the quote consists of two sentences joined by a linking word such as *and, or, for, but, so*. For example:

'Well, he told me to go there,' she said, *'but he wasn't there.'*

'Audiences are used to it now,' she said, *'so we'll have to do something else.'*

Extended quotes

In news stories it is often necessary to use several sentences of direct quotation in succession. For example:

'I love him,' she said of her husband, *'he is a very important part of my life and has been for 25 years.'*

Sometimes one speech tag can do for two sentences, if it comes no later than the end of the first sentence:

'Last night we had some excellent food,' Susan said. *'For lunch the other day we had soup. This is my favourite place to eat out.'*

You can also use this kind of quote to introduce a whole paragraph of direct quotation. In such cases, however, the speech tag often ends with a colon and the direct quote is put in a separate paragraph:

The governor made the same observation about budget growth:

'I wonder when people are going to get angry. Budgets and taxes can't continue to grow at this rate.'

Verbatim texts or long excerpts from texts that run over many paragraphs are generally introduced by a speech tag such as

The text of the governor's statement: [followed by the full statement].

Extended quotes may run over two or three paragraphs but still need only minimum attribution. Note how in the next example the single speech tag in the first paragraph manages to support two full paragraphs of direct quotation:

'Sleep is much more of a problem with old people than with children', he said, 'A sleepy child will crash out anywhere, but older people just don't have the need to sleep as much so find it more difficult.

'Even a not very caring parent will try hard to get kids to go to sleep. No one will do that for an old person.'

Note: there are no quote marks at the end of the first paragraph. There are opening quote marks at the beginning of the second paragraph, but the closing quotes come only at the very end of the entire quote.

Checklist

1 Complete sentences make the best quotes. To be useful, a quote must be a complete thought.
2 Don't use parentheses within a quote when the quote cannot stand alone.
3 Be sure the major point of a sentence is entirely quotable.
4 Beware of pronoun ambiguity: when you use general reference pronouns in a quote (it, this, that) you often water down the quote and make the reader doubt whether the person quoted is actually addressing the writer's point.

5 When you have an effective word to quote, don't use the word in the text before your speaker uses the word.
6 Do not characterize the quote for the reader. Always leave the reader to decide what the quote means.

Attribution and sourcing of quotes

To give credibility to news adequate attribution is a necessity in most news stories. Every news story should include enough attribution to assure the reader, viewer or listener that the story is accurate and believable. Attribution should be subordinate to the facts of the story. Attribution that becomes bigger than the information the story is intended to convey damages the story by confusing the reader as to what is important. A three or four paragraph story with attribution repeated several times is a weak story. Excessive attribution wastes precious news space, and is seldom necessary in the lead to a story. This is particularly true when adequate attribution will follow in the body of the story.

In routine news stories, one attribution may be enough. For example, in a brief story about a traffic accident, 'police said' used once will probably be enough to support the story. The attribution should come after the lead, probably in the second and no later than the third paragraph. Get the attribution into the story before the reader starts to wonder where the story came from. Attribution in the lead is necessary when the source of the story is as important as or more important than what is being reported, e.g. 'President Clinton said today'. Attribution is a must here because the source determines the importance of what is being reported.

Not all stories need specific attribution, sometimes it is implied. Brief stories, for example the announcement of a special meeting or speech, may be acceptable without attribution. You do not have to attribute information to a source if one or more of the following is true:

● the information is a matter of public record
● it is something generally known by people
● it is available from several sources
● you are the eyewitness
● it is easily verifiable by people

- there are no assumptions
- it contains no opinions
- it is not controversial.

Anonymous sources

Sometimes we use a source for a story who, for excellent reasons, should remain anonymous. Anonymous sources should be used as infrequently as possible (everything should be 'on the record' wherever possible); when you do use them, you must attribute somehow. Try to preserve your credibility as a journalist by giving as much information as possible about the source without identifying it. For example, 'a source close to the governor said'.

Sometimes you may have to change someone's name for a good reason. Then you *must* tell readers that the name you are using for a quoted source is not the real name: 'Li – not his real name – said . . .'

Editing quotes

Direct quotes represent the exact words of the speaker, not the words of the reporter. This means you report what the speaker said exactly the way the speaker said it. But what if the speaker uses loose or awkward syntax, makes a mistake in grammar, or gets so wrapped up in pronouns or references that the meaning gets lost? Or you are translating from one language to another? The easiest solution is to use indirect quotes, when you can paraphrase. Put the quotes in *your* words – paraphrase – so you can straighten out or simplify the message. Leave out the bad bits. No one ever has to be quoted directly.

If the quote is a good one, then edit carefully and fairly. Unless you want to be unfair and show what a fool the speaker is (and we should never want to do that), you should always correct the grammar. We all speak colloquially, and the spoken language is not as precise and formal as the written language. Fix up colloquialisms that look strange on the page, and which might be fine in speaking but less acceptable in writing.

The quote marks tell the reader that what is said within them is not only what was said, but what was meant.

When editing quotations:

- quotations must be accurate
- never make up quotes and never change them
- never take quotes out of context; this may change the meaning
- never add quotes to one another if taken at different times; they may be out of context.

Identifying people

People must be identified clearly and accurately. Don't misspell names, for example. Know who people are, and ask them to spell their names for you.

Sometimes age is used as an extra identification, as in police stories. In most news stories, identify a person only once. However, don't use sexist identification of people (e.g. 'a woman') unless it adds significantly to the story. (Be warned about the: 'Woman does something for the first time' story. We're past that.)

TENSES

News stories about events that have already taken place are written in the past tense and call for active verbs. When you write in the past tense, you must couple the verb with a time element – for example, 'The speech continued on Tuesday'.

Some news stories contain no specific time references, such as feature leads or feature stories that put more emphasis on the story and less on timeliness. This is also true of stories about past events, where the fact that something has happened is important, but the exact time is not known or is relatively unimportant. For example, 'The Prime Minister has announced...'

When you use the present there is no need for time references ('The Prime Minister says ...'). Timeliness is sometimes emphasized by use of the present tense.

Stories about events that will happen (coming events) require specific time elements, both day and hour, as well as a different form of the verb. For example, 'will meet at 3 o'clock'. Future is usually expressed by the use of the auxiliary verb 'will'. Sometimes, however, you can use the present tense to imply the future: 'The team leaves tomorrow for the United States' or 'Legco meets tomorrow...'.

Normally, the main verb in the sentence determines the tense of the verbs that follow. For example, 'He tried to do a good job but failed' or 'he does a good job but fails'.

The verb in the second clause generally follows the first verb's tense, but not always. It depends on the meaning expressed in the second clause. For example, 'The governor said that Hong Kong *was* rapidly becoming overcrowded'. Here, the meaning is not that Hong Kong *was* becoming overcrowded but now it isn't any more. It's a past statement about a continuous event still happening. The governor is referring to the present, so the second clause should be in the present or future tense: 'The governor said that Hong Kong *is* becoming overcrowded'.

STORY BACKGROUND

Background to a story makes the story meaningful to the reader. It is the reporter's job to make sure that sufficient background is given in a story to let the reader understand what is going on. The skill of the reporter – and the sub-editor – is to give just enough information so that the average reader won't be weighed down with too much information. Usually one sentence will be enough in a normal length story (by normal length story I mean about five or six paragraphs). However, don't delay the news by giving the background. It's what's happening that readers want to know about.

The way to construct the story would be:

- para one: the news point
- para two: fuller info or quote to support the news point
- para three: background as to why the story is important.
- para four: pick up the news event again
- para five: what's going to happen next, or what it means.

Background is better for a story than interpretation; interpretation runs the risk of introducing too much opinion or bias. So, explain as you go along. Background can also be added for interest. A few extra words of detail add bite to a story. Instead of simply referring in a story to Tiananmen Square, add a few words to remind the reader that that's where the riots took place and when.

Story treatment

For hard news stories it is usually best to simply give the news hard and fast; what has happened. However sometimes, for variety, it can be done a little more like a story. For example:

Several soldiers were hurt yesterday in a landmine explosion in the New Territories.

They were following a 14-year-old boy who later admitted that he had planted the explosives.

The soldiers said he was a 'cute little guy' who hung around the camp gate asking questions. They had talked to him and answered his questions – on explosives.

Or:

Gurkha soldiers at a camp in the New Territories thought that the friendly 14-year-old boy was a 'cute little guy'.

He would hang round the camp asking questions.

The Marines told him what he wanted to know – about explosives.

Then one day the boy led a number of the soldiers into a minefield outside the camp – a minefield he had laid himself.

Some of the Gurkhas were hurt.

The boy, caught later, said he had been tortured by the triads to make him do it.

The source of news reports can also be delayed. For example, it is not always necessary to say right at the top that this is a court story:

Golfer Joe Bloggs lost his temper, took a swing – and broke a policeman's jaw.

It happened between the eighth and ninth holes on the Sydney golf course.

Bloggs, a 42-year old accountant of Paddington – a 'fairly quick golfer' – was playing the course behind Sergeant John Smith.

And Bloggs told the sergeant: 'Get a move on, you're slowing us up'.

The sergeant said: 'We can't go any quicker because of those chaps in front'.

Then, Mr K. Lawyer, prosecuting, told the magistrates court yesterday, the sergeant received a 'hard blow'.

He was taken to hospital with a broken jaw, concussion and amnesia. He has lost six weeks work, but is expected to return on December 1st.

Bloggs later told police Sergeant Smith had tried to throw him: 'I was out for a game of golf not a punch-up. I stepped back and hit him once'.

FURTHER READING

Bagnall, N. (1993). *Newspaper Language*. Focal Press.

Giles, V. and Hodgson, F. W. (1996). *Creative Newspaper Design*. Focal Press.

Hamlett, T. (1998). *TYR Style Guide*. HKBU.

Hodgson, F. W. (1993). *Modern Newspaper Practice*. Focal Press.

Hodgson, F. W. (1998). *New Subediting*. Focal Press.

Hough, G. (1994). *News Writing*. Houghton Mifflin.

Itule, B. and Anderson, D. (1997). *News Writing and Reporting for Today's Media*. McGraw-Hill.

Keeble, R. (1998). *The Newspaper Handbook*. Routledge.

Laakaniemi, R. (1995). *Newswriting in Transition*. Nelson-Hall.

Mencher, M. (1991). *News Reporting and Writing*. Dubuque.

Stone, G. (1992). *Newswriting*. Harper-Collins.

8 Writing features for print

News is the story. The feature is the story behind the story.

In a feature you let your imagination flow around the facts. There are two kinds: news features and timeless features. The news feature is usually written to a tight deadline associated with the news story, and will probably be a sidebar to the news story. It can appear as a 'follow up' to the news story, perhaps the next day. The timeless story does not have to be used immediately and can sometimes take several months, but it still needs a 'peg' for it to be written or published.

Sources for features include records, contacts, interviews and newspapers.

STRUCTURE OF A FEATURE

Every feature has:

- a focus (what it's about)
- a lead
- the body of the story
- an ending.

First organize your thoughts, which will give you the focus for your story. Do this before you do your detailed research, otherwise you won't know what you're looking for. Then decide:

- what is the story
- what is the lead
- what facts will go into the body of the story
- what is the ending.

The focus

The focus must be specific, not general (e.g. 'Jenny the ship cleaner' ... not 'A story about the Navy'). The focus must make readers comfortable with the subject of the story, making it easy for them to see the word picture you are painting. Having decided on the focus and the story, and having got all your facts organized in some kind or order, you then think about writing.

The lead

You always look for a new angle on an old story, a new twist, a different way of saying something. Unlike a news story, where the lead usually writes itself, the lead for a feature story is something that has to be searched for. It's got to be different. Unlike a news story, where the lead will certainly be one sentence, the feature lead may require several sentences. After all, you can afford to take longer because the story will be longer. It often needs 'setting up'. For example:

1 *Jenny never set the world on fire. But for more than half a century she was one of the best known people in Hong Kong.*

2 *Up on the thirty-third floor of City One there's one of the most active men in Shatin. He's 98 – or at least he thinks he's 98 – but he beats people half his age at being active. But there's one more thing about Joe – he's blind . . .*

The lead has intrigued the readers, providing them with an air of mystery, which will make them read on. For example:

There's nothing on the surface that makes 22 Sui Wo Road any different from thousands of other highrise blocks of flats. Like many other places in Hong Kong, it's on a hill, and it has all the usual means of getting to and from the places you want to get to and from . . . But 22 Sui Wo Road has a nickname . . . it's called . . .

and so the story goes on.

So leads can be a summary; they can be intriguing; they can be descriptive. The descriptive lead gives the reader a clear, simple picture of a scene from which the story will then flow:

Imagine a Summer day with the temperature in the forties. The lawns are turning yellow; and most of all . . . what you really want is a drink of water . . . But that's the problem: there isn't any water.

There is also the direct approach lead. This is the easiest for beginners, so you have to beware of overdoing it. This is the gimmick where you address the reader directly:

Is your garage like an overstocked warehouse?

Finally, there is the quotation lead. It can be an excellent way to lead off a feature story, but you have to be careful because the quote can't just be an ordinary quote. It has to be grabbing, and it has to have some twist in it. For example:

'If you want to get sick, go to a doctor.' Sounds OK, except that the woman who said that was 92 last week.

The ending

There are two types of endings: summary and twist.

Whichever you use, don't fall into the trap of editorializing. Editorials are for the editorial page, not for a feature. Reporters report what they have seen or heard, not what they think they have seen or heard or felt. There's a big difference. For example:

So Joe doesn't expect to do great things with his life . . . he just drifts along, thinking maybe that one day he'll go back to counting flowers again.

The body

Having got all the facts and written your lead (and possibly even thought of an ending), write the body of the story. That means tying it closely together. You write the story as a whole, not in parts. There has to be a smooth transition from the lead to the body of the story, and from the various facts within the body of the story to the ending. In the body of the piece you have to keep the reader interested. It's like going up and down mountains; you reach a peak (major point of interest) then go down into a valley (explanation of the major point you've made), then up another peak etc. The way to keep a story lively is therefore to have a series of major points with some kind of explanation, then a transition to another fact, and so on. Interwoven throughout, of course, must be quotes from people you've spoken to about the story. Quotes give colour to the story and help the reader 'see' more clearly.

Feature writing must be tight and well edited, with just the right number of words. This is the major difference between academic writing, essay writing and journalism. Needless words are out. For example, rather than 'have you ever met a person who is very important in the world? If you have, what did you experience?', why not use 'Have you ever met a VIP? What was it like?'

Show people doing things. Let them talk. Underwrite, rather than write too much. This way you keep the piece moving, and the reader interested. To keep the story moving quickly, keep the quotes vivid so the characters are real. Don't over-report. One good quote per point is enough. Give an accurate, complete and balanced account, and don't put in too much background. A year-to-year, day-to-day account muddies the point and is boring. Remember: something specific is better than something abstract. If you ask someone about drugs and kids, get specific examples such as: 'John, the boy who delivers the papers . . . he's on drugs and needs help'.

Instead of writing about the lack of eating places, make it interesting by talking about the number of dim sum restaurants. Break up a big idea into small ones; break up paragraphs. This is a way of giving advice or suggestions in small doses. Lists are a problem because they look long and dull. You can also sometimes use overlapping paragraphs; it's a great hook to keep interest. Use the same words or ideas at the end of one paragraph and at the beginning of the next. For example

There was nothing to do but wait.

And wait he did. All through the afternoon.

When writing the feature:

1 Keep sentences short, but vary the shortness. A series of short five-word sentences can be boring. Vary the length.
2 Prefer simple ideas/words/constructions to complex ones. Break complex ideas into simple ones.

3 Use basic sentence constructions.

- Simple: has one subject and one statement (eight robbers held up a train yesterday)
- Compound: has two simple sentences joined by a conjunction (eight robbers held up a train yesterday and stole all the money)
- Complex: has one principle statement and one or more modifying statements or clauses (eight robbers, who were seen by a railway worker, are still being sought by police after trying to rob a train yesterday and steal all the money).

4 Be active in the use of verbs.
5 Be positive. Readers don't want to be told what *isn't*; tell them what *is*. Try to express a negative in a positive form.
6 Prefer familiar words.
7 Avoid unnecessary words.
8 Write informally.
9 Write as you would talk to a friend.
10 Use words the reader can picture.

Use one thought per sentence; one sentence per paragraph. Have something to say, and say it as clearly as you can. That is the only secret of style. Also remember: edit your own material, once, twice, maybe even three times. Feature writing is a longer, more complex and more conversational type of writing than news. It tells about people, personalizes issues and explains dramatic trends in human, people terms. It takes news and expands, analyses, personalizes. The structure is less formal than the news inverted pyramid or news formula stories. This doesn't mean it's easier to write. You have to:

- find a focus
- develop an interesting lead
- get enough sub-stories and quotes and background to make it a good story development
- find the 'right conclusion' that somehow makes readers satisfied that they have kept reading.

The feature lead doesn't give the news; it gets the reader interested in reading the rest of the story. The feature ending is not like the ending of other news stories. It is a 'reward' to the reader for having read the whole story. It generally has a 'bang' of its own. It hits us between the eyes; makes us think; surprises; makes us want to know more.

Above all, a feature is a story, an example of a person or incident that needs to be retold so people can understand what is happening to other people. Features are longer, looser and less structured than news stories, which have to give the facts quickly, simply and succinctly. We should be looking for the 'people stories'; the ones readers can relate to, the ones that tell the story behind the story even when doing a news feature. They should also somehow illustrate a point of concern to society and people. They often have a news 'peg'. You cannot simply list the facts you have found out in an interview; you have to put them together selectively as a story. The first draft you do will help you think the story idea through and it can be complicated. The feature can look more deeply at news and help the reader understand the background to a story or an event; it provides detail, word pictures and insights not available in the inverted pyramid news story. However, even in features we do not provide our own opinion: writers and reporters report the facts; readers provide the opinion.

In writing a feature you have, somewhere near the top, to tell the reader why you are writing the story. You have to show the reader why this person or issue is worth talking about. You have to explain the reason for your story. Examples of types of features are:

- backgrounder
- personality
- anniversary
- seasonal
- news analysis or explanation.

Suspended-interest

This is one particular way of writing features and is best used to tell short, humorous stories. These are difficult because you have to save the best until last and keep interest throughout right up to the last paragraph. It's like telling a joke; give away too much too soon, and you've given away the punch line. For example:

Joe Bloggs wants a dog that bites.

Bloggs was taking his labrador for a ride in his car when he was stopped by a young innocent-looking boy.

'Does your dog bite?' asked the boy.

'No,' said Bloggs.

'Great', said the youth, pulled out a gun, ordered Bloggs and the dog out and drove away.

In these features you have to write a lead, develop the story, bring the story to near climax and then reveal the outcome.

STORY DEVELOPMENT

The story can be developed in several ways. It may be chronological – logical from beginning to end with some blocks of explanatory matter thrown in. If, for example, the feature is about a new law, after the 'happening' feature lead you might like to explain how a bill is made into law, the process in the steps etc. If a story has two sides – an explanation of some controversial policy – you could list four or five points and present both sides of each topic. Presenting both sides of a number of points can be done either by presenting one side of the topic and then the opposing view alternately, or by reporting several points on one side of the argument, then all the opposing views.

Always be logical. Finish one stream of thought and logic before starting on the next one, otherwise the reader will be confused. Features can then be arranged in 'blocks'. Each block may have a different structure: one might be a summary in the writer's words (using research, quotes etc.); another might be direct and indirect quotes (mixed) introduced by a summary paragraph; another might tell a story; another might be an itemized list. Good features combine general propositions written as explanation or factual background in your own words with specific examples or quotes. For example, if you are doing a story about employee theft from a factory, you might give examples of what's been stolen; then follow with comments from employees, their bosses and unions.

Every feature must be based on factual background and good research, which should be written entertainingly and interestingly in your own words and combined with relevant quotes (direct and indirect). Remember, you aren't writing a news story, where you have to give the news point straightaway. Features are different. In the lead, give the reader enough of the story to stimulate interest and curiosity but don't completely satisfy it. You set the stage and hint at the type of story that you are telling, but hold back enough of the details to make the reader read on.

Use vivid language. Good storytelling – good features, in other words – needs good illustrations; ways of painting word pictures for the reader. These include description, examples, anecdotes, dialogue and quotes as well as figures of speech – metaphors, similes, allusions, and so on.

In developing a story, allusions can be very useful for maintaining interest. Sometimes a literary, historical or topical allusion serves as a good starting point for a feature. Sometimes an allusion can provide a theme in the development, a link between sections. However, the allusions and references must be instantly recognized by the reader; they are a kind of shortcut to understanding between writer and reader. Allusions to the words of a song, for example, can be very good – assuming your readers know the song. Allusions must either be very topical or current, or they must refer to something that is part of our common language or culture.

Perhaps the story development is not chronological but starts with the climax, followed by background and explanation. This requires an imaginative and creative lead. Some examples:

1 *Anyone can forget where they parked their car for a day. Or maybe even for a week. But for one year, six months and 22 days?*

2 *Justice is supposed to be swift. But a high court jury was so swift yesterday that it delivered a 'not guilty' verdict before hearing defence testimony.*

3 *One of the last great nonspenders, Alfred J. Tennyson of Tai Po, is about to retire after almost 20 stingy years in the Hong Kong budget office.*

4 *Noisy cars entering the tunnel . . . 9280*
 Quiet cars entering the tunnel . . . 6.

5 *All the camel was doing was standing quietly on the road in the middle of nowhere minding its own business when it was hit by a motorcycle.*

Features hang together better if they have a neat close and a well thought out conclusion. Often the conclusion will swing back to reinforce the beginning of the story in some way. This is a circular development of the story. Lead and conclusion bind the story together and emphasize the feature angle, the human interest, the vivid picture. Conclusions are one way of achieving a very important part of feature writing: involving the reader and getting reader reaction. For example, the final paragraph may say: 'Oh boy, so would I'; and the reader says to himself: 'so would I . . .'

SOME TIPS FOR WRITING FEATURES

1 *Know how to research/collect news first.* Once you can report and write short news stories confidently and accurately you will be able to write a feature. Not before. Learn how to dig for facts, how to interview and how to collect and write a news story to a very tight deadline, then you will be able to write a feature. Remember, however, that a feature is different from news: it has a different type of intro lead; different approach to quotes; different approach to background and context and a different type of ending.

2 *Do your homework.* Before you start collecting information for the feature, know something about the people you will be interviewing or who might help you. Know the direction that the interview and the story will probably (or should) take.

3 *Observe and describe* the house or the office, what the people are wearing, how they talk, whether they gesture. Are they wearing jewellery? Do they take a lot of time to answer a question? What are their clothes like?

4 *Use a tape recorder* whenever possible (the small cassette variety that can be put on the table in front of the two of you). Taping is good because it provides a precise record of what is said. It allows you to give full attention to what is being said, rather than missing some by having to take physical notes. It also reveals how a person answers the question. For example, it might help to write that a person paused or took a deep breath

before answering. Also, of course, if later you are accused of misquoting, you have the taped record as proof.

5 *Ask questions.* Ask as many as possible of as many people as possible. Sometimes you will have to say 'can you explain this to me, I don't understand'. Good. Neither will the reader. Sometimes what you ask won't help. Never mind; it's better to ask than not to ask.

6 *Maintain contact* with the source. Additional questions may come up while the story is being written. At the end of the interview ask the source where they can be reached, and alert them to the fact that you may contact them again to check a fact or ask some additional questions. However, never give away your editorial control.

7 *Transcribe handwritten notes* as soon as possible. This helps to organize thoughts and prepare an outline of the story so far. The longer a reporter waits to transcribe notes, the more difficult it becomes.

8 *Write a rough outline first,* then write a rough draft. Revise it, write another draft, revise it, and so on until you are satisfied. Writing is a process of refinement. When you start out feature writing, the more drafts, the better the end product will be. It will never be perfect the first time. Show it to someone else for their comments.

9 *Look for the best lead.* When you write the draft, although you may *think* you know the lead, you might find that actually the best and most interesting intro is somewhere in the middle of the story.

10 *Look for the best ending.* Again, when you reread and revise your story, the best ending might not be at the end. You may find that the best and most dramatic, interesting or memorable ending is somewhere in the middle of the story. Change it to the end.

11 *Do not overwrite.* A feature should be as long as it is worth. Don't write too much, or more than you have the material for. Stop writing when you run out of things to say, or when you think the reader will lose interest. That's more important than filling a required space.

12 *See it afresh.* If you have time after you finish the story, try to leave some time before you read it again before finally sending it to the editor.

FURTHER READING

Bagnall, N. (1993). *Newspaper Language*. Focal Press.

Davis, A. (1998). *Magazine Journalism Today*. Focal Press.

Giles, V. and Hodgson, F. W. (1996). *Creative Newspaper Design*. Focal Press.

Hennessy, B. (1997). *Writing Feature Articles*. Focal Press.

Hodgson, F. W. (1998). *New Subediting*. Focal Press.

Keeble, R. (1998). *The Newspaper Handbook*. Routledge.

9 Reporting for broadcast

Veteran British Labour politician Tony Benn once said, 'Broadcasting is really too important to be left to the broadcasters'. Broadcast journalists have a responsibility and a trust: they must be aware of the legal responsibilities that affect their practice; the wider ethical issues that have a bearing on decisions about what to broadcast and how topics should be treated. The language of broadcast journalists must sound responsible and professional and serve the best interests of listener and viewer. The language they use must be objective and neutral. Broadcast journalists use the language of speech – of conversation. Naturalness has to be relearnt both in writing for speech and in speech itself. The language they use is important because, by its use and in its meaning, the broadcast journalist is accountable:

- to the listeners and viewers
- to the law
- to the management of the station
- to the ethics and values of the profession.

The broadcast journalist must be objective in reporting facts. This is a higher responsibility than in print. Reporting must be impartial, even-handed, fair and honest. The purpose of news in a democracy is to satisfy the right of people to know what is going on around them. That's the job of every broadcast journalist. Broadcasting has been impartial since it was started in Britain in the 1920s by Lord Reith. Broadcasting was set up in Britain, and elsewhere, as a 'public utility to be developed as a national service in the public interest'. It became known as public service broadcasting. Reith founded the BBC as a 'cultural, moral and educative force for the improvement of knowledge, taste and manners . . . a powerful means of promoting social unity . . . an essential part of a democratic society'. Impartiality does not mean absolute neutrality or detachment from basic moral and constitutional beliefs. Reporters are not neutral about truth and untruth, justice and injustice, compassion and cruelty, tolerance and intolerance, law and lawlessness.

News judgement is by definition personal and subjective (everyone makes individual judgements), and the listeners or viewers also listen subjectively. They reach their own conclusions. Facts to one person are lies to someone else. News judgement must therefore always be based on fair, objective, truthful decision-making concerning story importance and treatment.

Pressures on broadcast journalists include:

- advertising (the company for which they work might try to stop a story that could lose advertising revenue)
- personal (pressures not to report a story because of friends' or relatives' involvement).
- moral (personal, religious or moral beliefs may make the reporter angle a story in a particular biased way)
- government/politics (pressures from officials not to run a story, or to do it in a particular way favourable to government or a political party).

NEWS MANIPULATION

This destroys professionalism in one stroke. Beware of it at all times. Politicians, public relations officers (and press releases) will try to pull the strings. Don't let them.

The increasing importance of information media in the political process (particularly of radio and TV) is seen when the leaders of the opposing sides use the news media, and the access it gives them to each other's supporters, to communicate their diplomatic and military propaganda.

In domestic politics too the ability to use and manipulate news media to set agendas and shape debates with the aid of photo opportunities, soundbites and professional image consultants is now generally accepted as a prerequisite of success. Political parties and pressure groups compete with equal vigour to manage the news, because they believe that, for the majority of the audience, news and current affairs is the key point of contact with the political process.

CHARACTERISTICS OF RADIO

Radio is a blind medium; it is also a personal medium. Radio appeals to the imagination. Radio is distinctive because it involves the imagination in a different way to TV, creating its own pictures.

In literature, everything is imagined. In TV, things can be seen and heard, and much less is left to the imagination. In radio, many things can be heard, and so verbal descriptions of a physical setting or a person's thoughts or appearance are more economical. Radio is about what is happening; it's a medium of the present. Radio is what everyone listens to in an emergency. Radio is about words and sounds. Since the medium is blind, the words cannot be seen by the listener. The linguistic code of radio approximates more closely to that of speech than writing. However, radio talk is usually first scripted, so it is premeditated rather than spontaneous. It is also much clearer and more explicit than general speech, and more fluent, precise, and orderly. It doesn't spread itself over many thoughts. It doesn't repeat itself the way conversation does. However, scripted speech on radio must never admit to being scripted. Aspiring broadcasters should see the script as storage of talk. Scripts should contain frequent use of conversational expressions: 'Well now'; 'Come to think of it' and so on. This kind of colloquialism discourages the flat, expressionless tone of the unskilled broadcaster, who concentrates on the words of the script rather than on the content or meaning. Reading tone should not be detectable to listeners.

How much do we understand?

A BBC survey tested a group of people on how much they could understand of a talk. The average listener correctly answered only 28 per cent of the questions. Radio speech and radio news writing does not pose questions. It interprets answers, and it puts into plain language the complex or specialist responses of the expert so that the ordinary listener will understand. It is a waste of time to broadcast news unless it is listened to and understood. The aim is intelligibility, immediately. Newspaper readers have time to reread; radio listeners can never do that. Therefore:

- know what you want to say
- say it in a direct, simple, precise way
- say it *naturally*.

Radio news writing

Radio news writing should be conversational so that the style is crisp, economical, direct and colloquial, but should never use slang. Prefer short words to long words; simple sentences to complex sentences; concrete to abstract words; direct subject–verb–object sentences. However, always look for the added detail that brings the story alive; the remark that reveals a personality, the phrase that makes the scene vivid. The good, simple, clear radio story is constructed by answering the questions, one sentence at a time:

- WHAT   has happened?
- WHERE   did it happened?
- WHEN   did it happen?
- WHO   was involved?
- WHY   did it happen?
- WHAT   does it all mean?
- HOW   did it happen?

Good radio news writing tells listeners all they need to know to understand the story, then stops.

Intros in radio writing are short, snappy, to the point: they are closer to a newspaper headline than to a newspaper intro. The first sentence has to establish in the mind of the listeners what the story is about, but must never say too much. The first sentence in a radio news story has to 'sell' it to the listeners to keep them listening.

The radio intro:

- tells us the most significant point
- grabs our attention
- makes us want to know more
- gives us the direction the rest of the story will be taking.

It should also be short. Radio has to be logical in its thought processes, so the story should follow with logical points. A good radio story starts with what has happened. The next sentence usually expands this by telling how it happened, explaining the immediate background. The next sentence amplifies the intro and fleshes out the main points in order of importance. Finally, tie up any loose ends and give any additional background information. Remember: you only have about 60 words to tell the story, so the trick is what to leave out. Radio gives impressions rather than facts.

Radio news writing:

- tries to explain the facts
- doesn't use figures if at all possible, and when it does, gives examples: *as big as a football pitch*
- uses contractions to help the understanding and the speaking: *He can't go* not *He cannot go.*

Beware of clichés such as 'fires rage' or 'ambulances rush'.

Radio writing means you:

- decide what you want to say
- list your points in logical order
- have a grabbing, short opening sentence
- write for *one* listener, and visualize the person you are talking to
- speak out loud what you want to say, then write it
- use ordinary conversational language
- write in short simple sentences
- use punctuation that helps the reader, not necessarily literary punctuation.

Remember: KISS: Keep It Simple; Keep It Short.

Broadcast news stories can be written in different ways, but there are some basic techniques:

1 Consider what the story is about; what is the point you want to get across to the listener?
2 Ask how much the listener is likely to know of the background to the story. You may want to relate this particular story to another, or it may be an important development in a story that has been running for some time. You may have to explain various technical terms and references; people, places and organizations may have to be identified. Do not assume the listener knows all about it.
3 Don't clog up the story with figures. Listeners find it hard to understand and remember them. In a story based on a set of

statistics, quote the really significant figure and express the others in a simpler way: *half, double*. Round figures are better than precise exact ones. *Nearly two hundred thousand* is better than *one hundred and ninety-three thousand*. However, sometimes precise figures have to be given (e.g. if the inflation rate was 7.8 last month and this month it is 7.3, then say so).

4 Too many *todays* and *yesterdays* get in the way and are usually unnecessary. News is reported when it happens, always on the same day in radio, so *today* isn't needed.

5 Be careful about the first word of the story. Listeners often miss the first word; their attention isn't fully with you for the first couple of words. Therefore, it is important not to begin with a key word or unfamiliar name. *Rice is to cost more* is a simple direct statement, but listeners might miss the first word and never know what is going to cost more. In radio it is sometimes better to be a bit more longwinded and have a lead that says, for example *The price of rice is going up*. The words *the price of* will attract attention, and we will listen. It is also worth repeating the key word 'rice' if the story is a long one, in case people have missed or forgotten it.

6 If you give a name (particularly an unfamiliar one) at the beginning of a story, the listener might miss it. While you tell the rest of the story, they'll be wondering who you are talking about. So repeat the name in the body of the story.

7 If you have to switch ideas in mid-story, remember not to confuse the listener. Your story might be about a new development in China, and you might want to include a quote from a Washington spokesman. So use a 'signpost' word at the start of that sentence: *In Washington . . .* This helps the listener adjust to the change of scene.

8 Check the facts. Check anything of which you are suspicious: a figure, a title, a piece of geographical information, a historical reference.

9 If you can, read your story aloud to yourself before handing it in. If you find something is difficult to say, so will the newsreader.

Inserts

In radio news, stories usually have actuality inserts – either a voice or soundbite. Despatches from reporters and extracts from speeches and interviews as well as *live* sounds like music supplement the word pictures of the story. Inserts can make the bulletin much more interesting (they are the 'picture' of radio). They also bring the listener closer to the event. It's always best to hear something in the words of the speaker. The reporter can describe a scene, but the eyewitness standing amidst the chaos of the disaster can do it better. Unnecessary hesitations in extracts from interviews you want to use as an insert can be cut out. However, remember that 'cleaning up' the tape has its dangers. A pause before a speaker replies to a penetrating question may be editorially significant, so it should be kept; if it is something else, remove it. A man with a stammer is a man with a stammer. Some of it should certainly be kept, otherwise we are distorting reality.

Remember always to remove references to any material you have edited out. You will confuse the listener if you leave in things like: *As I said before*, *I tell you again*, and *secondly* when the comment isn't there to hear, or if you use an extract with the wrong stress on a name that has been mentioned earlier but cut out in the insert.

Insert introduction

Every insert must have an introduction (a cue or a lead), which is read by the newsreader to introduce the insert. It will usually be the first few sentences of the news story, and lead into the voice or the insert. The lead helps sell the story to the listener and keeps them listening. Such intros will usually end with a phrase like *This report from* or *X reports* etc. Try to use different phrases, such as *explains why; gives the reasons for the decision; outlines the problems involved'; 'was told the full details of what happened* etc.

Prepare the listener in the introduction for anything out of the ordinary, such as distracting background noise. A line in the intro saying that John X spoke to the union leader in a busy works canteen will prevent listeners being distracted by the clinking of crockery, and will enable them to concentrate on what's being said.

Background

Journalists report the events that matter, that are happening now, that are important. Part of that reporting duty is also to explain the background of events. The reporting of an event, the reporting of comments on that event, and an accompanying analysis of the background to that event are all the proper tasks of a news programme.

Major news reports should contain or be accompanied by enough further information to allow listeners to understand what is going on. It is easy to skim the surface of the story, but then listeners won't understand what the story is really about. A story about a faraway country or an unusual event somewhere else must be set up for the listener. In other words, it has to be adequately introduced. With stories that have been running for several days, every now and then there should be a recap of the main idea. Remember, journalists are very familiar with the story and what it means. Listeners may not be, or may have forgotten.

Each news report should be self contained. No listener should need to know what was reported yesterday in order to understand what is said today. This further information includes background of a straightforward kind, the wider context of events and expert perspective, not only what has already happened. Sometimes you should think forward, suggesting to the listener what are the likely consequences of an event or a series of events. However, be careful that it is not mere speculation; facts are the most important part of a story.

One final thought: newspaper journalists will generally top a news story with the latest developments and follow with a reminder of earlier events. The reader is told: 'Stop reading when you begin to recognize the story'. In radio, listeners can't do this. They have to listen to the whole story or bulletin. They have to hear every item, however familiar many of the details might be. Radio newswriters must therefore structure their stories to maintain interest. Background material should never be put as a final paragraph at the end; it is better incorporated into the body of the story.

Writing for the ear

Ten points to remember about good broadcast writing:

1 Use simple, straightforward spoken language. Ask yourself, 'If I were chatting to a person I'd just met, is this the way I'd tell them what's happening? Are these the words I'd use? Are these the

phrases?' Always remember, you're not creating great prose; you're talking to people, not literary critics or academics.

2 Find a strong start to attract the listeners' attention. Follow it with a simple, logical progression of ideas, and finish strongly as well.

3 Be personal. Use *I* and *You*.

4 Use simple sentences whenever possible.

5 Try not to use adverbs and adjectives. Great economy of language is needed on radio.

6 Watch out for 'ing' verbs. Don't say: *on entering the building*. Say: *when you enter the building* or, even better, *when you go into the building*.

7 Turn passives into active verbs. It's more direct and more vivid.

8 Contract verbs. Try to say *he's*; *it's*; *isn't*; *there's*.

9 Names and positions. If you mention someone's name and official title, always give the position first: *The secretary of the golf club, Mr . . .,* not *Mr . . ., the secretary of the golf club.*

10 Avoid figures. If you can't avoid using them, then simplify and relate them to something your listener will know (football pitches, jumbo jets etc.).

TELLING THE STORY FOR BROADCASTING

Broadcast journalism is about telling stories that are true and important. They matter to the viewer and the listener. Watch your friends listening to the radio or watching TV at home. It's little more than background noise, something 'turned on' in a busy room. If they are watching or listening at all, it's usually whilst doing something else. They point, comment, do something else, miss what's being said. Communication by radio or TV is not like being in a movie theatre or reading a book. Communication by radio or TV is person-to-person, one-to-one. It's not a lecture; it's not a movie performance. It is intimate. The reporter's job is to break through the noise, to get over the distraction so as to make the listeners and viewers look, listen and go with the reporter to the world being reported. Reporters take a real-life event, convert what they see and hear to tape (audio or video), broadcast it through the airwaves or by satellite or cable, and hope to make a lasting impression on the listener.

So:
- set the scene
- establish a mood
- bait the hook.

Visualize and then construct. Get the intro right, and the listener is hooked.

Humanize the story. News is people, and people are interested in people. Stories about people, however dry the economic or political story may be, will always make people listen and watch. There's nothing wrong with a story having heroes, villains, main characters, comic relief. Ask:

- who does the story affect?
- why?
- how?

Try to characterize the story. Connect the viewer with a real person. The more dimensions you give the character, the more the viewer will watch, care and remember.

Strive for spontaneity. Good reporters supply the basic facts. Good interviews expand these facts with opinions, emotions and moments in time. Soundbites should work for, not against, the reporter. How many times, when doing research, has someone you speak to on the telephone been terrific, only to become shy and not say anything when the camera is rolling? The reporter's job is to put the subject at ease. Remember that, although reporters do interviews every day, it may be the first (and only) time that the subject has ever been interviewed. Great soundbites do not just happen. They often require hard work by the reporter to ask the right question to get the best answer.

- Forget the technology. Battery lights and mikes rarely bring out the best in an interview. Whenever possible, use a wireless mike rather than a stick mike; it looks better. They also give better sound when shooting cover video and, perhaps most importantly, your subject will forget you've got one.
- If it's a formal interview, ask your subject where he or she feels most comfortable and try to accommodate this. Put subjects at ease.
- Beware of the person who wants to tell you everything before the camera rolls. Rehearsal rarely helps. If a subject insists on talking, steer the conversation away from your interview questions. If the

subject wants to know what questions you plan to ask, say: 'Just what we've talked about. In any case, my questions will follow your answers so I don't know what I'll ask yet'.

Bear in mind that it might take more than one interview with a person to make the story. Often we get our best bites when the person feels relaxed or forgets the tape is rolling.

Create illusions of intimacy and depth. The viewers do not know the reporter only had about 20 minutes to do the story.

Seek the simple truths. Reporters spend too much time trying to do the story they think they should be doing, rather than simply telling the truth, telling the story like it is. How often have you described a story one way to friends and quite a different way to the viewers? Think before writing the story; ask what the story really means. Good stories:

- do not all have to come out of the morning newspaper
- do not have to feature officials acting like officials
- do not have to follow any standard line.

To be memorable, however, most stories must relate to people in one way or another.

Do not be a statue. Hopefully, everyone quickly progresses beyond the stage of being in television to being on television. Good stand-uppers (pieces to camera) advance the story and give it perspective. They are not simply to get the reporter on screen. Good stand-uppers:

- let the viewer connect with the storyteller
- help the storyteller describe things that pictures might not be able to show
- may help the reporter confide in the viewer to make a point
- do not get in the way of the story, stop it or slow it down.

Unless the reporter is more important than the story (and that is very rarely the case), there is nothing worse than starting with a piece to camera. Unless it is an abstract hard news story requiring a closing summary, the next worst thing is to finish with a stand-upper. Such things tell the viewer that the reporter has failed to develop a strong story line. The most effective stand-uppers take the form of a bridge between aspects of the story. They may provide some perspective, history or background, help the reporter fill in details that have no pictures or serve as a transition. Above all else, when appearing on camera:

- be natural
- do not pontificate
- use your body
- gesture
- refer to your environment, move within the frame, or have the camera move with you. However, do it for a good reason, otherwise it will distract.

Whenever you appear, you are just another talking head. As such, make sure your head and that of the interviewee are not different sizes or facing in different directions. TV cameras have two sides; use them. Some reporters get into the habit of always interviewing from the same side of the camera. The drawback to this is that, on screen, all the talking heads then face the same direction. That's boring, and it doesn't work if you have several soundbites in succession from the same or different interviewees. The head-to-head technique works well when editing separate talking heads together without the interviewer appearing on screen inbetween. It helps aesthetics, clarity, balance and pacing. For example, two heads facing screen left would cut awkwardly, especially if they were arguing two opposing points of view. Let their juxtaposition advance the story.

Be active and avoid extra phrases. The best broadcast writing is active writing. In other words, the simplest possible English sentence: subject–verb–object. For example, use *The cat sat on the mat* rather than the passive *The mat was sat on by the cat*. We don't talk that way so why write that way? Remember:

- active voice is more immediate
- active voice takes less time
- active voice prohibits lazy reporting; passive voice provides an easy crutch for overlooking facts.

Think pacing and remember the rule of threes. Listen to a script while you are writing it. Flow with it in editing. Pay attention to the rhythm. If a voiceover track runs more than four short sentences, try to break up the sameness with some sound on tape. Anything will do; perhaps a short soundbite or some actuality.

Break the script into sections. In longer stories especially, open it up. Let the natural sound play and the piece will breathe. That's why we do shot lists. Spend time in the viewing room beforehand and you'll save time later. Often, when listing things or writing clauses, three is better than two, than four or any other number. It has something to do with timing, cadence and the natural order of things. The ear likes threes.

How to tell the story

There are many ways to tell a story. Think about prologues, flashbacks, climaxes and denouements, just like Shakespeare. When possible, use drama, suspense and humour. Remember to build your characters. Every story should have a distinct beginning, middle and end. This may mean setting the scene or leading with the strongest video, then working back later. Every story's different. Be creative, and every story will sound different as well. In the same way as an intro is crucial, so is an ending. It does after all make the final impression. Too many times reporters have strong stories that don't end properly. The only way to end it seems to be a sign off after a soundbite. Closing the piece should be compelling. To work well endings must provide a better bottom line than you could ever write. However, do not let the technique get in the way of a story. Many times especially in hard or breaking stories, the pictures and story are so compelling that all the viewers really want is a clean, clear recitation of the facts.

Be conversational. For print journalists making the change into broadcasting, the hardest adjustment can be the break from a literary approach. The emphasis in print is on the written word, while the emphasis in broadcast journalism is on the spoken word. Broadcast reporters write only to speak; newspaper reporters write for the eye, not for the ear.

Good broadcast writing:

- translates ideas
- translates words from the complex to the simple
- translates from words that look good on the page to those that sound good to the ear.

Ask:

- what is the story trying to say?
- what is the point of the story?

Then rewrite in your own words, making sure you understand what you're trying to say first.

Look for the simple meaning of a word before using it. Don't use jargon, technical or academic words. People don't speak like that; neither should broadcasters. Beware of police-speak, politician-speak and economist-speak. They all have to be translated to words that listeners can understand the first time they hear them. Nothing must disturb the logical flow of what reporters are trying to say. If it does, listeners start wondering what is being said and stop listening. Broadcast journalists have to do the work for the listeners. They have to provide listeners with all the answers. The detailed steps on the way are the boring bits that don't work in broadcasting, and listeners lose interest. They don't want the detail, the steps in the process; they want the answer, the result, without having to work it our for themselves. Broadcast reporters provide the answers.

Writing for a mass audience

Broadcast reporters don't write for a mass audience; they write for a single listener or viewer. Broadcast journalism writing is always one-to-one. Try to visualize the person you're writing for, speaking to. You are talking with, not at. Write accordingly. Reporters on radio and TV have to learn to tell a story. Remember that broadcast listeners have no second chance to hear, to understand. They have to get what you're saying the first time, which is the only time. Therefore, use simple clauses, simple words and no inverted sentences.

Listeners and viewers have to hold in their memory what has been said, so never invert sentences. Subject–verb–object is the simplest way to understand. State the point first, then explain it. Listeners can never refer back. Use plain language and familiar words, and keep language concrete, not abstract.

Beware of information overload. Precise instructions, complex abstractions or statistics don't come across well in broadcasting. Such abstract facts have to be translated into expressions that the mind can easily grasp. TV can use graphics, captions and illustrations to bring home a point, but even then it is easy to overload with information. The listener or viewer can take in only so much. Half of what you say is forgotten; the rest gets twisted.

Lead sentences should be short, snappy, memorable and easily understandable. They should provide the answer to: 'Why am I listening to this?'.

Remember: one idea per sentence.

Clear simple broadcast writing

1 Make the sentences active, with active verbs (this makes the sentence stronger and shorter and clearer).
2 Let the verbs do the work. Don't change the verbs into nouns; that's too abstract. For example not *Authorisation for the absence was given by the Boss*, but *The Boss said it was OK to be away*.
3 Be concise. Cut out the excess baggage. Worry if a sentence goes much longer than a line and a half.
4 Be specific. Use concrete terms; not generalizations or abstractions. Abstraction is the enemy of clear speech and clear writing. Gobbledygook, the language of jargon, pomposity, politicians, civil servants, is *out*.

   - Not: *Such preparations shall be made as will completely obscure all Federal buildings and non-Federal buildings occupied by the Federal Government during the air raid for any period of time from visibility by reason of internal or external illumination. Such obscuration may be obtained by blackout construction or by termination of the illumination,*
   but: *In buildings where work has to carry on during an air raid, put something over the windows: and in buildings where work can stop for a while, turn out the lights.*
   - Not: *We are endeavouring to construct a more inclusive society,* but: *We want this country to have something for everyone.*

5 Use words with a sensory base, that is to say, words that represent objects the audience can see, hear, touch, taste, smell. That's real understanding. Remember the ladder of abstraction. The lower rungs represent the concrete terms the audience can easily identify in terms of physical senses. Going up the ladder, you'll find each word becomes more abstract than the one below. At the same time, each reference grows more general, more vague, more open to different

interpretations. Take the word 'armament'. What does it mean? As you go down the ladder of abstraction from the most abstract (armament) to the least abstract, it goes something like this:

- armament
- arms
- weapons
- firearms
- guns
- handguns
- pistols.

6 Keep related sentences and ideas together (preferably in their own sentences). Keep unrelated elements apart, and be careful of 'dangly things'. There are several types of dangling constructions in English, but they are all faulty in pretty much the same way. Phrases dangle when they don't clearly and logically refer to the appropriate noun or pronoun. For example:

After climbing the mountain, the view was beautiful. Of course the view didn't climb the mountain. *We* climbed the mountain and saw a beautiful view, didn't we? Why not say it that way? . . . *We climbed the mountain and saw a beautiful view.* Again, *To save money, the thermostat must be turned down to 18 degrees.* Why not *If you want to save money, turn the thermostat down to 18 degrees*?

7 Avoid unnecessary shifts of numbers, tense, subject, voice or idea. Put it positively, not negatively (if you write a negative sentence it's more difficult to understand than if you turn it round yourself into a positive statement; after all, it's what the listener or viewer will have to do, so why not do it for them). The basic principle is: don't throw your audience off the point. Keep going straight ahead and, if you have to make a turn, at least do it at a signpost.

- Not: *The project was not successful,* but *The project failed.*
- Not: *The company says it will not now proceed with the plan,* but *The Company says the plan's off.*
- Not: *Joe Bloggs has still not been caught,* but *Joe Bloggs is still free.*

Prefer the simple to the difficult.

8 Arrange your ideas logically. If you really have to present undiluted difficult material (and by and large it isn't necessary), then take it one step at a time. Try to do the work for the audience so that they don't have to do the work or ask 'what does that mean?' The journalist should ask, *what does this mean; what am I trying to say?*; you can then tell the listener or viewer what it means. Remember that no writer can ever tell the whole story about anything. Some books take hundreds of pages to describe a single day. You haven't got that much time or space, so you have to decide right at the start of the report what to put in and what to leave out without harming the meaning. So:

- Stick to the essential facts, and only those facts, and cut out all else. Always strive to put the facts in a logical order. Start with the basics that everyone will understand, then move one step at a time until the listeners or viewers can take in more difficult concepts because you have prepared them. You've given them a map.
- The easiest way to have the audience follow what you're trying to say is to start with a generalization of some kind and then move to more specific facts. The general statement is then followed by additional facts that explain it. They follow step by step. Start with something that is familiar and interesting, then move on one step at a time. Don't skip any steps. Lead them gently at a comfortable rate from the known to the less known.
- Use analogies, comparisons, contrasts, examples.
- Use illustrations to explain difficult concepts.
- Use the same system all the way through. Never make your audience do the sums; that's your job. All the listeners want are the answers.
- If you're discussing, say, four animals, a cat, dog, horse, an elephant, then there is a logical sequence, usually from smaller to largest. Don't mix up the sizes. Or progress from the better known to the least well known.
- Prefer the familiar to the unfamiliar.

Never write this way: *This passageway has been made non-conductive to utilization for an indefinite period* (a sign in the Pentagon); how about: *This passage is out of use.*

The soundbite

Soundbites offer great opportunities to report facts. Use soundbites to communicate feelings, ideas and emotions.

Good, compelling soundbites make the viewers or listeners think they are at the scene of the story. Soundbites should be about 20 seconds, not much longer. Of course you can have several short soundbites throughout the story, adding to the overall impact. As you select a soundbite, listen carefully for names or terminology that need to be explained. You must either explain them fully, or pick another soundbite.

Selecting soundbites

Be sure they convey information that advances your story's focus.

Lead into your soundbite by talking about the subject that will be mentioned in the soundbite.

The lead-in should flow into the soundbite (SB). For example:

The Governor says he hates the Bill. SB: *The votes aren't there.*

This doesn't make sense and doesn't flow. Instead:

The Governor doesn't think the Bill will get through. SB: *The votes aren't there. It won't be passed.*

You should lead from intro to SB seamlessly, with a transition that continues the flow of the story. For example:

The Governor says the Bill benefits the wealthy and he won't support it. SB: *I want a Bill that will help the poor. The Bill is a blank cheque for the rich.*

Never lead into a soundbite by using the same words as the speaker does. For example:

The Governor says he'd like to see Company B get the contract. SB: *I'd like Company B to get the contract.*

The way to do it is to paraphrase loosely the soundbite in the lead:

The Governor says he's made his choice. SB: *I'd prefer Company B to get the contract.*

BROADCAST PACKAGES

When you go out on a story, you can never be sure how it will turn out. You may have been told to get a *package* (a story that includes soundbites, reporter's voiceover, stand-upper, pictures for TV or actuality sound, interview soundbites, reporter voice piece for radio). Sometimes you can do all this, sometimes it has to be less; maybe a simple reporter's piece to camera or just an interview. As with all broadcast journalism, a package involves pre-production (when you plan the piece); production (when you do the piece) and post-production (when you put the various elements of the piece together in the studio before transmission).

Bulletins are mostly made up of packages. They bring a story alive; good pictures, interesting soundbites, well-written and presented script. The quality of the pictures and the soundbites usually dictates the length of the package.

At the scene

Good organization is essential. Decide quickly the shape of the piece, at least how you are going to start (whether with you or pictures), where you will appear (if at all) and how you will close (with you doing a summary tailpiece or with voiceover and pictures).

Opening the story

You have got to get the viewer interested with the first pictures and the first sentence of the script. Take time over these; the rest usually then falls into place. The first sentence is dictated by the first pictures; the first pictures are dictated by the best pictures. Find the best pictures to start the story, and then find the best sentence that best fits those pictures.

Good pictures

In television, it is the pictures that are most important. Get the pictures, then write the script. Don't tell the story in words and not worry about how the pictures are being seen by the viewer. Never write a script until you've seen the pictures. Spin through the tapes, make notes in the left-hand column of the script and start to tell the story visually in your mind. Tell yourself: 'this is what happened, this is where it goes, this is how I'm going to finish it'. With a shotlist you can then easily write the words to go with the pictures.

Writing the script first does *not* work: you end up with a script that doesn't flow properly, and suddenly you find you have words where there are no pictures.

News writing for television

The writing is different. Write well, in conversational, colloquial form, after you've got the pictures. Ask: how can these pictures tell the story on TV? Underwrite rather than overwrite. Sometimes, in a complicated story, you have to add graphics. If you are on a news story with a crew, always take notes yourself of what is being shot for later.

Organizing the story

Keep the story short. Short stories are more difficult than long ones. Organize your thoughts; think the pictures through in your head.

Selecting sound

As well as good soundbites, look for good natural sound to set the mood. Good TV stories try to get people to experience what a story or situation is like for themselves, without them being there. Sound helps the viewers experience the sensation for themselves. Sound also brings their attention back to the TV screen because so much of what we call news just washes over the viewers. Sound is an exclamation point. Sound should never explain. For example, rather than have the soundbite say: *We're going to have a picnic on Friday at one o'clock and we're going to have music and it's going to be a great time and we hope you all come and it's sponsored by the local football club*, just take the best bit: *we're going to have a great time*. Then you, as the reporter, can fill in the information that leads up to the soundbite. The SB should prove what you have said; support it, not explain it.

Video editing

This is where you can 'rewrite' the story. A good editor can make your story a thousand times better; a bad editor, on the other hand . . . Everything you edit and leave in must move the story forward. Only the pictures you have time for, and that are essential, are left in. Everything else is thrown out.

Voiceover

The reporter or newscaster reads copy as the video appears on the screen. Normally voiceovers aren't very long, because they are generally used to break up a series of packages or to give the anchors some exposure. Most newscasts use voiceovers together with read stories to fill in the time around the packages; voiceovers are always short (maybe 20 seconds). They are usually separated by some technical device such as a wipe, which is an electronic technique that slides one video picture off the screen as it replaces it with another.

Reporter involvement

Reporters should be seen within their stories if at all possible. Usually the stand-upper piece is at the end or in the middle rather than at the start. The theory is that the viewers should think of the reporter as their family, in the room with them. The more on-air exposure the reporter gets, the more the viewer identifies and likes him or her. However, stand-uppers should only be used when necessary and when they add to the story. Wherever possible, let the pictures and other people's words tell the story. The best reason for a reporter appearing on screen is to help explain. Sometimes the reporter does a stand-upper in the middle of the story to provide a bridge tying two parts of the story together, but this can also break up the flow and should be avoided if it might do this. Good writing is what good journalism is all about. Good packaging of the writing is what good broadcast journalism is all about. Good writing makes news come to life. It makes radio a magic medium of wonderful visual pictures and imagination, and it's what makes television a compelling source of news and information.

Matching words with sound and pictures

Radio news

In radio news, integrate words with sound and actuality:

- do not repeat word-for-word what the tape will say
- be close enough to the topic so the tape doesn't come as a surprise.

For example:

...the governor says he's not worried.

Tape: *I have complete confidence the situation will work out OK.*

Use wild sound in radio pieces, but *never* fake the sound. Credibility applies not only to facts, but also to the means you use to communicate your story.

Don't overlay the sound on tape so as to mislead. Don't distort reality. Use the right cheering for the right reason. Actuality is best in radio. The soundbite is best when it expresses something other than straight facts; you can put the facts in the copy. The actuality has to add something extra. Use the facts from your recorded interview to write your script, that's the background. Choose as actuality soundbites the part of the interview that says something personal or controversial, or an opinion that you can't use without sourcing in your copy. Also try to use a soundbite that won't go out of date too quickly. Use the time-sensitive material in your script, which can be easily changed.

TV voiceover copy

Write without distracting from the picture.

All that has been said above for radio applies to television, but there are some extra points:

- the voice and video must be reasonably related but not too closely related; at the same time, they cannot be at odds with each other
- the central thought of the script must relate to the basic theme of the pictures.

For example, you can't have a close-up shot showing only construction workers while the copy talks about massive traffic jams created by the construction work. The traffic jam is the story, so you've got to see the traffic. If there isn't video, you have to script it for the anchor to read to camera.

Never write voiceover copy that repeats what people can see for themselves. For example: don't say *This is the room where the university's computers are kept. There are computers at each desk which each student can use* if the shots include a pan of the room clearly showing a room full of computers, a computer at each desk and a superimposed graphic that says 'Computer centre'. The way to do it is to use the voiceover to tell more of the story while you use visuals to illustrate the obvious things (everyone knows what a computer is, what a desk is etc.). For example: *This learning centre with its 30 computers is the university's way of being at the forefront of new technology for future journalists* ... You can 'point' to the picture with the words (*this learning centre*), but you don't have to. Viewers will understand. It can be done even better without any pointing to the pictures at all – *Some universities say computer technology is the way to teach journalism in the future. And at this one, the lecturers are spending millions of dollars to prove that their new learning centre will be the best . . ..*

Soundbites can be voiceovers as well; it isn't always just a script. The news writes itself then.

Timing

This is important in writing to video pictures. The tape and anchor might have to hit the spot together and, since it's live, there's only one chance. Sometimes you deliberately want to write the opposite of the pictures ('away from the pictures') for some special effect, usually humorous or dramatic. If you're writing a story about cockroaches, you might use pictures of big cockroaches with anchor voiceover saying something like: *Everyone loves animals, and most people would like at least one pet* (you've caught the viewers attention both with pictures and audio, now you can lead them into the joke bit about *but not this type* etc.).

Continuity

Pictures should tell as much of the story as they can without the words; therefore, you need to lead viewers logically from scene to scene. First, place the viewers in the scene. Give them a view of the environment in which the event occurred. This usually means an establishing shot, a wide shot that presents as much of the location as possible with the newsmakers within the frame. Then, introduce the viewers to the newsmakers in the event; show the newsmakers in juxtaposition with their surroundings. Use medium shots to introduce the newsmaker participants into the story. Show the viewers the relationship between newsmakers; let them see the newsmakers' physical positions and their reactions to each other. Use wide shots for this. Finally, let the video footage tell the story. Let it unfold in a logical sequence, so you can carry your viewers smoothly from one shot to the next as if they were moving through the story with the camera. You can also use an opening discovery shot to introduce the story where necessary; this is sometimes used to open a telecast of a big event like a football match (or indeed the start of the news). Viewers get a wide overall city shot, then zoom in to show, say, the football stadium in the foreground of the earlier city shot. Viewers discover where they are. The discovery shot is the opposite of the way you write for broadcast:

- focus first on the specific aspect of the story you want the viewer to remember
- expand to include all the supporting elements

Here you expand the overall scene rather than narrow it.

Composition

Good picture composition will focus the viewer on the important elements. Viewers focus their attention a bit away from the centre of the screen, to the left or the right, above or below. Most shooters believe that viewers focus their attention about a third from the top or a third from either side (so they work to the 'rule of thirds'). If you set up an interview and shoot the interviewee in close-up, head and shoulders, think about the position. If the person is looking slightly to the right of the lens, frame them slightly to left of centre. If slightly to the left, then frame slightly to right of centre. Leave a little space on the side to which the interviewee is looking. It's called 'looking room'. Frame the head slightly above centre so the shoulders can be seen but not so the top of the head is cut off. Leave some space above the head, but too much space there makes the space obvious and detracts attention from the person speaking.

Be aware of distracting background. Be aware of background colours and lighting. If you do the interview in front of a window, the camera will absorb more light from the window than from the person, so the face will be darker. The reporter usually positions with the back to camera, face-to-face with the interviewee, and the camera is generally positioned looking at the interviewee over the reporter's shoulder.

Help viewers visualize the size of objects by positioning them in relation to people.

Movement

Movement is essential, but not for the camera; restrict pans, zooms, tilts and walking dollies to special occasions when they show the scene best. Natural news action should occur within the picture frame, not in camera movements. Viewers will follow you if the action keeps flowing in the same direction on the screen. It's called 'the line', and you should never 'cross the line'. For example, joggers are running along a path. If you shoot them running from the left side of the screen towards the right side, and then you move to the opposite side of the path to shoot again, they will appear to the viewer to now be running in the opposite direction. This doesn't make sense, because the viewer expects to see runners turn before they run in another direction. The same applies to interviews. There is a mental line between interviewer and interviewee. When the interview is finished, the cutaway shots must not cross the line, otherwise you and the guest will appear to be looking away from each other instead of towards each other.

Reaction shots can help if you have to edit or change direction, for example, crowd watching etc.

SCRIPTING FOR TELEVISION NEWS

The art of TV writing tells the viewer what the story is about, not what they can see. First, decide whether to write the script to fit the pictures or match the pictures to the script. You should write to the pictures because TV is a visual medium, so:

- always shotlist first
- if you've got good dramatic shots the words will spoil the effect, so be sparse with your script (maybe you only need words to fill about half the picture time)

- let the pictures speak for themselves.
- don't over-script: this reduces the impact for the viewers.

See how few words you can use, not how many.

Structure of TV news scripts

The cue (or lead or link or intro) is your way of preparing the viewer for what is to come. You are saying: 'Hey, listen to this'.

Try not to use adjectives in broadcast writing, but particularly not when you simply describe what you can see or hear on the screen:

- *screeched to a halt*
- *deafening blast*
- *dramatic siege.*

These adjectives aren't necessary, particularly if there is *sound on tape* (SOT) of them. If there's no sound, still don't tell the viewer; if you do and they can't hear it they'll wish they could and feel cheated. Let the viewer decide whether something really is dramatic.

Soundbites are good, and reporters should always be on the lookout for them. However, they really are bites, short and sweet.

A throw line is the line of the script that leads immediately to the soundbite itself; for example *said the situation was . . .* which is followed by the interviewee saying *Dire and must be fixed immediately.*

When names are given in the intro, the one mentioned last should belong to the face that next appears on screen. If you cut from the intro to an interview done by the reporter with the interviewee, the first picture you see must be the name you hear. But why give names and titles? They clutter and confuse. Just go to the video tape with names superimposed.

Avoid writing so many words that the video tape ends ahead of the commentary. Always have fewer words and be certain of pictures at the end of the report.

Visuals illustrate and clarify a report, not add to the general clutter. A visual should contain just enough information to get the message across; the fewer words and detail the better. Too much detail swamps the images and saturates the senses, so be simple if you want viewers to retain what they see.

Commentary

The commentary is only half the story. The viewer gets information with two senses: the eyes and the ears. Your script therefore is only part of the information the viewer gets. If the words and the pictures disagree, the pictures will win and the words (which usually contain the hard information) lose. Your script should add to the information that the viewer receives with the eyes by:

- complementing it
- supplementing it
- or, sometimes, simply explaining what is happening.

The words should counterpoint the action on the screen. The pictures are the melody, the words the harmony.

Commentary has its uses. The pictures tell the story, but the commentary can have hard facts, numbers etc. It's the bit of the information over which you have most control. So commentary should

- expand and explain the visuals
- give the story pace and direction
- highlight the pictures, sync sound and music.

Commentary should be done last: it's the easiest to alter, to shorten or lengthen to fit the other elements of the storytelling process. Commentary is also important in stitching together the different sequences to make the story logic flow better. That's why it's written last, after the cutting is complete, and when the strength and impact of all the other elements in the story can be assessed.

Make the visual story flow. Intrigue then inform. Consider the junction of two visual sequences: you might be able to make the join between them on the basis of a neat conjunction of two pictures, then let the commentary pick up from there. More often than not you've got no choice but to join up sequences with no real continuity in the pictures, and you have to cover the join with a neat phrase to make the logic flow properly.

It's important to cue precisely. You'll need to start a commentary so that the picture cut comes at the right place; otherwise the joins will begin to show.

Introducing new elements

Commentary can introduce new elements, like an interviewee for example. Instead of scripting a bad introduction, *We talked to Swiss cheese maker Jason Emmenthal about cheese prices* (boring), why not make it flow much better by losing the question at the start of the interview: *Mr Emmenthal why are you so interested in cheese?*, and starting at the part of the answer that says: *There are all sorts of cheeses . . ..* You could use a commentary link like: *But the price increase isn't seen by everyone as a bad thing.* There's no need to introduce him by name; it's much better to superimpose his name and title on the picture a little while after he's begun his answer. It's then that the viewer wants to know who and what he is and what his relevance is to the piece.

Commentary is also useful at the end of a clip of a speaker. It can help smooth what otherwise might be a very jerky transition to the next sequence. You have no (or very little) control over the way your interviewees phrase their sentences, so you have to craft yours to suit theirs to keep the flow of logic in the story.

Commentary checklist

1 Don't speak at the same time as your guest.
2 Don't make the viewer fight to hear you. If you really must have the commentary over voices, you've got to be very careful with the levels; especially if the 'in shot' voice and the commentary are the same sex. Try not to speak over vocal music (if you must use it).
3 Don't tell viewers what they can see for themselves. The one cardinal rule of commentary writing is, don't describe things. If the shot is of a red bus, don't tell viewers the bus is red or, worse, say: *This is a red bus.* Tell the viewers about the driver, the route, the special brakes; anything, but don't tell them what they can see. That's radio, not television.

4 Don't patronize. Don't tell the viewer what people in the video are thinking. Even if it's a crowd shot, it's better to have a cutaway of a man saying that he is so happy the Berlin Wall has been pulled down because he can visit his 90-year-old mum who he hasn't seen for years. If people really are happy, get them to say it for themselves and show happy pictures. Use the voices of the people in the film. It needn't be in a formal interview situation, just the voiceovers will do. For example, a shot of a lone man walking along the seashore with his voice (recorded separately) telling you how he felt when he heard he'd got cancer or AIDS can be very effective. In a case such as this you would need a short commentary line to set up the fact that another voice was coming up (the sick person).

5 Don't speak over the exciting bits. Reserve your commentary for the less exciting parts of the programme. You can help bring these shots or sequences to life with a neat phrase or visual pun, but don't be tempted to do the same to a picture that has great life and colour of its own. You'd spoil a car chase or a music sequence by putting words over it.

6 Don't clog the commentary with too many hard facts. Numbers are especially difficult. The result can be total chaos. The words will become a mess, and the pictures will win, every time.

7 Don't overwrite. Practice ruthless economy of words. If you haven't got anything to say, don't say it. Don't cover everything with commentary; leave room for music, effect and for the viewers to catch their breath. If there is good action or dominant sound, don't write anything at all. Let the viewers see and hear for themselves what is happening. In general, keep the commentary to the duller parts of the film. **Let the pictures speak for themselves; they do it much better**.

CAMERA ANGLES

The camera is like the eye, except it can also zoom in and out of a scene. This zooming happens all the time. The mind doesn't zoom in like a camera, but it does zoom in on a detail of a scene to bring it more closely to our attention. The TV camera imitates this automatic mental approach by three basic shots: long, medium and close-up.

These expand into about six different shots in everyday use:

- The long shot (LS) takes in the whole person from head to foot
- The medium long shot (MLS) cuts in closer, revealing the head to just below the knees
- The medium shot (MS) reveals the head to hips
- The medium close-up (MCU) gives head and shoulders
- The close-up (CU) shows head only
- The big close-up (BCU) fills the screen with the features of the face.

On location, where the camera is also taking in the surroundings, the LS would give a view of the whole picture. The MS reveals more detail, and the CU focuses on the action in detail, for example, the strain on the face. Another common shot is the general view (GV) or very long shot (VLS), which gives a panorama of the entire scene.

Camera positions

Another set of shots describes the relative height of the camera to the scene:

- the top shot (a bird's eye view)
- the high shot (looks down on the scene from the front)
- the level shot (in line with the subject's eyes)
- the low shot (the camera is looking up)
- the low-level shot (takes a worm's eye view of the world).

Single shots, two shots, three shots and groups shots all refer to the number of people in vision.

Cutaways

These are sometimes called 'noddies' when it is a reporter or a person being interviewed. They help bridge two different pictures (taken at different times, or when there is only one camera to record the interview). Common cutaways of the reporter, for example, are of a nodding head, listening hard, or of a two shot, where the camera pulls out to show the reporter and subject. There are ethical problems with such an approach for cutaways. If the reporter uses them wrongly, the interview could be reassembled in any order to produce any effect.

Revoiced questions for cutaways may also differ in tone or content from the original, giving a distorted impression.

Some news organizations, the BBC and CBS for example, have a rule that reverse shots are only to be made in the presence of the interviewee, if they are necessary at all, and the questions should be identical with the original, with no distortion. Others insist that no cutaways ever be used for ethical reasons, or that the edited answers be kept strictly in the order in which they were given in the interview.

VISUALS

Visuals are stills, slides, captions, charts, graphs and full-screen images that fill the wall behind the newsreader (windows). They are vital in giving the viewer easier information about facts and figures and in making news reports more interesting and watchable.

Pictures from newsagencies come into the electronic picture store, which holds them in a computer. The pictures can then be changed for use on screen. Most TV stations have a stock of coloured slides of major politicians, businessmen etc. Video freeze-frame techniques mean that stills can be used from videotape.

Graphics

Graphics can be very important to a story. They allow you to put a lot of information on screen rather than in your script.

Visual Production Effects machines now make it possible for the graphic artist to create graphics that are stylish and limited in their creativity only by the electronic memory of the machine and the designer's imagination.

The Paint Box is a means of painting with light using an electronic graphics machine. A light pen is moved over the screen to draw pictures in different colours.

Captions give the names of people and places.

Charts, maps and diagrams are often essential.

Overlays

Chromakey is the electronic means of displaying still or moving pictures behind newsreaders. All you see in the studio is the newsreader at the desk sitting in front of a brightly coloured back wall (usually blue). At home, viewers will see the newsreader with pictures behind him or her. The same applies for weather forecasts. Chromakey eliminates one colour from the screen and replaces it with a picture or graphic (if the colour is replaced by blue and the newsreader is also wearing blue, guess what happens!).

THE MECHANICS OF SCRIPTING FOR TV NEWS

The basis of all good script writing is the shot list. Don't ask an editor to do it for you; do it yourself. All good reporters should do them, and you can then use your own shorthand descriptions to remind you of the exact picture. Starting at the beginning, write down the timing of every shot and the specific occurrences in it. For example:

0.00 VLS car drives to camera and out left.
0.08 MS driver. Turns on radio.
0.11 LS car.
0.14 LS boy and ball. Moves slowly right.
0.18 MCU boy.

Continue to the end of the piece, noting everything in the action or shot you might need to refer to.

Now go off somewhere quiet with your notes, shotlist, reference books and telephone numbers of contributors, interviewees etc., and start writing. You'll have had a good idea of what you were going to say over each picture when you shot it. You might have altered that idea to a greater or lesser extent during editing, but the basics of the piece are there. Now you're just crafting the words.

Timing

Working to the formula of three words a second, start timing; but beware:

- don't cue to pictures: it never works
- stick to numbers.

Numbers are precise and allow you to do things you can't do if you try cueing to pictures. Some things are obvious, like making a person's name coincide with his or her picture, especially if it's the first time the person appears. For example, if there's a shot of a general of a regiment at 44 seconds, you might well want to introduce him with the words *The last general of the British Forces in Hong Kong was General Bloggs, commandant of the Black Watch . . ..* There are 11 words before the name, and 11 words take about 4 seconds to say, so the cue for that paragraph should come at 40 seconds.

You might find you've cut the video in such a way that it's inappropriate to cue at 40 seconds. You might be on a shot of a Chinese junk until 41, so modify the sentence to something like *Hong Kong's last British Commander.* That's just five words, 2 seconds, which will finish nicely before the shot of the general at 44 seconds. If, on the other hand, you've got plenty of time and find that without commentary the pictures drag, make the sentence longer: *Already many of Britain's soldiers have left the Territory, with more to go soon. But the last general of the British Forces in Hong Kong, the commandant of the Black Watch, is General Bloggs . . .*

Interviews

There are similar conventions for introducing a clip from an interview. Unlike studio interviews, which are often shown whole, an interview as an insert to a news item might just take a 20-second soundbite from a much longer interview. The interview insert will expand or explain the news story commentary. For example:

Commentary: *Mrs Lim still goes to the park every day to feed her hairy friends.*
Mrs Lim: *Well without me they'd starve . . .*

Or you might need to signal that there's a different point of view coming up:

Commentary: *But not all scientists agree that the speed of light in a black hole is infinity.*

Scientist: *That's just a simplistic view of the situation. People rely on these theories . . .*

Or add a fact to point up a personal reminiscence:

Commentary: *And from base camp it's 5 miles vertically, but 500 gruelling sweaty miles by road, and that's very long way on a bicycle.* Cyclist: *When I took my boots off at the top there were blisters everywhere . . .*

Names

Name mentions are better left until after the commentary intro, when the person is on screen, so that you can superimpose the name then. The general was introduced by name in the example above, but he's not going to speak. The name super is a better way of introducing who the interviewee is because it can be made to appear just when the speaker is making an important point. It's then that the viewers want to know the speaker's name and title or function.

Getting out of sync

A similar problem to that of introducing a speaker presents itself when the interviewee finishes and the commentary begins again. A good tip: ease the change of voice by taking a word or phrase that the speaker uses to finish, and let the rest of your sentence flow on into the next subject. For example:

Interviewee: *. . . next time I think I'll go by motorbike*
Commentary: *A motorbike would certainly ease wear and tear on the feet, but an internal combustion engine has its own problems at high altitudes.*

Script layout checklist

Do:

- double space your text. This gives you room to write in changes, and there will certainly be changes in dubbing.

- write on the right-hand side of the paper only. The left half of the paper is for the shotlist, visuals, times etc.
- include the studio intro (if there is one) in the script so the reader/reporter can understand the why and wherefore of the first few lines.
- be clear about when to expect a cue, and when the reader should stop or go straight on.

Convention says go until the end of the paragraph then wait, so make your paragraph breaks big (about six lines). Don't go over the page with a paragraph unless you really have to.

Don't:

- put cues so fast on top of one another that the reader feels the need to speed up to finish in time. The viewer will be similarly overloaded.
- put a cue in the middle of a sentence. If you want to get to a picture at a certain time, use the three words a second rule to get you there.
- finish a paragraph at, say, $43\frac{1}{2}$ seconds and cue again at 44. Half a second isn't even long enough to draw a breath and begin a new sentence. Your script will sound rushed and messy.

Four golden rules

1 The words and pictures must go together.
2 The commentary must not describe what the viewers can see for themselves.
3 Punctuate the commentary with silence.
4 The commentary must not be overwritten. To put it another way, the best script has the fewest words.

FURTHER READING

Alten, S. (1996). *Audio in Media*. Wadsworth.

Boyd, A. (1994). *Broadcast Journalism: Techniques of Radio and TV News*. Heinemann.

Crissell, A. (1994). *Understanding Radio*. Routledge.

Crook, T. (1998). *International Radio Journalism*. Routledge.

Gage, L. (1999). *A Guide to Commercial Radio Journalism*. Focal Press.

Gibson, R. (1991). *Radio and TV Reporting*. Simon and Schuster.

Hausman, C. (1992). *Crafting the News for Electronic Media*. Wadsworth.

Hilliard, R. (1997). *Writing for TV and Radio*. Wadsworth.

Holland, P. (1998). *The Television Handbook*. Routledge.

Hyde, S. W. (1991). *TV and Radio Announcing*. Houghton Mifflin.

Itule, B. and Anderson, D. (1997). *News Writing and Reporting for Today's Media*. McGraw-Hill.

Mcleish, R. (1999). *Radio Production*. Focal Press.

O'Donnell, L., Benoit, P. and Hausman, C. (1993). *Modern Radio Production*. Wadsworth.

Seymour-Ure, C. (1997). *The British Press and Broadcasting since 1945*. Blackwell.

Shingler, M. and Wieringa, C. (1998). *On Air*. Arnold.

Utterback, A. (1990). *Broadcast Voice Handbook*: *How to Polish your On-Air Delivery*. Bonus Books.

Walters, R. (1994). *Broadcast Writing*. McGraw-Hill.

White, T. (1996). *Broadcast News Writing, Reporting and Producing*. Focal Press.

Wilby, P. and Conroy, A. (1994). *Radio Handbook*. Routledge.

10 Broadcast presentation: looking and sounding great!

If listeners don't like what they hear they won't listen, or listen only with difficulty for a short time. Good broadcast journalism gets the listener to stay with the news for as long as possible. The language used is fundamental, and so is the way it is used both on radio and TV. Good broadcast speech must be conversational, intimate, one-to-one and credible, and transmit clearly and simply facts and information. However, the language of broadcast news is not just verbal. It's non-verbal as well. News is determined by a set of values, and the kind of language in which news is told reflects and expresses those values, and also the values of the journalist collecting, analysing and writing the news or information.

The way we use language affects content and message. For us all the language is always accompanied by the voice; the vocal quality and style of presentation affects the listener or viewer, sometimes more than the language itself. In broadcasting, news consists mainly of a number of brief items of hard news gathered into a short bulletin or, a couple of times a day, a longer bulletin (often 30 minutes). In the longer bulletins there is a combination of short and long items, giving background to the news, interviews and colour packages. However, there isn't much. On a 24-hour news station, for example, only about 10 per cent is actuality news. The rest is comment and information.

BROADCAST LANGUAGE

There are two types of broadcast language:

1 *Prepared* (scripted, can be a talk, a piece of news copy or a scripted reporter's piece).

2 *ad lib* (a piece of unscripted, unrehearsed conversational reporting or speech on radio or TV; it can also be an interview, both questions and answers).

Broadcast journalists may have to shift without pause from direct newscasting to interviewing a newsmaker guest in the studio or 'down the line', talking off air to guest or technician or answering phones. Broadcast language needs to be appropriate for individual newscasters to read aloud, adapting the language style to individual vocal styles within the tight constraints of difficult pronunciation and familiarity of vocabulary for the audience, who get only one chance to hear and understand.

If the first few words get the attention, listeners will keep listening. Clarity, shortness and colour (interest and enthusiasm) are needed to grab attention.

Good broadcast language is made simple by the use of various formulas:

1 Delete unnecessary or complex information (remove details of place, age or time).
2 Generalize whenever possible (a list becomes a category: a dog, cat and canary become 'pets'; there is no need to give all the names).
3 Use lots of concrete words and verbal actions (active not passive verbs – people *do* something. In broadcast language there has to be lots of action, so there must be action verbs, and they should be active not passive).

Go for certain facts to lead with, followed by an explanation of the action of the event (adding perhaps some conflict or criticism) in as short a timespan as possible.

Other aspects of broadcast language include:

- time and place (the where and when)
- facts and figures
- talking heads
- high rate of speech verbs (*say, tell, according to, announce, declare, refuse, threaten, warn* etc.)
- direct quotes (soundbites)
- lots of modifying expressions (*according to; speculation* etc.).

Good broadcast language has lots of soundbites. It is also full of sound effects that show the listener particularly that the reporter is really at the scene. Lots of good pictures replace these sound effects on TV.

The most common speech verbs include said, told, reported, asked, called on, expressed, spoke to, confirmed, issued and noted. Verbs also often appear in the present tense or in some form that shows that the action is happening now.

Examples of two types of good broadcast language are:

- narration: the words spoken by the newscaster working from a script
- actuality: the words spoken by the newsmakers (the electronic equivalent of print quotations; in radio news, the audio equivalent of newspaper pictures or television illustrations).

Soundbites take on additional functions in news; they call attention to non-verbal aspects of the story and are used so that the listener can hear or see the speaker's emotional reaction to the words being spoken more than to the language itself. They also refer to the sound of the story, and this forms a part of overall broadcast language used by journalists.

The language of broadcast news, therefore, is much wider in impact and interpretation than the words used. All news stories on both radio and television require a use of verbal and non-verbal language, which can also be seen in the way presenters speak and in their own non-verbal language. News reporters have to sound and look credible. The language and look are the basis of this authority. The pronunciation has to be acceptable and accurate and the vocal delivery pleasant and approachable. Broadcast credibility is a combination of the right language and the right speech for the medium and the occasion. Ultimately it is the presenter, the newscaster, the anchor, who is responsible for the success or failure of a news operation. The newscaster is the one people believe. News is not background noise. When listeners put the news on, they want to listen. The newscaster therefore has a responsibility to the listener and viewer, and news credibility hangs or falls on their words.

DELIVERY

A presenter or reporter who stumbles, corrects words and has to apologize, or just doesn't know how to communicate properly, is irritating and annoying to the listeners and viewers. They give up and switch off. They say to themselves: 'If this reporter is making so many mistakes, how can I be sure that the facts aren't also mistakes?'

Delivery shows the newscaster's confidence in the truth and importance of the message. The sound and the look need to be relaxed, without being too chatty or cosy. Chattiness detracts from the importance of what is being said. Suit the style of delivery to the story; deaths and tragedies need a different approach from good news. At the same time, the delivery must remain impartial and neutral and personal convictions, likes and dislikes should not show. However, detachment should not be taken too far. Newscasters are human, and every now and then their humanity should show through, particularly if the piece is a light-hearted one. However, the change of tone should always be subtle. Often all that is needed is a well-placed pause.

Phrasing

This means putting words together that belong together, in sense groups. Careful grouping of words can help you say exactly what you want to say. For example, read the following sentences and pause at the spaces:

He won		the right	to		vote	
He	won	the right	to	vote	
He	won	the right	to vote		
He	won	the	right	to	vote

The first sounds confusing, because the second phrase seems tacked on as an afterthought. It sounds as though you have announced a victory, then suddenly remembered that you ought to explain what the victory was. The second reads well, if the intention is to distinguish the victor. It tells two things: who and what. Number three reads even better if the intention is to identify three things: the person, the victory, the nature of the victory. Four sounds choppy and singalong.

Phrasing involves not only identifying word groups, but also speaking the groups smoothly. Usually it is unnecessary to come to a complete halt between phrases unless a sentence is so long that breathing is essential. In each of the above sentences you can easily say all six words in one breath and with continuous tone. By varying the speed, you achieve a sensible, natural, meaningful phrasing. If you understand what you are trying to read, the phrasing will follow automatically. Understanding is the key.

Emphasis

By emphasizing something you give it increased importance; you point your speech to bring out as much detail as you can. There are four ways of emphasizing something:

1 Volume: more breath gives a louder, fuller tone. Don't shout, simply use more volume in the word or phrase you want to emphasize. It doesn't, however, work in broadcasting, and is by far the least imaginative or creative way of emphasizing something.
2 Pausing: this is a change of rate to arouse the listeners' or viewers' interest. Whenever they hear a pause, they immediately prick up their ears to find out what's happening. Silence is a most effective means of emphasis and of getting the attention of listeners or viewers.
3 Rhythm: this is the indefinable something that makes speech musical, alive, interesting, exciting, listenable. Rhythm brings together phrasing, pace and emphasis. Try to throw your voice around, so that it has a musical quality. Monotonous delivery results from a lack of rhythm. However, at all times it must be natural speech rhythm. Don't think that rhythm is letting your voice go up and down like a ship on a rough sea.
4 Pitch: variation of pitch, so important for good speech and reading, is called intonation. This variation of pitch is controlled by the speech patterns, family and regional, unconsciously acquired from your surroundings and background, and by the meaning of what you are saying. Again, as with rhythm, there is nothing worse or more unnatural than a speaker who tries consciously to throw the voice around in an attempt to be interesting, without any reference to the meaning.

Broadcast speech

Broadcast speech is like a one-way conversation with an individual person, the listener or viewer. In other words, you are talking to a person, not to lots of people. The words you use should be written conversationally, but spoken with authority and interest. In order that broadcast speech will reach out to the listener and inform without displeasure, there must be two things: good articulation and good voice production. Otherwise people will have difficulty following what you are saying, and won't find it interesting to listen. Good articulation means using the lips, teeth, tongue and palate properly. These are what we use to form both vowel and consonant sounds. Specifically, good articulation means good consonant sounds. Careless articulation results in speech that fails to meet the one great demand made of the broadcaster: to be easily understood by the viewer or listener.

Pace is also important. Everyone has heard speakers who speak too quickly or too slowly; too fast and it's difficult to understand, too slow and it's boring. Pace, speed, is important. The overall impression that a reporter is speaking fast can be given by a proper use of pauses and phrasing. That way you don't actually have to speak fast, but just give the appearance of doing so. If there is a reasonable pause between sentences and stories, the listener can catch up with the thoughts you are expressing. Try to go from the beginning of a sentence to the end without stopping – hence the importance of short sentences. That way the listener stays with you. If you break up the sentence, and therefore the meaning, the listener gets annoyed and stops listening.

Once you have digested the theory of good speaking on radio or television, the techniques and practices, and have made them a habit, then forget the theory and just speak. It will come out right. If you spend the entire news bulletin or report thinking about all you have been told and learnt about voice production and breathing, consonants and vowels, your newscast will be unintelligible and meaningless. You will be far too worried about the sound of your voice and not worried enough about the message you are trying to get across. The emphasis, inflection, speed and the sense will all be wrong. You will be emphasizing all the wrong words – verbs and adjectives, for example – instead of letting the meaning speak for itself. Before you can tell the listener what has happened, you must know yourself. As a test, sit down and read a story to yourself. Throw the page away and try to repeat it in your own words. If you can, then you understand it and can communicate it. If you can't, then you haven't got the faintest idea of what you have just read, and the listener or viewer won't either.

The presenter is the focal point of any news programme and introduces, reads the stories and is responsible for the smooth running of the show. If anything goes wrong the viewer thinks it's the presenter's fault, although it often isn't. Viewers look at more than the words spoken, or the pictures around the news story: they are impressed by major presenter characteristics such as dress, facial expressions, gaze (eye contact) and sex (of the presenter). Audience perceptions are significantly altered by physical appearance. Eye contact is usually direct because the presenter uses a teleprompter and appears to be looking at the viewer. These non-verbal aspects are all part of broadcast speech.

Audiences are unforgiving of presenters who make mistakes in their speech. Research shows that errors such as:

- slurs in pronunciation
- repeated words or phrases
- mispronunciations
- hesitations in responding to an on-camera cue
- looking off to one side of the screen when the shot returns to the studio

are all considered negatively by viewers, and the programme suffers a severe loss of credibility.

Language speed

Experiments show that listeners and viewers need a certain amount of time to understand what is being said. If the word rate is too slow (or if the words don't connect together naturally and sensibly) they get bored. If the word rate is too fast they can't understand and get lost. They need time to catch up (full stops). The delivery rate also has to be right for individual presenters. It is clear that delivery rates and the language used interrelate. The words have to be simple and easy enough for the presenter to say them fast, without fluffing.

Broadcast journalists must be aware of two problems with language:

1 it can easily be misheard
2 it can easily be misunderstood.

Listeners tend to hear what they want to hear, and interpret what they hear in terms of what they think and believe. Therefore, if the speed of the language isn't right, the listener doesn't understand or gets a meaning different from the one the reporter wants to convey. Listeners only recall about 25 per cent of what they hear in a news bulletin. Recall of stories improves when they are written logically according to the who–what–when–where–why – how technique and spoken in natural, conversational language at the right pace and with the right pronunciation. Listeners have greater difficulty in understanding longer sentences with too many clauses. Simple sentences have the most impact. It is much easier for the presenter to speak at the right speed (in English, about 180 words a minute) if the sentences are simple.

Conclusion

The language of broadcast news is very different from the language of print, that of newspapers, and is both verbal and non-verbal. Non-verbal language, particularly on TV, can incorporate meaning that may differ from the words spoken. It is also evident that listeners and employers look for a good, fast pace of delivery (in English, about 180 words a minute) with an intimate one-to-one approach. Radio and TV are tools, and will be no worse or better than those who use them. Technology doesn't make things better; if reporters can't write, they can't write, whether with quill pen or computer; if they can't report, they can't report, and all the technology in the world won't save them. Reporters who can write, report, analyse and ask the bright, right question are needed in radio and TV today more than ever. The vocal tools of the broadcast journalist are as important as the literary, journalistic ones. The ability to construct the news story so that its message is spoken with the maximum vocal credibility and conversational intimacy is of paramount importance. It's not a question of public speaking, elocution or of speaking 'properly'. It's a question of being able to report with the necessary authority, and this means vocal quality and intimacy linked with the right kind of professional language.

THE NEWSCAST

Radio newscasts differ from TV newscasts. They are shorter, and are repeated with greater regularity during the day. Lead stories are changed and all stories are shuffled around a lot between bulletins. The lead of the 0700 bulletin might not be the lead at 0730 hrs.

Story order

Radio changes story order a lot so listeners don't think they're hearing the same things over and over, and to give a more immediate sound. Don't lead with an unimportant story and bury the important one down the bulletin just to make a change. If you need variety, rewrite the important story (and many others as well if time permits). Use different actuality and soundbites. Always try to present stories in order of importance; the more important stories are those that have the greatest listener impact on the largest number of people, which means usually the most local stories. Live stories are usually better suited to being lead stories. The important story, the lead, for a radio bulletin is usually the story that is most important or relevant at that particular time.

Bulletin stories are better remembered when they are grouped in some logical order, usually by subject or theme or geography. International, economic, crime, flow more naturally within the newscast when they are in similar blocks. Groups focus the listener's attention on one general theme and the newscaster can write logical transitions between stories in a group . . . *another sign of bad economic times* . . . Geographic groupings may be local then overseas etc. Actuality groupings may be a group with soundbites, then a group of newscaster copy etc.

Lighter (*and finally*) stories are good at the end of a bulletin or before a commercial in the middle of a bulletin.

Radio actuality

The radio newscaster has a great advantage over TV: you can handle a complex newscast by yourself by just pushing buttons (either cartridges or digital). Radio is great at using live material at the last moment, but the live material must be perfect and accurate to be credible. Remember: 30 seconds is a long time in radio. In an unplanned live report remember to cue the reporter at the other end: *Charles, what did the jury say?*

TV appearance and dress

Successful dress on TV is mostly knowing what *not* to wear. Don't ever wear anything – clothes or jewellery – that is distracting and gets the viewer's attention. You want their attention on you, not your clothes. You want them to listen to the news, not watch your earrings or latest tie.

Remember:

- Avoid anything bulky or patterned; heavyweight clothes tend to make you look chunky and big patterns have the same effect
- Small patterns make the camera strobe, a wavy pattern on the screen
- Suits (men and women) shouldn't be too dark or placed very close to a light shirt or blouse; black with white is difficult for the camera to handle
- Clothes should fit
- Frilly blouses or collars can cause distraction
- Bulky jewellery or earrings or rings appear awkward or can jangle
- Wear clothes that are comfortable and look good but are not over-stylish or dressy; you have to be accepted by the ordinary viewer and are not a model (male or female)
- Stick to basic clothes that don't have to be (in fact should not be) very expensive (particularly reporters).

Navy is a good colour, and lightweight jackets are good too. Light-coloured outfits are fine, but stick to the darker shades of beige and don't choose the extremely light varieties of blue and grey. Very light clothes tend not to photograph well. Remember the seasons. Men should avoid too colourful, ostentatious ties. Open-collared blouses and those without a collar are fine for women, but not plunging necklines.

For men, haircut choice is simple. Women have a wider choice, but keep it natural and simple. Don't be too flashy. News anchors are news people, not top fashion models. Your clothes should never say 'I can afford expensive clothes'. Most viewers can't.

Talking to the camera

Look directly into the lens when you look up; even a small deflection of your gaze will be obvious to the viewer. It takes practice, because we don't normally look straight into the eyes of the person we're talking to, and certainly not for long. Side-to-side movements of eyes on camera look terrible; the camera vastly magnifies such movement. It's fine to look down from time to time; in fact it is necessary to break the monotony of looking straight at the camera (through the autocue). Viewers expect you to look down at your script every now and then. If you are not working with an autocue but with cue cards, have them held beneath the lens and not to either side.

Movement of head and body is fine when the shot is right. For example, with a CU you should hold your head very still, but with a medium long shot you *must* have some restrained movement and gesture of body.

Facial expression is difficult. Avoid stiff, mechanical expressions. Don't look concerned every time there's an accident story (the same applies in radio with the voice). This colours the story and takes away your objectivity. Likewise, don't overuse your beaming smile when someone's won the lottery. When you do use an expression, hold it for a fraction longer than you think is necessary. Dropping your expression immediately you complete your line is amateurish and distracting.

Working with a microphone

These tips apply to both radio and TV.

Keep a standard distance from the microphone. Don't move your head in and out or move the mike closer and further away. It changes the sound level. How close to the mike? That depends: but about 20 cm (the length of an outstretched hand) is fine.

In noisy situations you must move much closer to the mike so that your voice is more obvious than the background noise. Wherever possible use clip-on mikes on TV when you are doing pieces to camera. These are usually clipped about 15 cm below the chin, and they are less distracting than hand-held mikes. Be careful of noise if you use a hand-held mike. Cables transmit noise too, so don't touch, kick or jiggle them. If you are wearing a clip-on mike, be careful not to brush hands or papers against it or wear any jewellery that will knock against it. Remember: with a clip-on mike, take it off before you leave the set or location. Otherwise you'll break it, and they're expensive to replace.

Using the Autocue™

Autocues (teleprompters) project the image of the script onto a
one-way mirror that covers the lens of the camera. You can dictate the
speed at which the autocue rolls; get it right for you. This allows you
to maintain eye contact with the viewer. Using an autocue is a skill
that requires practice:

1 Pick the same line and read that rather than work your way down
   the page.
2 Maintain a reasonably steady pace throughout.
3 Make sure you can see the autocue. You must have the camera
   positioned so you can comfortably read the screen. You need to be
   able to read with precision, and not have to stare or peer or frown to
   read the words because they are too far away.
4 If you can't read the words, ask for the camera to be moved closer
   (that's fine). Make sure it is at the right height so you aren't looking
   upwards.

Moving between cameras

1 When you shift your look from one camera to another, make the
   transition smoothly and naturally by looking down and reading from
   your script while the director switches cameras. If you look down on
   cue before the switch, then after a phrase or two look back up at the
   other camera, the switch will happen without you appearing to have
   moved too early or too late.
2 If there are two of you, remember visually to acknowledge each
   other.
3 If the anchor is leading into a story that you will report live on the
   set, look at the anchor. Only after the switch has been made
   from the two-shot to the CU should you look again at the
   teleprompter.
4 If you are co-anchoring a newscast and the director begins with a
   two-shot as you read the headlines, look into the camera lens, then,
   when your co-anchor begins to read, turn your head to look and
   listen to the other. If you look steadily at the teleprompter while the
   co-anchor is reading, your audience may think you don't like each
   other; it looks unreal.

Reading from scripts

If you're reporting live with a script it will be less obvious if you hold it where it can be seen. Hold it away from you, at arm's length. Then when you look you only have to drop your eyes, not your head. Don't hold it close to your chest because you then have to drop your head. You can gesture with your notes, and you can visually punctuate by lowering and raising them. Sometimes, in a court story, you should actually be seen reading the script word for word. Discuss camera movements before you shoot. Decide in advance where you'll look when you lead into tape or a live report. If a monitor is placed so you can see it to the left or right of camera, you can look directly towards it to anticipate video footage. Your eye movement in this direction gives a visual cue to the viewer that something is about to happen, and it also saves you the embarrassment of staring at the camera when you have nothing to say. Concentrate on what you're doing, both in the studio and in the field. Don't let things distract you. In the studio, concentrate when you're not on camera. React to unexpected happenings.

REPORTING LIVE

Reporting live is one of the most profound differences between print and broadcast. Reporting live is usual and daily for radio reporters. Immediacy has always been the big advantage of radio. New technology now means that TV can do this too. It can put a live signal into the home almost as quickly and easily as radio does.

Organize your thoughts. Broadcast reporters have to learn early in their career to organize their thoughts quickly and say them fluently and quickly. They also develop *ad lib* skills. Broadcast reporters are expected to report from the scene of a breaking news story, often without a script. The best way to organize your material is with a notebook. You must also learn to take notes quickly (speed writing or teeline). However, never get so involved in taking notes that you lose track of what's happening. Reporting live, radio reporters work alone. TV reporters need a crew and a microwave truck or a satellite phone. TV reporters going live will sometimes send the news conference or individual interview back to the station unedited as it is actually happening. Someone at the station will monitor the feed and make notes of good soundbites or pictures etc. When the feed is over, producers can talk with the reporter and decide which soundbites etc. will be used to go with the reporter's live piece. The reporter then does a live opener from the scene and cues in the soundbites, which are played from the control room, followed by a cut back to the reporter live for the closing scene/words. Today it is also common to do it all from a mobile truck. New technology allows TV crews to record and edit video in the truck, add the reporter's narration and play the story live without using any of the support station equipment.

For the live report, it is common with a big story for the anchor to continue the story for the 'latest' by asking the reporter live at the scene for additional answers to questions or comments. Today in, say, an earthquake disaster, reporters can be at the scene within hours, together with a portable satellite earth station, and can put on a wireless mike and report live as soon as they are ready. They use a digital sky phone that connects to the satellite and is then downloaded to the earth station and to the TV station. The satellite dish and antennae now fit into a box slightly larger than a briefcase. ENG is great, but it also increases the risk of one-sided, inaccurate reports.

The stand-upper

Stand-uppers are also called pieces to camera. Reporters in TV can enhance their reports, and their reputations, by appearing on camera. These short stand-uppers usually feature the reporter standing in front of the scene, talking. If that's all that happens, it's boring. If it is a story with lots of colour and movement, the TV reporter should never indulge in motionless speech looking at the camera. Use the action as the backdrop and, whenever possible, take part in the action; you are there and the viewer isn't. Viewers want to see the face behind the voice, doing things they aren't able but would like to do. This kind of reporting adds variety and shows viewers that the reporter is where the action is, reporting the action. Otherwise, you may as well do it in the studio.

The piece to camera (stand-upper) may be used at the beginning of an item to set the scene, in the middle to act as a bridge linking the threads of the story or at the end as the reporter's way of signing off in a human way. Stand-uppers are usually short.

Stand-uppers should never be static, motionless. Television is the movies, so move. As you talk, move, look, show the viewer what you are talking about. Don't worry what your hands are doing; let them look after themselves. However, try not to clasp them in front of you. Gesture in a natural way.

Very often in stand-uppers reporters are in shot holding a huge microphone in front of them, with trailing mike cable in shot as well. It's distracting, looks untidy and stops the reporter from actually doing things in a normal way. Try to get some other type of mike, such as a radio mike or an out of vision mike held by someone else.

FURTHER READING

Boyd, A. (1994). *Broadcast Journalism: Techniques of Radio and TV News*. Focal Press.

Chantler, P. and Harris, S. (1992). *Local Radio Journalism*. Focal Press.

Crook, T. (1998). *International Radio Journalism*. Routledge.

Gage, L. (1999). *A Guide to Commercial Radio Journalism*. Focal Press.

Holland, P. (1998). *The Television Handbook*. Routledge.

Wilby, P. and Conroy, A. (1994). *The Radio Handbook*. Routledge.

11 Interviewing for print

Interviewing is the only way to get quotes. All stories need quotes; therefore, all stories need interviewing skills. Before you interview someone you need to do as much background research as possible. First, decide what it is you want to know from the interview:

- do you need a particular fact?
- do you want a date?
- do you need a phone number?
- do you need an expert name?
- do you want background?
- what statistics do you need?

Make a list of the research you need to carry out, then decide why you want to know this information:

- is it critical to your story?
- is it secondary?
- is it interesting but optional?

Rank your list of research items, least to most important, then work out how you will use the information:

- will you quote the information, the source or both?
- must you include the statistic or the date to make your story complete?
- will you use the information to frame interview questions?

Reporters usually don't have the luxury of much time to do the research. For a quick deadline, use the phone. With more time, you might be able to go in person. Set a realistic deadline to start the story. Sometimes you get so involved in trying to get exactly the right people to interview, or to answer the questions you've decided need answering, that the story deadline gets close without anything actually being done. This is a fatal flaw. Set a realistic deadline after which you stop researching and gather the facts for the story, or change stories if the research is proving the story angle you've adopted to be too difficult. When you have done your research it is time to create the questions, remembering that every question will depend on the answer given to the previous question when you are doing the interview itself. However, it is still a wise precaution to create your own list of possible questions before you go to the interview; and indeed before you actually ring people to ask them to be interviewed.

Put the subject's name in the middle of a piece of paper, and all around it put points learned through research plus every other source you can think of. All the facts. Put these into a kind of logical order. Start with easy questions, where the subject doesn't need to think too deeply and can relax. Then work up to more substantial questions when there is a warm rapport. Circle each fact and link it separately with a line of thought, so you've got trains of thought. Ask the questions in your head. Note down, in as few words as possible, every query you have connected with the topic. Include solutions. When you ask a particular person to be interviewed, it is sometimes difficult to get their agreement. You have to convince the person to agree to an interview. Always be prepared for a 'no', but use psychology and charm and hope for a 'yes'.

THE INTERVIEWEE

You have to decide who initially will be your best interview and why. You may want to interview someone because:

- their job is important
- they do something important
- they are charged with a big crime
- they know something or someone important
- they have watched something important happen
- something important has happened to them (accident victim etc.)
- they represent an important national trend (traveller caught at airport during typhoon; working couple who can't buy a house because prices are too expensive etc.).

The type of person you will be looking for may be ordinary (a member of the general public), a specialist or a celebrity.

A good interviewee needs to be accessible, reliable, accountable and quotable. However, you need to be careful about the rent-a-quote politician who will say something about anything at the drop of a hat.

If a particular interviewee you really want won't talk, you can still do the story; you just have to do it differently. You can write the story anyway without the quotes. You can write the story saying that you tried but couldn't get a quote. You can convince the interviewee to talk. People refuse to be interviewed because of:

- time
- guilt
- anxiety
- protection (shielding someone)
- ignorance (doesn't want to admit they don't know)
- embarrassment
- privacy (doesn't want to share a personal catastrophe with the public).

Obtaining the interview

You can sometimes be lucky and simply be in the right place for an interview at the right time. Sometimes you get the interview you want by focusing on what people want to talk about, rather than what they won't discuss. Sometimes you get the person you want not by going through the Public Relations department but by managing to contact the newsmaker by yourself, perhaps at a place other than their work. People decide to be interviewed for various reasons. Sometimes it is out of a sense of pride and fairness. Others feel they must speak out because of something they feel is unjust. Others just like the attention, or feel they want to represent a particular point of view. Further reasons include a sense of professional or personal prestige, or a desire for community good. All of these can be used in an attempt to get someone to say something.

Meeting the interviewee

Arrive on time. In fact, try to arrive a few minutes early. There is nothing worse than arriving late and flustered, and not being cool, calm and collected.

Be in control. This is very important. You are the professional; expect the interviewee to realize that (even if this is your very first interview).

Act like a professional. This requires self-confidence. Self-confidence is a state of mind; it is also the product of being adequately prepared for the encounter and looking and feeling well. The first few minutes of any interview situation are vital; it is then that rapport can be achieved. Spend a few minutes warming up the interviewee – that's not wasting time, but saving it. Get the interviewee calm and chatting to you in a relaxed manner before you start the interview proper. Be careful of body language and don't appear to act in a threatening way. Friendliness is what achieves best results and opens up the thoughts of the interviewee.

INTERVIEW TECHNIQUES

Interviews are an exchange of information, opinion or experience from one person to another. Interviewing is different to a conversation; in an interview, the interviewer keeps control. First define exactly what you need, then plan the questions to get that information. Use open-ended questions that can't be answered by a simple yes or no. Getting the interviewee to say yes can sometimes be difficult. Be warm, friendly, quiet. You'll get your answer if you're charming, and if you make the interviewee think he or she is the expert. Questions can range from cordial to antagonistic (sometimes all within the one interview). The type and approach you adopt depends on the information you want and the circumstances of the interview. Remember: the best interviewer gets the best quotes and the best story. There are two basic types of question:

- those from your research
- those that come up in the course of the interview by listening to answers.

Both are very important, and both will be used during the course of the interview.

1 Don't write out your questions; listen and respond to the answers. You can, however, have trigger words (for example, photos – where?).
2 Don't ask predictable questions; they give predictable answers (e.g. 'How do you feel?').
3 Avoid general questions; don't ask 'What's the meaning of life?' or 'How would you solve the world's problems?' Be specific.

4 Don't be shy to ask questions. That's why you are there, so ask whatever you want to know.

Interviewers must

- listen
- observe
- enquire
- respond
- record.

During the interview, be in charge. Never let your subject take over. Demeanour and appearance are both important, because they determine the way your interviewee will react to you. The interviewee is probably feeling nervous; put him or her at ease.

Achieve a rapport, a sympathy, with interviewees so they will think of you as a listening friend to whom they can talk. Be a good listener. Give them time to think after you've asked a question. Listen for important and meaningful pauses when interviewees are merely considering the next words. Be able to differentiate between this kind of important pause in the conversation and a full stop. Be casual and chatty at the start; don't get down to business straightaway. Set an agenda (but don't give away the questions). Under no circumstances tell interviewees what precise questions you are going to ask, even though they will almost certainly want to know. Give them general guidelines, but not precise questions. That is your editorial right; don't allow it to be taken away.

Good questions make the interviewee want to answer them. Ask a question that is clear and cannot be misinterpreted and asks precisely what you want the interviewee to answer. Focus on 'how' and 'why' questions. Remember:

- define terms
- consider the interviewee's viewpoint
- ask questions the interviewee is qualified to answer
- separate yourself from criticism of the interviewee
- ask questions to which you know the answers
- if you don't ask, you won't get an answer
- ask follow-up questions to clarify
- restate the answer (if you aren't sure, say something like *are you saying that . . .*)

- clarify generalizations (ask what evidence there is for calling two robberies a crime wave)
- translate jargon (ask for a definition or explanation)
- verify statistics and dates (ask after the interview where you can find a record of the statistical information given; you should check)
- determine sequence (did you get married before or after you became a politician?)
- ask for specific sources (if the interviewee can't answer, ask who might know)
- follow up questions that expand
- try not to ask questions to which the answer is 'yes' or 'no'.

- ask *why do you say that?*
- ask for specific examples
- ask for a chronology (*what happened after that?*)
- display your ignorance (then the interviewee will explain and give new information)
- repeat the question if it isn't answered, either deliberately or unintentionally
- be critical and suspicious of what is said; don't just believe everything.

THE INTERVIEW

During the interview:

- ask the easy questions first and save the difficult ones for later
- relax
- let the interviewee talk and don't interrupt unless you have to
- display empathy and concentration
- listen
- be willing to show your ignorance
- avoid arrogance
- be selectively silent (an unfilled silence lets the interviewee collect new thoughts or expand on an idea).

The interviewee will expect you, the professional, to end the interview. Put away your notebook, but keep listening. Deny requests to preview the story. You keep editorial control. Say thank you.

Interviewing checklist

1 Know the subject:

- seek specific information
- research the subject
- list the question areas.

2 Know the person:

- know relevant biographical information
- know the person's expertise regarding the subject matter.

3 Set up the interview:

- set the time (at the interviewee's convenience), the length of time needed and possible return visits
- set the place (interviewee's or neutral, whichever is more comfortable).

4 Discuss arrangements:

- will you bring a tape recorder or just a notebook?
- will you bring a photographer or just a camera?
- will you let the interviewee check the accuracy of quotes?

5 When you arrive:

- control the seating arrangement if possible
- place the recorder at the best spot
- warm up the person briefly with small talk
- set the ground rules (put everything on-the-record and make everything attributable)
- use good interview techniques
- ask open-ended questions
- allow the person to think and to speak in his or her own time
- don't be threatening in voice or manner
- control the flow but be flexible
- take good notes
- be unobtrusive
- be thorough
- use a tape recorder (check that it works, and note digital counter for important bits).

6 Before you leave:

- ask if there's anything the interviewee wants to add
- check facts – spellings, dates, statistics, quotes
- say you may ring again to recheck possible facts
- let interviewee know approximate publication date.

7 After the interview:

- organize your notes – immediately
- work out a proper lead
- write a coherent story
- then sub your story into better writing.

COMMON INTERVIEWING TRAPS

1 *The source agrees to an interview but keeps postponing.* It could be just a busy diary, but if it continues you should recognize that the source has no real intention of coming to the interview. Confront your source; be persistent without being unpleasant. Use charm to get what you want.

2 *The source keeps wandering off the topic during the interview.* Try putting your pen down. If that doesn't work, wait for a pause and ask another question. If the source is giving you non-pertinent information and doing so in a long-winded manner, you may have to interrupt and steer the interview back onto the topic. Recognize that some sources try to tell you what *they* want you to know, not what they know you want. Your backgrounding should alert you to this.

3 *During the interview the source says: Now this is off-the-record.* Immediately hold up your hand like a stop sign and reply: *if it's off-the-record, don't tell me.* If you allow a source to tell you something off-the-record, you can't publish it. The source is probably relying on that. Giving a source off-the-record privileges compromises journalists and the free flow of news. Your first response should be *no.* You may find that the source willingly tells you the information anyway, on-the-record. If not, at the end of the interview ask your source if they want to tell you now, on-the-record.

4 *After telling you something, the source says, 'now that was off-the-record.* You say, *sorry, no it wasn't.* Then explain that when

you set up an interview, all your sources are told that they are speaking for publication. Once the interview begins you must give your permission before a source can go off-the-record, and you never give it.

5 *After the interview the source asks to see the story before you publish it.* This is *always* a definite no. You don't have time to show stories to sources, and you don't need the hassle of being edited by a source (you have enough hassle being edited by an editor). Simply explain that your editor doesn't allow you to do that (get your editor to make it a policy for you – it always is). However, if the story is highly complex or technical it is acceptable to ask the source to review your finished piece for accuracy before you publish it. This is your decision and is being done under your control. Sometimes you may say you'll ring to just double-check a fact or quote. That's different to giving them the whole story to change as they wish. You must always keep editorial control.

6 *The source asks for a list of the questions that will be asked.* The answer is *always* no. There are several reasons you can give: *I don't prepare questions in advance . . . I ask questions arising out of what you say in your answers* (which should always be true); *It is not editorial policy to give a list of questions in advance.* Sometimes the source will say: *No questions, no interview.* In this case, find someone else. It is, however, perfectly acceptable to give them a general idea of the kinds of questions that you might ask about a topic. That's a pre-interview briefing, which is fine. Never give the actual questions. Apart from anything else, if you do, and then don't ask a question at the interview or ask different ones, you'll be accused of not telling the interviewee beforehand.

7 *The source asks for money.* The answer to that is *sorry, we don't do that kind of journalism.* Never get into the situation where you have to pay for interviews. If someone wants to be paid for doing a story, you will always mistrust the motives behind speaking to you (if doing it simply for profit, interviewees might not be truthful). Remember, in most cases you are giving them free publicity, which is good for them, so you are doing them a favour by interviewing them. They should always do it for free.

8 *You can't break the minder barrier.* Often you are trying to get to a particular person for a quote for some facts, and you can't get past the secretary/PR person/personal assistant/ spouse etc. You know that, if only you could get to speak to the person, you'd get your

quotes. It's breaking through the minder barrier that's the problem. Public figures can avoid an interviewer or journalist simply because someone else answers their phone. Some suggestions:

- Be charming. Cultivate the person shielding the source. Try to remember their first name, and treat them like a friend. Your aim is to get the buffer person to like you and say so to the boss, then you'll get your story.
- Try to find a reason for the person to let you through. 'I know everyone is calling you and you're about to go out/go crazy/go into a meeting' ... *I'm very sorry, but I promise if you give me two minutes of your time I won't bother you again ... I promise it really will only be two minutes.*
- Call after normal working hours. Sometimes you can be lucky and the person, working late, will answer the phone.
- Ask for the person by name, or by a familiar nickname: *Can I speak to James please?* (they'll think you're a friend).
- Say: *It's a personal call.* Only tell the person who you are when you get through.
- Call the person at home. In casual conversation or through research, find out where the interviewee lives. A surprising number of important people are in the phone book.
- Find the interviewee in an informal situation (in a lift, at a car park, in the pub, in a restaurant) and ask for a short chat.
- Ask someone who knows the person to ask for you.

Finally, convince the interviewee that he or she is the most important person in the world, and you want to tell the world about how good he or she is.

FURTHER READING

Biani, S. (1992). *Interviews that Work: A Practical Guide for Journalists.* Wadsworth.

Clayton, J. (1994). *Interviewing for Journalists.* Piatkus Books.

Hennessy, B. (1997). *Writing Feature Articles.* Focal Press.

Keeble, R. (1998). *The Newspaper Handbook.* Routledge.

12 Interviewing for radio and TV

Broadcast reporters don't have much time to prepare and research their interviews for radio or television. The interview itself is also shorter than it would be in print. A good broadcast reporter must be able to interview not only people prepared to be interviewed, but also people who have never been near a microphone or television camera. A good broadcast reporter must have something worthwhile to put on air and want the interview to be interesting to watch. The worst sin in TV news is to be dull; the worst sin for a TV reporter is to do a dull interview. If you are dull, it doesn't matter how responsible, accurate or unbiased you are. If no one is listening, what is the point?

All news comes from an interview of one kind or another, whether a chat, an informal phone call or a formal recorded interview. The appeal of radio and TV interviews is that the listener or viewer can hear and see the facts straight from the source. The speaker's own words give greater authority than print quotes.

The aim of the interview is to provide, in the interviewee's own words, facts, reasons, opinions on a particular topic so that the listeners or viewers can form their own conclusion as to the truth of what's being said. The interviewer has to:

- match the goods on offer with the customer's needs
- tease out the story in the teller's own words
- report so that listeners can make up their own mind
- expose viewpoints to public debate.

An interview is a conversation between two people to get as much information as possible, and a performance in its own right; a mini-programme with a beginning, a middle and an end. It is made up of questions and answers and information.

Questions must sparkle, be lively, interesting and sound enthusiastic.

The interviewer:

- must sound spontaneous
- must be interested in what is being said
- must be a good listener
- must be a watchdog for the listener/viewer
- represents the listener and should ask the kind of questions the listener would like to ask
- is the bridge between non-expert and expert; between the person in the street and the official
- never turns into a public relations officer or stenographer.

A good interview tests the truth of an argument by exploring its points of tension or controversy.

TYPES OF INTERVIEWS

An interview may be:

1	Informational	(to give the listener or viewer information); these are the short, hard fact news type, or the longer current affairs type
2	Interpretative	(the interviewee comments on facts supplied by the interviewer)
3	Emotional	(provide an insight into the interviewee's state of mind).

Within these three types are the various categories of interview:

• hard news	(short, to the point, dealing only with important facts; for major stories)
• information	(not restricted to major stories; can be about events or provide background, and explain the facts – the how and why)
• adversarial	(a kind of 'cross-examination'; don't clash head-on with the interviewee)
• interpretative	(can be a reaction or explanation)
• vox pops	(short gathering of answers to one question)
• personal	(revealing a personality and motivation, a profile; intimate and penetrating, can make fascinating listening)

- entertainment (the lighter side)
- actuality (interviewee alone with reporter's voice removed)
- telephone (avoid whenever possible because of bad quality; if you have to use it, keep the interview as short as possible)
- investigative (gets behind the facts to discover what really caused the event; often for a documentary)
- emotional (lays bare someone's feelings so the listener or viewer can share in a personal tragedy; tread carefully)
- grabbed (getting an interview when people don't want to give one; obtained by pushing a camera/mike in front of them and asking the question).

Interviews can be live or on tape, on the telephone, in the field or in the studio. You can be covering a breaking news story or preparing a news feature. All broadcast interviews share the need for succinct questions and answers, good pacing and interest.

TELEPHONE INTERVIEWS

Telephone interviews are only used when the event happens so close to airtime that pictures or actuality aren't available. In radio, telephone interviews are very common. It's an easy way to get a comment from an expert or eyewitness. Telephone interviews, either live or on tape, also give an interviewer access to a world of experts and issues outside the local community. A taped interview gives more freedom because you can edit later. A live interview is sudden and unchangeable.

When doing telephone interviews, develop familiarity as appropriate and smile through the phone; seem interested and appear to be listening. Interviewees can't see your interest, so they must hear your interest. Your voice must sound enthusiastic and interested. Explain the process: you should always tell interviewees that what is being said might appear on air. If you are doing it live explain that you will need short, sharp, interesting answers, and that you may have to interrupt occasionally. Tell them not to worry; reassure interviewees and tell them not to be nervous. Explain the way the interview will go beforehand; explain the focus but don't tell them the questions.

Remember:

- watch the *uh-huhs*
- vary the sequence of questions: one question–answer after another is not as interesting to the listener or viewer as a question–answer followed by something different, like *what do you mean?*
- listen: in a telephone conversation especially you can easily ask a question that has no relationship to the comment the person just made because you are preoccupied. Take notes to help maintain your interest.

FIELD INTERVIEWS

Most broadcast reporters spend a lot of time out of the office doing interviews in the field. You should look for the following kinds of interviewee when doing a story:

- established experts
- lower level, less official people who make the system work; they won't be in positions of authority, but understand or live in the circumstances you are looking at
- the person who is different; not part of the system, not an authority, but a fluent, interesting observer whose view is a bit more informed than the ordinary person in the street.

The interviewee

Getting someone to agree to an interview can be very difficult. Telephone ahead if possible to organize a time and place (unless you are doing a telephone interview, when you can do it on the spot). If someone says no, ask again before getting someone else. However, if you really need that particular person, then wait. Find out where he or she will be when it is convenient for you and catch them unexpectedly (door stopping). Be persistent, but not pushy. Whenever possible, try to visit the potential interviewee without the camera crew to set the interview up.

Remember:

1 Talk with the person for a while to assess what he or she knows and feels; look for someone who is a fluent, clear speaker, outspoken and willing to say something controversial.

2 Focus the topic and prepare the interviewee quickly; remember to explain how the equipment works and put the interviewee at ease.

3 Talk the interview through in a general, not specific way. Don't ask too many questions before the interview starts because the on-air interview will then seem rehearsed and the person might say, 'as I told you before'. Even worse, you might forget to ask a question because you think you've already asked it.

4 Phrase the questions carefully so that you will be able to use the answer with a voiceover introduction.

5 Anticipate the answer to your question. Don't make it a leading question, putting words into the interviewee's mouth so that all you get is 'I agree'. Phrase the question with the possible answer in mind so that the interviewee will respond with the answer taken from the hint in your question.

6 If you have to ask the interviewee to repeat an answer, try to ask the question differently the second or third time, or you will lose the interviewee's spontaneity. Responses have to be fresh.

Live interviews

Your interview in the field can either be live or recorded and edited for later use. A live interview in a breaking news story has some special problems. You can make mistakes, respond to rumour rather than facts, make libellous comments unwittingly and react too quickly to your own emotions. Once you've said something in a live interview, there is no escape.

'Live' is once only.

Remember:

1 Try to do your report in a location away from background noise. Some noise is great – and necessary (otherwise you will sound as though you're doing it in the studio). However, the background noise should not compete with your interview. Avoid a spot where onlookers can stand behind you and wave or make faces.

2 Attribute official comments to their official sources so that you are not reporting unattributed rumour. If possible, interview a qualified official for comments rather than summarize the situation and editorialize yourself.

3 Remember the laws of libel, contempt and those relating to giving names of victims. There will be laws and station rules; know what they are.

4 Avoid a 'teaser' that might inflame or increase the size of the crowd. Reports of fires and other tragedies done live will gather people to watch, and they can hamper the rescue operation. Take care.

5 Beware of emotion-charged verbs and nouns.

6 Avoid overstated, unconfirmed guesses about the number of people affected or the amount of property damage (it will almost always be a guess at the start, so make it clear that you are reporting unconfirmed and say that there are various figures rather than stating one as a specific).

7 Double check facts and statistics before you go on air.

8 Take a deep breath. You are the detached observer, not the involved participant. If you are wheezing anxiety, your audience will infer a holocaust from your statements, even if you're reporting a simple two-car accident.

The interview

Pre-chat

The reporter and subject establish rapport, and the reporter sounds out the interview direction and puts the interviewee at ease. Use a pleasant greeting with a firm handshake and lots of eye contact. *Never* rehearse an interview; just discuss it. Agree to a run-through only if there is no other way, and make sure your tape/camera is rolling; if the rehearsal goes well, you're fine anyway. The best punches are delivered when your opponent's guard is down.

The questions

Good questions give good answers, so think ahead to the answer you think you'll get before you ask the question. Use notes, but don't write out your questions. Listen to the answer and ask what you want to know. Construct questions so that there has to be a proper answer: not just 'yes' or 'no'.

Remember:

who, what, when, where, why, how:

who = a name or response
what = a description

when = the timing of the event
where = the place
why = explanation
how = opinion or interpretation.

Questions beginning with such words give the interview a forward pace and direction:

- who was hurt?
- what caused it?
- when did it happen?
- where did it happen?
- why did it happen?
- how did you save them?

General rules concerning questions include:

1 *Avoid yes/no questions.* Sometimes they can be useful, but normally don't ask them. For example, 'Do you think the shares are good?' will get a one-word answer. If this is the importance of the story it's fine, but if you want the person to say more, ask the question differently.
2 *Avoid questions that will lead to a monologue.* Questions need a broad scope. Make the question too narrow and your interview keeps on stalling; open it too wide and it will run away from you.
3 *Use short, single-idea questions.* If a question is to be understood by listener and interviewee, it must be clear, simple and straightforward.
4 *Progress logically from point to point.* Maintain logical flow so each question naturally follows the previous one (you do this by listening to the answer, not thinking of the next question).
5 *Avoid multiple questions.* Ask one question at a time (otherwise the interviewee will choose one, the easiest, and forget to answer the rest).
6 *Keep questions relevant.* Any examples you give should be concrete and real. Don't ask abstract questions.

Question fluency

An interview is a contrived social conversation, the purpose of which is to elicit factual, analytical, informational or human details. The interviewer should know the purpose of the interview, background about the subject and about the person being interviewed. However, the interviewer must never give the impression of talking down to the audience from a level of knowledge that makes the whole interview appear patronizing. Asking TV questions is a habit that requires confidence and thought, but mainly confidence. Like all habits, good interviewing technique improves with practice. With practice comes the art of sounding informal and conversational in a situation that is contrived, unnatural and formal.

Question formulation

The style of language you use is important. It has got to sound spoken and conversational, not literary and stilted. Interviewers are often worried about how they are saying something when their major concern should be about what they're saying. Leave the actual speech process alone; it'll work normally if you don't worry about it. Just let the words come out naturally as you would if you were listening to someone and wanted to ask them a question. Be yourself.

You and the interviewee are talking not to each other but to the listener. Any chatting or giggling together, any 'in jokes' that exclude the listener, are no good. Questions are important because they refocus the listener's attention; one voice is difficult to listen to for any length of time. Questions in an interview break the flow and make the listener concentrate once again. Questions are part of the total sound of the interview. Never be afraid to ask embarrassing or potentially embarrassing questions. Don't think you have to be too respectful to the interviewee and ask only the kind of questions that won't offend or embarrass.

The silent question

During an interview, learn to communicate silently with the interviewee – with your eyes, with expressions of interest. Nod enthusiastically if you want more from the interviewee; look a bit bored if you want the answers to liven up; make a silent sign such as opening your mouth or lifting your hand if you want the interviewee to stop. Never say such acknowledgements out loud; 'Oh yes', 'how interesting', 'really' etc. 'I see' is a favourite with beginners. Just keep quiet and formulate your next questions. If you are commenting, you aren't thinking of what to say next. Make use of the silent nod; it really works. Nodding silently at interviewees spurs them on to further revelations; it encourages them and means you don't have to waste time with a question that will sound forced. The nod can also be effective when you are trying to get interviewees to say something and a question might put them on guard and make them suspicious or cautious.

Differences between broadcast and print interviews

Broadcast reporters are part of the interview in a way that print journalists never are. The listener or viewer will hear or see the questions being asked; newspaper interviews are never like that. Sometimes an interviewee will talk easily to a print journalist but not to a broadcast journalist, so the broadcaster must be able to get the subject to speak naturally, and coherently. Interviewees might be self-conscious about looks or how they sound when answering questions. They might stutter or need a haircut. The broadcast interview is normally on-the-record, for everyone to hear and see. There are exceptions such as the no-name, faceless anonymous interview for specific reasons, but it isn't usual.

In a TV interview, the interview shows more than it tells. The audience hears or sees unfiltered reactions from the interviewee, so description of the interviewee or of the interviewee's reaction is unnecessary. The first shock of a tragedy or the first response to a pointed question is instantly available. Broadcast interviews give an immediate personal emotion. Reporters in radio and television are looking for and giving the living quote. Broadcast offers immediacy and access; print gives reflection and review. Broadcast compresses; print expands. Broadcast offers information; print adds explanation. A newspaper reader can read a print story several times; broadcast gives the listener or viewer less time to think and to absorb because the stories move quickly and so do the pictures on TV. Broadcast interviewers use sounds and pictures as shorthand to enhance a story; print reporters only have the words to convey sights and sounds.

Get a focus

Ask yourself, what is the one topic to discuss? What is the one issue to explore? It's also a good idea to practise to yourself beforehand, on the way to the interview or the previous night.

Develop a question sequence. This is helpful to yourself and also for the interviewee, to order their thoughts. However, never tie yourself to a list. The biggest mistake is coming with a list of 10 questions and then not listening. Always, always listen. The questions should logically follow the previous answer and their own line of thinking as well.

Interviewing tips

1 Don't wear patterned or fussy clothes on television. Some small patterns can cause a weird effect called strobing. Black and white are not TV colours. Plain, happy colours are best (pinks are particularly good psychologically on television).

2 Whether in the studio or on location, always sit forward rather than lean back. Stick your bottom right back into the corner of the chair.

3 On location, brief the crew properly as soon as you arrive. Television is a team effort. Don't just tell them what shots you want; tell them how the story is to go together with other shots from elsewhere. Do the interview in a place relevant to what your guest is saying. The desk with the purple curtain behind doesn't make good television. Offices are often small and have noisy phones.

4 If you're going to do a stand-upper, remember it should be in a relevant place (otherwise, why bother?). The interview might well be the next sequence, so make sure the edit will work. In the case of a new sculpture, for example, you certainly couldn't get away with a shot of the presenter in front of the statue, then go directly to a shot of the sculptor in front of it. At least a close-up of the statue is needed. If in doubt, do a storyboard. It will almost completely eliminate jump cuts and awkward joins.

5 Remember the sound person. Their problems are often forgotten, especially on location. An interview in traffic will be difficult to cut, unless the traffic is constant and distant. A camera is selective about what it sees. It can concentrate on the beautiful river scene, and completely miss the motorway just out of shot. A microphone is far less particular. In fact it will hear things that we miss. If in doubt about the sound, listen to the sound recordist's headphones and close your eyes.

6 Try never to use a hand-held mike with trailing cable.

7 Always do cutaways, even when you're absolutely certain you won't need them. You probably will.

Using the interview in a story

Editing a taped interview is easy; throw away the bad quotes and keep the good ones. Use the same criteria you would use when choosing quotes for a print story. It will probably be shorter and more to the point than a print quote.

When writing the story to use the quotes, remember:

1 When you incorporate your interview into your live copy, you don't need to use quote marks.
2 Use attribution before, rather than after, the person says something, otherwise the listener or viewer will not know who is talking until the person finishes.
3 Remember that broadcast quotes for on-air copy rarely run more than two sentences because your viewer cannot grasp more than two sentences at a time.
4 You can introduce a quote that you read verbatim by saying 'in her own words' to help listeners understand that you are quoting someone's words, but don't say 'quote . . . unquote'.
5 Be careful to use someone's exact words in your copy or in an interview if the quoted words could be at all libellous.
6 On television, to emphasize a quote from an official source that you don't have on tape, you can superimpose the words on the screen for impact. You can also use superimposed quotes if the sound is somehow garbled, but you want the audience to hear the person's voice. Use this approach very selectively, however, because an audience can grasp only a sentence or two at a time. Whenever possible, your interview should stand by itself.
7 Read the copy aloud before you broadcast. Remember, the language of radio and TV is spoken.

STUDIO INTERVIEWS

With these you lose the impact and excitement of being at the scene, but you gain time and preparation can therefore be better. You can be briefed better. They are fairly short if they are part of the news programme (they can, of course, be much longer if in the current affairs programme). The choice of interviewee is crucial. Studio interviews can be less spontaneous than those in the field, because the studio guest has more time to consider what is to be said but much of the field interview section still applies. Celebrities and stars are used to being interviewed and need to be carefully controlled. Public figures want to take control; also to say what *they* want to say. Guests have their own reasons for being interviewed. You have to make sure your motives are the ones they follow, not their own. The guests should appear, and be, relaxed, and sound and look spontaneous.

The interview

Before the programme:

- prepare the interviewee
- outline the programme
- make sure you have the names and titles absolutely correct
- stop a guest who starts to tell you a good story before the programme; save it for the real thing (a programme can die in the pre-interview stage)
- advise guests to keep answers short and to the point.

During the programme, remember:

1 Pay attention to the interviewee and listen. Maintain eye contact.
2 Begin with easy questions that put the guest at ease.
3 Succinct questions are best, delivered in a logical sequence.
4 Be conversational but not too familiar. Always be polite. If you are interviewing a friend, forget it during the interview.
5 Don't pretend. Don't try to pretend you've done research if you haven't. Don't pretend you've read the book if you haven't. You should have!
6 Clarify on the spot. Give background when someone mentions something new to the audience. Ask the interviewee to define or explain jargon or abbreviations. Avoid too many numbers, because your audience can't absorb them fast enough.
7 Ask the interviewee for the point rather than the statistics.
8 Rephrase a rambling answer. Ask the interviewee, 'Are you saying that . . .'. This gives the audience time to pause with you to understand the answer.
9 Interrupt. The danger in live interviewing is a guest who won't stop talking. The result can be a boring monologue with only a few questions. You *must* interrupt and get the interview back on track.

10 Pursue difficult questions. If someone says, 'I don't want to answer that', you have two choices: accept, or get them to talk about it. Rephrase the question or come back to it later in the interview. If someone is giving yes–no answers, then rephrase the questions.

11 Use the immediacy to your benefit. Someone on a live interview can't turn back and you can expand or capture the spontaneous slip of the tongue.

12 Use silence; never fear a pause in an interview, particularly a TV interview. A pause can indicate you have asked a very good question that someone can't answer easily. Don't talk too much.

13 Don't be rude. Be careful how hard you push the guest.

14 Ask questions without apologies, and in a matter-of-fact way. Avoid starting a question with 'Sorry to have to ask you this'.

15 If something goes wrong, acknowledge you've got a problem. Tell the audience.

16 Remember to conclude with some kind of summary or signal that you are finished. If you have to interrupt and say 'we're out of time', then at least give a quick thanks to everyone for taking part.

All interviewers on radio and TV are looking for the quote or look that is special, the moment when the purpose of the interview seems clear and valuable. On TV, viewers are not only listening to the words. There is also the picture to show emotion. If you see someone grappling with a particular thought or emotion, let it happen and don't interrupt. Let it evolve. Don't follow your format, follow the moment.

Remember the equipment

Broadcast reporters never work alone. There is always the equipment and, in TV, a crew. You must adjust to the equipment. A TV reporter has to manage the equipment and the people as well as be a reporter. In the studio interview there is makeup, a set, hot lights, Teleprompter, the crew etc. Always be sensitive to the interviewee's possible fears and hesitations. Explain how it all works and how long the two of you will talk, and that will reassure the interviewee and show that you care. Never rush the interview or yourself. There's a lot of hanging around while others do things in television.

Remember your goal

The interview is an artificial conversation, but your aim is always to capture the interviewee's attention so well that the person forgets the equipment and the audience and talks just to you.

FINAL TIPS

Remember:

- don't get drawn into answering a question from the person you are interviewing
- never provide the questions in advance
- always keep control of the interview; you are the broadcasting expert
- decide beforehand on the key questions you are going to ask, but always be ready to discard them if the answers take a surprising or more interesting turn
- don't be afraid to put the opposing view, even though you don't believe it, to test the case of the person you are interviewing.
- the art of interviewing is listening.

FURTHER READING

Boyd, A. (1994). *Broadcast Journalism: Techniques of Radio and TV News*. Focal Press.

Crook, T. (1998). *International Radio Journalism*. Routledge.

Gage, L. (1999). *A Guide to Commercial Radio Journalism*. Focal Press.

13 Feature and documentary production for radio and TV

Documentary, feature: what's the difference? The words are often interchanged, but they don't really mean the same thing. Documentaries are basically factual. Features can be factual or entertainment. Documentaries are extended treatments of a single subject; they tell of real events, of real people. They include all the ingredients of first-rate news reporting.

There are two types of documentary: news and cultural or lifestyle documentaries.

Documentaries should always be angled at the human side of the story; great political events have to be analysed, but from the point of view of the people involved. That's what makes a documentary interesting and worthwhile. Radio excels at one type of documentary; TV at another. In making a documentary you are a reporter, an interpreter, explaining complex issues. Research is vital. Consult everything and everyone you possibly can for background: press cuttings, relevant books, reports, experts, eyewitnesses, and video of other relevant programmes or interviews.

Documentaries and features can be long or short. They can be on one theme that takes an hour or more, or they can be on one theme broken down into a number of specific angles, each lasting only a few minutes. Inexperienced producers often find themselves more interested in filling a time slot rather than producing a great programme (which may be short because there's only that much material). Remember: it's not what you can put in but what you can leave out that makes it interesting.

PRODUCING A DOCUMENTARY OR FEATURE

Research

This is part of the planning. First ask yourself, what am I trying to achieve? What do I want the audience to feel/know about my subject? List various topics within the main subject that you want to include, then decide how you will do the programme and how everything will fit within the allotted timespan. Next, set out a provisional running order. Don't worry about the title at this stage; that will emerge later. Put your thoughts down on paper and see how they relate to each other, then you'll see where the emphasis should be and what is unnecessary. Your aim is to finish up with a tightly edited, balanced, interesting programme that uses sound and pictures to the full.

When deciding on how to do the documentary or feature, list:

- the working title
- the aim
- the duration
- information you already have (probably what has triggered the idea)
- provisional content
- key questions
- interview sources: categories to interview etc.
- reference sources: cuttings, library, government reports etc.
- actuality: the pictures/sound that will form a big part of the programme.

You can then decide how much emphasis should be given to each and whether there are enough ideas to sustain the listener's or viewer's interest. You will soon realize that there is a lot to get into the programme.

Structure

The main decision is whether to use a narrator or not. A linking, explanatory narrative is useful to give the programme a forward drive that makes it logical and informative as well as interesting. A narrator can help a programme cover lots of ground in a short space of time, but can also give the impression of being unemotional. Narrators should link, not interrupt. There won't be the need to use a narrative voice between every insert or contribution. Inserts can be linked together, different voices following each other to tell part of the story, without the intervention of a narrator.

Collecting the material

Mostly you will do your interviews on location; seldom in the studio and hopefully never on the telephone. In documentary and feature programmes, because there is usually some time in which to do them, everything should be studio quality. If you decide there will be no narrator, it is essential when doing the interviews that you remember to have speakers introduce themselves in some informal, natural way: *speaking as a truck driver . . .*, for example.

You might ask interviewees for a lot of statistical and other factual information that you won't use in the final programme but will be useful source material for you. Also, decide whether you are going to leave the interviewer's voice and face in the programme. Sometimes it can be presented more as a personal investigation, with the producer, presenter, interviewer, narrator being one person. When you use a different narrator, all the questions should be removed, otherwise it looks untidy. The replies can then serve as individual statements, being careful in the linking script to preserve them in their original context. Don't take them out of order or out of context; they must always be exact reflections of what the speaker intended. Be consistent in the structure, once you have decided what it is. However, form and style are infinitely variable, and it is important to explore new ways of making programmes. Clarity and interest are the keys.

Impression and truth

You will probably want and need to use lots of actuality. This creates the right atmosphere for telling the story. People will also recognize the authentic sounds, if it is on radio, and what they see on TV. It all helps.

Take great care about using sound effects from discs. These days they are very good on CD, but they must be genuine.

Never stage manage: in other words, don't ask for something to be done again after the real event so that you can call it real. In these situations, a proper journalistic approach is to admit a simulation with a caption or voiceover.

Unless you tell the listeners or viewers otherwise, it is essential for them to be able to believe that you are telling them the truth. This applies to sound and pictures as well. What the listener hears or sees must be the genuine article; you must never deceive or confuse for the sake of a good picture or sound effect.

Music

Try to use it as little as possible, and only when there is real reason for doing so. Music must be used only when it generates atmosphere. It can be the easy way out, so be careful.

Assembling the material

After the research, do the interviews and gather the pictures and sound effects. Then you can edit the rough cut and write a basic draft of the script.

The start of the programme is crucial. It must get the attention by using a strong piece of sound or picture actuality, or a soundbite etc. The remainder of the programme will consist of a compilation of interviews, links, actuality, vox pops, music. You might use additional voices (actors or other reporters) to read official documents, for example. Always remember never to have one sequence too long. Break up the sequences into short elements. Don't have all the interviews together; break up a long voice piece or statement for use in several parts. Edit interviews so only the best part is used, with the less interesting bits put into the script.

The easiest way to assemble material is chronologically, using time sequences to tell the story. It will usually be better within this time sequence to stop and balance views with others on occasion before continuing. The programme has to make sense. That's the basic rule. Remember the listener must understand it on first hearing, whereas you, as producer/reporter, will have heard it many times. Structure is the most consistent fault with documentaries; not their content. You must have enough signposting. The listener in radio must know who's talking all the time; the same applies in TV.

The ending:

- allows the narrator to sum up
- may repeat some of the key statements, using the voices of the people who made them
- may repeat a single phrase that appears to sum up the situation
- may speculate on the future with more questions left unanswered so interest is maintained
- should end with the same voice and actuality that you used in the beginning, but with some small variation to show it's the end
- may do nothing, leaving it to the audience to form their own assessment of the subject.

Don't use jump cuts (an abrupt cut from one part of an action to another with no transition). If you join a shot of someone seated with a shot of them standing, that's a jump cut. You also see it sometimes in badly edited interviews. To avoid it, either insert a shot of the person getting up (a cut-in) or put in a shot of someone looking at them, thus giving time for them to get up (a cutaway). When doing a documentary, you must provide the editor with lots of cutaways and cut-ins to make all the sequences work.

When doing documentaries and features, learn to explain things visually. Remember:

- wide shot
- medium shot
- close-up.

The wide shot orients and tells us what's going on. The medium shot takes us a bit closer, tells us a bit more about the action and prepares us for the close-up. The close-up is usually the most exciting shot, and gives us a great deal of information about a small amount. The wide shot explains, and it's usually too much of a jump to move straight to a CU; hence the MS in between. Zooms can help, but don't overuse them.

Structure

The structure of your programme, the way the elements of the story are arranged, is difficult. Remember: your programme should have:

- a beginning
- a middle
- an end

. . . but not necessarily taken in that order.

The opening sequence sets the scene and gives the visual and verbal information needed to understand where the programme is going. Don't wait too long before getting to the point. The middle section involves the complete development of the story. Remember the original story concept, the essence of what you are trying to say. Endings are often very difficult. The film can't just stop when you don't have anything more to say; it must obviously come to a conclusion, tie up loose ends, recapitulate without telling the whole story again. The shots and sequences should somehow say 'end'. Wide shots, zoom-outs, tend to make good closing shots.

Juxtapositions

Look for good and interesting juxtapositions. One sequence cannot comment on another merely by being next to it. The same is true of interviews. You need to make the connection of ideas. One idea should be made to lead into another, not necessarily in the most obvious order. Sometimes areas need to be broken down into separate elements and distributed through the film. A good juxtaposition, a good connection, may occur to you that gives a whole new type of structure to provide interest.

Narration

Remember, the primary source of information in TV is the pictures, no matter how good the words or how ordinary the pictures. Viewers must understand something through the pictures, otherwise they will not understand the information. The information used in TV must be made visual, just as in radio the information has to be converted into sound. In TV you will do this with lots of graphic material. In radio it's the impression that counts, not the detail.

There are lots of kinds of information that you can use in a TV programme, not just facts and figures. For example, a shot of a man walking across a field can tell us how old he is, what he's like, whether he's a farmer or something else, whether the field is a good one or not, whether there's been a lot of rain, the season, etc. When you come to write the script for that shot, you must remember that there is already a lot of information unspoken in the shot. It's no good just repeating what can be seen, although the shot might need signposting to make sure viewers understand some of the less obvious things in it. The script must give extra meaning to the shot in story terms. Your aim should always be to give added meaning to the primary visual information. Good commentary does not merely point out what is in the shot; that's fine for a slide show, but not for professional television documentaries.

Remember to leave the occasional gap without words for the ideas to sink in and for the pictures and sound to tell their own story. Know when to keep quiet, and do it often. Wall-to-wall words don't work.

Sound

Sound is not a second thought in TV; it is very important. Sound provides the reality. It gives you people's voices, narration and music.

You can always include 'thought-tracks' (the voice of the subject used over appropriate visuals in place of narration). This provides a different approach, and the story is carried by someone within the film, who gives a sense of intimacy to it. Use thought-tracks to give someone's feelings or specific experiences. Basic information should be in the narration. Inexperienced reporter/directors tend to over-use thought-track, either because it's a new toy or because they have to write less narration (never a good reason for using this technique).

Music

Music can be a powerful tool, but only if used correctly. Music makes sequences seem shorter than they actually are, but it should never just be used to fill a gap on the sound-track. It should give extra meaning to a sequence. Don't always choose the obvious piece of music. Music provides you with an extra decision: whether music or effects are to be dominant in the mix. You must reach your decision with the editor and sound mixer. You cannot give everything equal prominence.
Remember: music does not have to be loud to work.

PRODUCTION HINTS FOR TV DOCUMENTARIES OR FEATURES

- don't overdirect
- don't give too many instructions: it will destroy what people are doing for you
- make sure people doing things on camera for you aren't self-conscious; it's always obvious even though they might only be walking in a wide shot
- tell them not to react obviously to the presence of the camera
- when you have people doing things in a documentary, have them doing what they do best every day. A farmer driving a tractor won't be self conscious; sitting behind a desk he will be.
- don't forget the long shot. The geography can be important for the viewer.
- give your interviewee head room in close-up shots, unless you're going for a very close-up shot.
- save the really tight close-up in interviews for when you want real visual impact.
- watch the backgrounds when setting up interviews. Avoid shots in which objects seem to be growing out of a person's head because they are on the same line as the subject and the camera.
- avoid shots that are wider than they need to be to contain the action. Even more rigorously, avoid shots that are too close to contain the action. It is annoying for the viewer to see someone reading something that can't be seen or pouring drinks that are out of view.
- in establishing shots or long shots, give some thought to foreground. Objects in the foreground give framing, interest and depth to the composition of a picture. Dress the set where possible and appropriate.
- try not to use zooms. If you do, hold the beginning and end of any zoom so the shots can be used without a zoom.
- in reverse questions, ensure that the camera frames you in much the same style as the interviewee. There can be variations, such as over-the-shoulder two-shots, but reasonably matching head and shoulder shots are best.
- in interview close-ups, keep distracting objects clear of the interviewee unless the object is relevant to the film and interview, in which case it shouldn't be distracting.

FURTHER READING

Boyd, A. (1994). *Broadcast Journalism: Techniques of Radio and TV News*. Heinemann.

Crook, T. (1998). *International Radio Journalism*. Routledge.

Gage, L. (1999). *A Guide to Commercial Radio Journalism*. Focal Press.

Gibson, R. (1991). *Radio and TV Reporting*. Simon and Schuster.

Hausman, C. (1992). *Crafting the News for Electronic Media*. Wadsworth.

Hilliard, R. (1997). *Writing for TV and Radio*. Wadsworth.

Holland, P. (1998). *The Television Handbook*. Routledge.

Itule, B. and Anderson, D. (1997). *News Writing and Reporting for Today's Media*. McGraw-Hill.

Millerson, G. H. (1993). *Effective TV Production*. Focal Press.

O'Donnell, L. Benoit, P. and Hausman, C. (1993). *Modern Radio Production*. Wadsworth.

Walters, R. (1994). *Broadcast Writing*. McGraw-Hill.

White, E. (1996). *Broadcast News Writing, Reporting and Producing*. Focal Press.

Wilby, P. and Conroy, A. (1994). *The Radio Handbook*. Routledge.

14 Public affairs reporting

Sometimes referred to as current affairs, sometimes as public affairs, these expressions mean the same thing. All the same principles apply to public affairs as to news, but there are additional responsibilities in these programmes. In public affairs the journalist has to explain, analyse and put stories into context.

Current affairs looks at reasons why the news of the day has happened. It isn't worried about the 'happening now' part of the news process, but is much more interested in drawing longer-range conclusions and analysing them. Current affairs follows the news and is involved with news that might be quite 'old'. Therefore, in these programmes studio links and stories must always be written and constructed with this in mind.

Good current affairs writing and production assumes the news point, and focuses on its importance, relevance and implications. It stops and takes a look while news runs on to something else, and shows why the story is important enough to be run. This requires a different attitude and creativity in setting up the story. The reporter's job is to expose the story within the story, not to show the story as it is today. News and current affairs is an essential ingredient of any free communication concept, and the 'mission to explain' role of broadcast journalism is therefore a vital ingredient of any broadcast journalism process. The reason for current affairs is to explain to the listener, so it has as its basic idea explanation in a simple, clear, interesting way, just like news. In any current affairs story, the reporter must continually ask:

- What is the point of this story?
- What am I trying to say?
- Will Mrs Jones of Southend understand?

Write for the audience, not for Professor Bloggs at the university.

Current affairs reporters try to demystify and clarify. This comes hard to most current affairs journalists because they usually have a university specialist background, while news journalists have at least the intellectual edges rubbed off by the day-to-day journalistic race. Even if you're an expert in a particular field (politics, economics etc.), be humble enough to make yourself simplify your expertise so that you are looking at it from the point of view of the person in the street. If you understand, you'll simplify easily. If you don't understand, you'll complicate your ideas. Never try to show off your intellectual ability in these programmes. You are still the representative of the people; act like it.

Current affairs programming also differs from news in that:

- subjects are usually covered in more depth
- items are usually much longer
- larger crews are required to put these longer items together
- there is more time to do the story
- there is more time for the programme
- detailed planning of coverage is necessary.

Basically, these programmes are the weekly investigation into the news of the day, often simply longer interviews or a single investigation of a topic maybe lasting from 30 to 50 minutes. There are also the longer-term documentaries or features. Decide on the treatment that will best suit either of these programme formats. In news, shots are often unplanned. In documentary and current affairs coverage, there is a great deal of planning before the shoot.

THE PROGRAMME

Working time on a current affairs programme is divided into pre-production (research), production (story treatment and shooting) and post-production (editing).

Research

In the pre-production stage the reporter:

- investigates the subject
- explores locations
- arranges interviews
- gathers background material.

Story treatment

A draft script will be prepared from the researcher's findings, listing the main shots that will make up the programme. This is the story treatment. You might well change your plans later, but the treatment offers a road map to show where the team is starting from, where it is heading and how it plans to get there. Producing a treatment gets your ideas out in the open where they can be examined, instead of waiting until you start filming to find they don't work. Once they are on paper, you knock them into shape. You can add things that you've forgotten and take out things that are no longer relevant or important. You can also see if you've got enough good ideas to sustain a programme.

Remember:

1 Decide what you want to say and what pictures you want to say it with.
2 Jot down the headings the programme will follow, with visuals on the left and commentary on the right.
3 Allow 15 seconds for each point, and a little longer for points made by interviewees.
4 Add time for opening shots, scene setters and pictures with no narration.
5 Cutaways shown over existing narration will take no extra time.
6 Work out the duration for each sequence of the programme and aim to run up to 25 per cent over length as the assembled programme will probably end up tighter and more polished after it has been trimmed down and things thrown out.

Shooting schedule

After the treatment comes a shooting schedule, to minimize time wasted. Every shot should be listed as it is taken (news can often dispense with this because of pressure of deadlines). This is vital, though, for longer programmes, otherwise you will never know where all the material is.

Editing

Once the shooting is finished an editing script can be produced, listing the takes that are to be included in the final programme. Then it's into the editing suite with the video or film editor who will translate your ideas into a finished product.

FURTHER READING

Boyd, A. (1994). *Broadcast Journalism: Techniques of Radio and TV News*. Heinemann.

Crook, T. (1998). *International Radio Journalism*. Routledge, 1998.

Gibson, R (1991). *Radio and TV Reporting*. Simon and Schuster.

Hausman, C. (1992). *Crafting the News for Electronic Media*. Wadsworth.

Hilliard, R. (1997). *Writing for TV and Radio*. Wadsworth.

Holland, P. (1998). *The Television Handbook*. Routledge.

O'Donnell, L., Benoit, P. and Hausman, C. (1993). *Modern Radio Production*. Wadsworth.

Walters, R. (1994). *Broadcast Writing*. McGraw-Hill.

White, E. (1996). *Broadcast News Writing, Reporting and Producing*. Focal Press.

Wilby, P. and Conroy, A. (1994). *The Radio Handbook*. Routledge.

15 Investigative reporting

WHAT TO INVESTIGATE

Investigate anything. Anything can be improved by a bit of investigation. The investigative story is often staring us in the face, waiting to be seen and looked into. The investigative story produces a story that is gathered and published or broadcast that would not have been revealed without your hard work. It provides a story of public importance that had to be pieced together from diverse and often obscure sources. It reveals a story that may be contrary to the version announced by the government or business officials, who might have tried to conceal the truth. It results in a story that is important and prominently displayed.

Investigative journalism is exciting. Consider an investigative piece as original work produced by a reporter, rather than a report on something. There will have been some attempt to conceal information, and the result will be very important to the audience.

Investigative journalists are always on the look out for corruption, mismanagement, unfairness and political secrecy. To be a good investigative reporter, you need to have in-depth familiarity with the way government and business works, how the law and the courts work and how to find out information from documents and from the Internet. You need to know how the police investigate graft and corruption, and about the civil service and criminals. You need to know how to find out about the latest drug scene, and all the rumours and gossip about who is controlling supply. A good investigative reporter has great knowledge and personal integrity, a balanced judgement, tenacity, a sense of justice and morality and a controlled sense of anger at injustice, unfairness or corruption in government or private institutions. The good investigative reporter also needs a wide general knowledge to pinpoint specific injustice and crime. Successful investigative reporters have to be fair and ethical in their investigations. If they aren't, or involve themselves in something illegal or unfair, this can undercut the whole story and destroy a valid journalistic inquiry.

It pays to be honest and ethical. Always use an honest, direct, balanced approach when dealing with sources and investigative subjects. Sources and the public will be disillusioned if the reporter misuses the power and privilege of the press and intentionally distorts the picture or engages in superficial sensationalism. You need patience and confidence that an honest and systematic inquiry will eventually uncover the full truth or establish the official responsibility for a cover-up of mismanagement, corruption or other malfunctioning of government or a private company. You need the ability to stand back occasionally from the details of the story and view the participants in human terms. Try to imagine how the people you are investigating will think and feel, and ask yourself if you have been fair to them in your story line and approach – both to those who are your protected sources and to the people you are investigating. Successful investigative reporters also need the courage to admit that they were wrong on fact or perspective and to take the steps necessary to correct the record immediately when there has been a significant distortion that reflects adversely on anyone.

GETTING THE STORY

1 Research the records and interview in depth.
2 Don't wait to be assigned to an investigative story; come up with your own. Develop small investigative projects on your own initiative. Be a self-starter on little projects that have little risk, and deal with simple record research, thorough legal research and in-depth interviews.
3 Look for as much corroborative evidence as you can. Get documentary evidence that will support the story. You have to do it cautiously and within your existing resources; you will quickly move on to bigger pieces. The foundation of effective investigative reporting is the dull, boring routine of repetitive record-checking at police stations, government offices, the courts, and on the Internet.
4 Develop a simple and accurate method of keeping records on an investigation that will give ready and quick access to the materials, and keep them safe for your later use but remember the Data Protection Act.
5 Good interviewing is essential. The technique you use will vary depending on the story and the people you are interviewing. E-mail

can be useful. Sometimes you might like to appear ignorant of the facts when interviewing someone (but you must always be fully aware of all the facts in the case before you do any interview about it). There is no excuse in important interviews not to have examined the records, all available facts and documentary evidence before you do the interview.

6 Be careful when dealing with the police, government investigators and crown prosecutors. You don't want to become an arm of the law enforcement; you must always be independent.

Write to the length of the importance of the story. There is a temptation to write very long, wordy pieces to justify the length of time taken on the story investigation. Resist. Don't over-estimate the audience, or their interest. Explain in clear simple language why a particular story is worth investigating and why it is against the law, but don't insult their intelligence. There's no need, for example, to tell them that 'lots of people like money'. Always relate the story to how it affects them. Comparisons and analogies are particularly useful to illustrate just how the wrongdoing is costing taxpayers money, or how it is destroying their neighbourhood. Or how, if judges worked a 40-hour week like everyone else, x number of extra cases could be sorted out in a year. However, not every story needs to be like this. Stories of sex, glamour and great wealth will always be read, however they are written.

Writing an investigative piece is not preaching a sermon or teaching a lesson. Don't assume the audience is on your side. Every allegation must be supported with as many facts as possible; every instance in which the subject of the investigation has violated the law or accepted practice should be pointed out. Even when this is done, reporters will find that many readers display a surprisingly high level of tolerance to corruption. Your job is to show why and how the corruption exposed is bad for them, for many other people as well, or for an individual the reader can relate to. Readers aren't interested in the trouble or frustrations of the journalist in getting the story; they want to know about the story itself. Unsupported allegations or insults directed at the subject of an investigation will always work against the reporter. Readers won't be interested in those opinions. They're interested in the facts the reporter has uncovered. But there's no need to use every single fact you have uncovered.

As with all reporting, it's what you can leave out that often makes the story better. You have to know by instinct and experience how to exclude irrelevant or uninteresting information from an investigative story. Most investigative stories are too long. No one reads a story if it's too long, except specialists, and reporters are not writing for specialists but for the ordinary reader.

Investigative reporters have to live by the law. Stealing information and trespassing on private property are violations of the law. You must never deliberately misrepresent the facts, do a story for personal gain, out of a sense of victimization or out of personal bias. Beware of being too aggressive, although it's better to be this way and get the story than not.

The methods used by an investigative reporter are mainly those used by all reporters:

- interviews: introductory interviews; interviews with the people closely involved; interviews with those being investigated so they have the opportunity to give their side of the story and answer all complaints or allegations
- documents: official and unofficial; you have absolute proof in a document, and it can't change its story. Use the Internet
- surveillance: you will almost certainly have to watch people; you must see the area or the people, a slum story cannot be written without you getting first-hand knowledge of what it is like
- surveys: take a car to several garages to check on charges or how well they repair, testing the case, investigating, getting facts and figures and proof
- following a tip, an unknown voice on the phone, a casual remark from a friend: make some quick phone calls to check it out, search for some documents to substantiate at least some part of what you've been told.

To develop an investigative story, first gather lots of information about the subject. Stockpile it, organize it, make it understandable. This all takes time. Start with an idea; one idea leads to another idea, and each idea leads to a new search. When looking for a story, keep an eye out for such things as problems with public or private transport; nursing homes, prisons or public housing; well-intentioned government schemes gone wrong. Look for possible fraud or wrongdoing or inefficiency. Look for bad salesmen who may be getting people to sign up for wrong things. In each case, look for performance and cost. Is the school bus safe? Are the schools being overcharged for the service? Investigating government wrongdoing can mean getting a look at the records. Most investigative stories are about political issues and social problems rather than individuals, but people tend to become central issues in a story. An investigative personal profile can therefore be useful. When you are writing, decide whether to write a straight news story, a serious feature or a lighter piece. Illustrate the story and break it up with graphs, pictures and photos, but only use real shots. Never stage them or make them up.

Check and double check your facts and always keep in mind that you will probably have legal and ethical constraints on your investigative reporting. You may, however, have a public interest reason to override these constraints. Another restraint in most countries is some form of data protection in which people have the right of access to electronically stored information about themselves. Therefore it may be wise for investigative journalists to limit what is stored on their computers. Always check the local laws in operation before starting your investigation.

FURTHER READING

Davis, A. (1998). *Magazine Journalism Today.* Focal Press.

Gaines, W. (1998). *Investigative Reporting for Print and Broadcast.* Nelson-Hall.

Harris, G. and Spark, D. (1993). *Practical Newspaper Reporting.* Focal Press.

Welsh, T. and Greenwood, W. (1999). *McNae's Essential Law for Journalists.* Butterworths.

16 Specialist reporting

THE EDITORIAL

All newspapers have an editorial page and take their editorials very seriously. Editorials inform, persuade, convince and conclude. As such, editorials are unique to ordinary print journalism. They are unique to newspapers and some magazines, and are not used in broadcasting. An editorial is about the opinions of the newspaper. It is what the newspaper believes, and is written in such a way as to convince the reader.

The editorial is about ideas and should present an idea or opinion concisely, logically and entertainingly. It should influence opinion and interpret events and news, mainly about serious issues, but not always. Sometimes an editorial is written to laugh at an issue. In the tabloid newspapers editorials are written in a very direct language; in the broadsheet newspapers editorials are usually written in more reasoned language. There is often more than one editorial; sometimes two or three shorter ones or, occasionally, one long one. The last of several is usually on a lighter subject.

Structure of the editorial

The editorial consists of three parts:

1 A statement of the subject, issue, or thesis.
2 Comment on the subject or issue.
3 The conclusion or solution.

However you write an editorial, always keep a grip on the argument throughout and never abuse people. Only abuse arguments. Begin with an unspoken question, then perhaps give various alternative answers. Assess and conclude and, in concluding, sum up somehow. Don't just give a jumble of facts and sides of the argument. It is up to you to come down on one side of the argument or the other. The message of an editorial always appeals to the intellect. The message can be its political or economic content.

Problem-solving editorials require a lot of research to get the solution right. You must recognize the problem, analyse it and solve it.

Editorials reflect the character, tone and style of the newspaper or magazine. They are the opinion of the newspaper. Sometimes this needs to be a single view; other times it should argue a case, illustrate an argument or opinion with facts and come to a conclusion. Don't just assert.

Leaders should be topical whenever possible. The language should be clear, vigorous and very simple. For example, don't say *Mr X has overstated the case*; say *Come off it, Mr X . . .* Leaders can state a conclusion crisply at the start, then justify it. For example, *Mr X has achieved the impossible. After much discussion, he has managed to get it wrong again.*

In newspapers there's a daily leader conference, when the leader will be discussed and its approach agreed. Remember that not everyone will automatically know the facts of the case. Never assume everyone knows the background. Leaders should give a single view, and they should be brief. Be careful of the *on the one hand . . . on the other hand* type of leader. Leaders that don't reach a conclusion or make a point are a waste of time. Argue in a straight line. Leaders should be provocative and catch the reader's attention. Once you have identified the issue in the opening, the body presents the argument logically. Don't make unwarranted assumptions.

COLUMNS

Columns are popular in both tabloids and broadsheets. They are a showcase for writing style, wit and discussion about topical issues. They are very satisfying, because writers can virtually say what they think about a subject in their own style. There are five different types of newspaper column:

1 The 'point of view' column commenting on a current issue.
2 The 'my say' column, the most popular type of column and perhaps the hardest to write. You have to draw on experience. It is the personal opinion of the writer.

3 The 'expert opinion' column. This is a column interpreting the news. It takes more expertise than a more simple 'my opinion' column.
4 The trivia column. A 'did you know' type of column, which requires a lot of knowledge of reference books.
5 The 'readers write, editors respond' column. This is a dialogue-type column in which readers write in with comments, opinions, thoughts and prejudices and get a reply from the columnist or editors. It's the print equivalent of a radio phone-in.

All news is subjective because it is selected from various possible angles. Personal columns are openly subjective, the result of 'I' journalism. There is no attempt to hide behind objectivity, balance or neutrality. A personal column is the work and thoughts of a signed individual, and must be seen and written as such. Personal columns need to be as original as possible. They may be witty, controversial, hard-hitting, quirky, whimsical or irritating, or all of these and more. The writer's personality is always obvious in a good personal column. Often the column has a head-and-shoulders picture of the writer, so the reader feels they are a twosome. Style, language and tone are also appropriate to the person writing and to the newspaper.

Columns may be in the following forms:

● straight opinion
● those with a small amount of journalistic research
● those that are a selection of short features or newsy stories reflecting the interests of the writer (gossip columns are like this).

Most personal columns take a significant news angle as their peg, but not always. The writing is always individual and personal to the writer. It can be a financial or politically-based column, or simply take something that attracts the writer's attention and which is then written about in as different a way as possible.

PROFILES

Profile writing is painting portraits in words. People are news, and the profile is the best expression of the people-are-news approach of all journalism. Profiles can be of:

● people
● organizations

- buildings
- cemeteries
- roads
- parks
- schools
- festivals, and so on.

However, most of all a profile is about a person. In a people profile you are satisfying the reader's curiosity about someone: what makes a person tick, what that person has done to get where he or she is, what the person is really like behind the public face.

Developing the profile

There are many kinds of profiles and there is no standard format. A short profile may highlight some newsworthy feature of the person. This is a profile that focuses on the person's views about a specific issue or experience or highlights their recent achievement or failure. A longer profile will aim to provide an overview of a person's life. The person will be chosen because of a newsworthy element (a new job, a new book, film, TV series, political campaign, a visitor). A person may be profiled because of an unusual feature of his or her life (an unusual job; the largest collection of . . .). It may be an obituary profile after an important or noteworthy person has died. There is also the type of profile that focuses on some aspect of a person's private life. The new financial secretary might be profiled in one paper focusing on past professional life or successes; in another paper the profile might be on relations with family and friends. A film star might be profiled based on recent love affairs or divorces and what the star has learnt from them – *I'll never do it again*, says famous film star. Special focus profiles build a picture of a person around a specific angle, e.g. 'my biggest mistake', in which a person is profiled each week about their biggest mistake. Others include 'a life in the day of'; celebrities going shopping, etc.

The more knowledge of the person you have, the better. If you are interviewing someone, always be aware of their previous achievements. Check with *Who's Who* first. Before and, if possible, afterwards, ask people about your subject. You may want to include some of their views in your profile, but it will all be good background for your questions even if you don't use it directly.

Profiles don't have to begin with a newsworthy introduction. You might want to highlight a particular significant or unusual event in their past to start with, or open with a particularly revealing or interesting quote. You might have a descriptive intro focusing on what the person looks like or the environment where the interview took place (running together through a park, for example). However, many profiles are influenced by the news agenda, and in these cases the news angle must be near the top. For example:

Coincidence is a word that Gillian Slovo uses often, so it must please her that a whole set of coincidences surrounds the publication on Thursday of her fifth novel, The Betrayal

(then go on to mention the coincidences and the book).

How about this beginning to a profile about the famous Russian conductor who is about to conduct a new work in London?

Ask anyone who knows Gennadi Rozhdestvensky – or Noddy, as he is affectionately called – for their impressions of this garrulous Russian conductor and you will get some unequivocal replies: clown, conjuror, modern Medici, a prince and protector of new Soviet music, a ghastly yet masterly, daring, wild conductor – and one of the strangest men you will ever meet. With that reputation to precede him, the grizzly bear of a fellow who turns up for his interview apologetically late, black beret pulled down over straggly grey curls, a single tooth protruding through thick, smiling lips, already holds a certain mystery – endorsed by his insistence on speaking through an interpreter, though his English is very good. Rozhdestvensky is here to conduct Boris Godunov, *the revival of which opens tonight at Covent Garden; a work he has performed, he says, 'one hundred times at least'.*

Most profiles carry the views of the person through the use of direct quotes. The language of these quotes is vital to showing their personality in the profile. A profile in which all the views are indirect quotes would be deadly dull. Hard news almost never starts with a direct quote, but profiles often do. For example:

'Any fool can father a child but it takes a man to be a father', says Larry Fishburne's character Furious Styles in Boys N The Hood. *And anyone who has seen it will confirm that Fishburne's performance is central to the success of the film.*

Some profiles will be based totally on an edited verbatim quote of the interview. Other profiles will merge direct quotes from a conversation (or several) into one long direct quote. Some profiles carry quotes from people about the interviewee, their personality and their work. Many profiles carry descriptions of the person, the appearance, mannerisms, asides, the environment where he or she lives, works or is interviewed. All this gives colour to the piece. It is not usual for a personal profile to start at the beginning and go to the end of a life; profiles change the chronology around quite a lot. For example, they might highlight a newsworthy aspect of the person at the start and then, in the body of the piece, take up a chronological theme. Sometimes it's better to carry a sidebar box with biographical details accompanying the general profile piece, which leaves the space on the profile to concentrate on more interesting and up-to-date matters.

The tone of the piece is vital. In other words, the style needs to relate very closely to the subject. Decide whether you are writing a funny, affectionate, respectful, mocking, damning, witty, or neutral piece. Work out the tone; it affects the questions as well as the background.

When you have gathered all your information, through the basic interview with the person being profiled as well as from comments and quotes and background about the person from others and from the library cuttings, close your notebook. The worst way to write such a story is to look through what you've written to get the information you want. You have been with this story for some time; you know the person very intimately. Sit at the computer and just write your impressions as a first draft. The story is not in your notebook; it's in your head. If you understand what you have just heard, and what the story is about, you'll come back and write the story from your head and from what you remember. What you remember will be what interests you, and what interests you will interest the reader. Listen to the tape, or look at your notes afterwards, to confirm what you've written and to check the quotes. Always write your story from what you know, understand, believe to be the case and observe. Be selective about the quotes you use.

Take this story from the *Wall Street Journal*:

Gastronome No. 1 isn't your usual Communist grocery store. Its pre-revolutionary hall has mirrored walls, a stained-glass window, 18-metre high gilded ceilings and chandeliers. Crowds give it the air of a baroque Grand Central Station.

The lure of the place has to do with the rare items for sale: fresh Brazilian coffee, ripening Nicaraguan bananas, Cuban rum, and a rich assortment of meats and cheeses. In the culinary desert of the Soviet Union, it is something of an oasis.

Gastronome No. 1 has a new director. The previous one, Yuri K. Sokolov, was executed for illegally selling rare delicacies – like black caviar and wild boar – out of the back door to certain special customers – Western businessmen, Communist Party big shots and so forth.

A firing squad might seem stiff punishment for a little pocket lining. But shoppers shuffling through Gastronome No. 1 on a busy Friday evening and the staff in their neatly pressed white uniforms shed no tears.

One woman buying tomatoes to make Saturday night's soup thinks Mr. Sokolov got his just desserts.

'He needed to answer for it' declares Mira, an attractive 58-year-old doctor. 'You can't allow corruption to live. It must be stopped . . .'

There is no quote until paragraph six. The rest is getting readers interested, sketching the background, describing the whole thing so they get the right pictures in their mind for what is coming. A profile is about a person. Effective quotes are selected pieces of the conversation between interviewee and interviewer. As a journalist, you have to deliver the quotation to the reader in its best form with proper placement and economical yet responsible focus. You also have to remember appropriate grammar, word usage and punctuation so that the reader understands the spoken words the way in which they were meant.

Once you've written the profile from the head and from the heart, reread what you have written. Look for clarity and conciseness. See whether you have chosen the best words to tell the best story.

Remember, the second draft will usually be better than the first, and that complexity in language is easy, simplicity in language is difficult. Examine each verb; are they mostly active? Examine each adverb; does the adverb clarify the verb? Instead of using an adverb, try to find a better verb: not *she moved slowly* but *she crept. She cried hard* can become *She sobbed.* Examine each noun: use the best, most accurate noun. *He is a young boy* can become *He's a first-former. She made a lot of money when she was young* can become *by 25 she'd made her first million.* Examine each adjective: ask yourself if you've used too many or too few. The right adjective helps a story; the wrong one doesn't. Get rid of extra words and try to make everything shorter; it's usually better that way. Be careful about statistics: don't let them get in the way of the story. If you need to show statistics, put them in a box or chart to give the whole list. In your writing you should tell the reader the result, not the workings that led to the result.

REPORTING SPEECHES

All reporters will spend a lot of time listening to and reporting speeches. They form a large and important part of the daily job. The speech given is not yet a story. The reader wants to know what is said, what it means, how important it is; not just that a speech has been given. If nothing new is said in the speech, don't report it. Normally you should summarize the main point made in the speech. It might have taken an hour or more, but you'll be covering it in about 400 words maximum. Speakers don't write their speeches in news form, and you will have to translate it into that form for the newspaper. Use the speaker's words when they are most interesting; there's no need to use them all the time. You are a journalist, not a stenographer. You're creating a story, not simply repeating the speech verbatim. Analyse all the speaker has said; find what is new, what is interesting, what is valuable to the reader. These then become the points of the story. There will sometimes be more than one issue of interest. If there is one main point, use a single-incident lead and then mention the other important items in the following paragraphs. Somewhere in the first three paragraphs or so give the speaker's background. The reader wants to know who is saying this and what his or her qualifications are. This paragraph should also mention any local tie-ups, such as the group to whom the speech is made. If you get a handout of the speech, be sure to check it against what is actually said. Speakers sometimes put things in or leave things out, and these can be important additions or omissions.

SPORTS REPORTING

Sports reporters are often thought of as 'underdogs', not doing a proper job. However, the sports page is usually what many people in general turn to first. The sports department usually has its own head, the sports editor. Sports and finance have similar approaches, similar problems and similar styles of individual writing. Like finance writing, sports journalism has a lot of comment and speculation – unlike news reporting, of course, which deals solely in facts. Sports news is often presented in an interpretative rather than objective way. Like finance, sports reporting also relies on a specific type of vocabulary and an assumption of special interest and knowledge by the readers.

Sport usually has its own specialist staff for each type of sport, though newsroom journalists are often recruited to help with the wide variety of match coverage on Saturdays and weekend evenings. The sports editor controls page planning, sub-editing and production.

Sport is news, and it is usually given a larger proportion of total editorial space in the dailies and Sundays than most other specialities. The popular subjects can take up as much as 15 per cent of available space in the daily newspaper. It is essential to have good journalists who can and want to write about sports so that newspaper sports coverage is improved, writing is tightened up, better graphics and pictures are used and local events get more and better coverage. Above all, sports writing must be objective, and not just PR for athletes and footballers.

Sports reporting should inform, interpret and illustrate; it should be fact oriented, background oriented (profiles of sports celebrities) and opinion oriented.

Sports reporting can be factual or can be opinions about the team or event. All sports stories should contain the following elements:

- the final score (usually at the top)
- names of the teams or people taking part
- when the game took place
- where it took place
- key players
- crowd details
- quotes from players/coaches/supporters
- injuries
- any records set during the game
- effect of the game on the team's standing in the league
- any oddities, length of game, etc.
- weather, if a factor.

Sports stories are often written in advance as features for publication on the day of the big game. Afterwards you would write a results story based on the above points.

Sports features

Guidelines for sports writing of an advance type include:

1 The significance of the game.
2 Tradition and history. How the teams' or players' rivalry began, and the most exciting and/or unusual contests they've played in the past. How they stand in won-and-lost figures in the series. The outcome of the last encounter is important.
3 Team or player records during the current season. Comments on the player/team records.
4 An analysis of comparative scoring records against mutual opponents.
5 Team/player conditions – physical and mental.
6 The weather. How possible changes may affect the outcome. How teams and players have performed in wet/dry/hot/cold.
7 A comparison of the way players/teams play, e.g. in tennis a player's volley, serve or backhand against the opponent.
8 The individual angle. In a team, the importance of one player to the whole – whether he or she is in or out of the particular game.
9 The local situation. The atmosphere in the city where game is being played (in soccer in the UK, the home side usually has an advantage).

10 The tickets and crowd. Is it a sell-out? Will extra seats have to be brought in? Are tickets being sold on the black market?
11 Statements by captains/coaches etc.
12 Who is the favourite? Who are the bookmakers and betters favouring?

Writing style and special vocabulary

The special style can be seen from the following examples:

Clive Rees cut inside from Dacey's pass with Scotland in turmoil. The ball switched magically between Dacey again, then David Richards, Eddie Butler and then to Robert Ackerman. He completed the break, Mark Wyatt surged through on the over-lap and gave the final transfer to Rees . . . (rugby)

Kevin Reeves had one solid 20-yarder touched wide by Mick Leonard and centre-back Caton found the net with a seventh-minute header only to be ruled offside. The tricks and illusions misfired and when Hartford and Bodak combined at speed, centre-forward David Cross hit his close-range return embarrassingly 10 feet over Bodak's head . . . (soccer)

Soon afterwards, Brewgawn raced clear and it became a Dickinson monopoly as the chestnut's four stable companions followed on. Captain John looked a big danger but made a mistake at the third last and had to settle for second. David Goulding said: 'He was very unlucky – nearly on the floor – and it took the stuffing out of him'. Jonjo O'Neill produced Wayward Lad to perfection to have every chance at the last but the eight-year-old could do no more, finishing third . . . (racing).

REPORTING LIFESTYLE

What is a lifestyle story? It's about people and how they live, and about our culture. Lifestyle reports in newspapers can include lots of things and be about all kinds of stories. They can be about business, news, sport. However, they all have one thing in common: they relate the story to the way people live. Included can be such things as:

- food
- entertainment
- drama
- reviews
- television and the media
- sports
- business (from the point of view of shopping, fashion etc.)
- weather
- pollution
- new ways of spending leisure time
- medical breakthroughs that help our way of living
- travel.

In other words, these stories are about anything connected with the way we live. This therefore needs a different approach. Whereas other forms need a highly critical, factual or newsy approach, lifestyle stories can simply be soft and explore current and future living and lifestyles.

REPORTING BUSINESS

Business and economic news is news, not something specialized. It can be specialized, but only for the finance/money pages. This is why there are techniques for both the specialist and the general reporter. The trick is not to make it an advertising feature but to have enough interest and a specific story angle to cover all the business facts you want to write about. You must have facts and background, not just quotes from the people involved in the business; that's just a public relations advertising story. Business stories are about new trends in business; profit and loss, fashion trends, comparisons of old and new business practices, not just about what a good brand of tea a particular shop sells. The business story has a major problem that must be addressed when writing it; it can be complicated and boring because of all the facts and figures and money terms it might contain. The goal of the business journalist is to report, accurately, the financial news (and remember, a misplaced decimal point can cost a fortune). Reporters have to make business news understandable and interesting.

In order to achieve this goal, every business story must be interesting and it must explain. To explain, you first need to understand, and this often means admitting to yourself that you don't know. Business news has to be made understandable to the ordinary reader as well as to the highly-educated business tycoon. To make the story interesting, it is a good idea to focus less on statistics and more on people. Changes in the economy affect people's lives; business is full of human dramas and reporters often forget to write about the people affected by or behind the statistics. There must also be well-developed and interesting background, full of comparisons, facts and figures.

Guidelines for reporting business affairs

1 *Avoid economic jargon.* Don't use the jargon of the economists and financial specialists. Translate.

The official called on indigenous producers of industrial, consumer and other products to engage in local sourcing of component materials

really means:

Officials are urging local manufacturers to use local raw materials

so write it that way.

Using economic jargon is a sign that the journalist has fallen victim to the real danger of economic jargon; hearing it so often that it sounds normal. It isn't to ordinary people. There is a danger of oversimplification and distortion in translating economic jargon into normal language, but it can usually be done by stopping and thinking what the jargon really means. If possible, a good technique is to ask speakers to summarize what they are saying in everyday language, so the speakers (not you) do the translation.

2 *Define economic terms.* When you have to use economic jargon, then explain if possible. For example:

Volatile inter-bank interest rates, which have been relatively stable in the past three months, shot up by about three percentage points yesterday.

Later in the story, where it fits, it might be a good idea to add:

Inter-bank interest rates are the rates at which banks lend money to and among themselves, and which are usually a fundamental factor taken into consideration when banks arrive at their final interest rates for loans to their customers.

The *Wall Street Journal* and the London *Financial Times* always do this. The *Wall Street Journal* usually explains gross national product when it first appears in a story (the total value of a nation's output of goods and services). Explaining can take more words but, if they add to the story and make it more readable, so be it.

3 *Use statistics sparingly.* Reporters usually use too many figures. Important figures give authority and precision to an article; you should try to get rid of those that aren't crucial to the story. Find your lead and then find the figures that will support what you are writing about. Forget the rest. The ordinary reader doesn't need the data; the specialist reader already knows. Statistics can be put in sidebars or boxes outside the main text. Let the text of the story develop the why and wherefore of the statistics, not be used to provide the statistics.

4 *Compare statistics.* When you use figures in a story, put them into context. Numbers have little significance on their own; their true meaning comes from their relative value. When you write figures, ask yourself, 'compared to what?'. Most statistics can be compared to equivalent statistics from another time, such as last year or the last financial quarter. They can be compared to equivalent statistics from another place, such as a neighbouring country or a competing company.

5 *Turn statistics into stories.* You, as a journalist, need to do more than report the figures. You have to turn them into stories by explaining their significance and saying what they mean. Ask: what's going on here, what does this all mean?

6 *Get the other side of the story.* You get a routine company announcement. Don't just write up the press release or the announcement: that's PR. There's usually another side to the story. Find it. A single source rarely gives a complete picture. Find other sources to give other views. Be sceptical. Don't believe everything you are told.

7 *Humanize business news.* Business news is about numbers, so the numbers have to be turned into people – not just government officials and business executives, but real people. Look for the human angle. Show the readers how they relate to the news or the story; how they are affected.

8 *Show the significance of the story.* Ask: *so what?* This is an important test when writing any story; particularly so with business stories. You have to explain to the readers what the consequences of a news event are likely to be; why the news is important for the company, workforce, industry, nation and, particularly, for the readers.

9 *Go beyond the press release.* The release is only the starting point. It is where you get an idea from which you develop your own story. Flesh it out. Company press releases should always raise questions that require answers from the company itself. Find out the significance of the announcement. Ask what impact the development will have on the company, and on other companies. Will it have an impact on the workforce? How will it affect the industry? Or the nation? Or the readers? All these questions need answers, and all spring from the simple press release. Never trust press releases, and never just copy them.

10 *Generate unusual business story ideas.* Find new angles on business developments. Find the business angle in important general news stories, and look at the human angle of business news. Examine trends that grow out of and have long-term importance for particular events. Look for trends. Look for case studies that illustrate a trend. Business isn't just about big business; it's also about small business, and small businesses are about people. To write financial or business stories, it's important to know the rules of the game.

There are two types of business journalism:

- that intended for the experts
- that intended for the ordinary reader.

Sometimes finance/business journalism does not appear on the general pages but in its own section. However, business and finance generate a lot of good news and feature stories that can and should interest the general reader. Journalists need to have some knowledge of it, even if they are just going to be ordinary reporters.

THE PHOTOPAGE AND PHOTO NEWS

Words alone don't tell the whole story; pictures and other visuals are also necessary. All reporters need to have good photo ideas, whether they take the pictures themselves while doing the story or whether they ask a photographer to take them. The same applies with other visuals. Reporters need to be aware of the importance of charts, graphs and illustrations, and to be able to suggest ideas to editors and graphic artists. Print reporters need to present a complete package of information: words, photos and illustrations. That's the way print journalists compete with television. A good story without any pictures might be run somewhere in the paper; with good pictures, it might be on page 1. Stories for the photopage need to combine the best words and the best art (photos, illustrations, charts, cartoons and other visual elements).

Newspaper reporters must add 'visual' to their list of story requirements. Visuals are not possible in every news story, but whenever they can be used, they add to the story and help the reader understand. Reporters must respect the importance of visuals; be prepared to understand the news requirements of charts, photos, illustrations; and understand the needs of and be willing to co-operate with photographers, artists and graphic designers. Photos make the reader stop scanning and read. They're that important. Reporters need not only to find the facts and write the story; they also need to find statistics that can then be converted to an easy-to-read chart and identify people who can be used in accompanying photos. The best photos provide their own messages, whether emotional or intellectual. The best illustrations add impact to the story by simplifying difficult facts and figures. Always be thinking of ways of taking the difficult statistics out of the body of the text and making them simpler to understand by graphics or a box.

Pictures need some kind of identification, usually called captions. The job of a caption is to explain the subject of a picture. There are two kinds:

1 Self-contained photostories built around the subject of the picture with extended captions providing the text.
2 Pictures used to illustrate a story, with simple line captions.

Writing a self-contained caption story is a skilled job. It gives scope for fun and imagination, since it often has to give a reason for using a picture that in itself may be decorative or visually attractive but not necessarily newsworthy. A line caption is simply for identification, although a quotation on a news point should be used where possible – for example, *After the ordeal, Jane Smith considers the decision* or Jane Smith: *I'm lucky to be alive.*

All pictures need captions. Readers see the picture first and are therefore entitled to know who or what it is about. They will then want to read the story. Captions are always written in the present tense, even if the picture isn't a 'now' one. The caption should normally identify everyone in the picture. Using (left) is acceptable, but try not to say, for example, *Mr Li (sitting)*. It means you have to look too closely at the picture. If this is the only way of identifying those in the picture, choose another, clearer picture. There must be a better way of writing a caption than, for example, *Ms Li enjoying a joke* (which you can see anyway). Try to write the caption as you would a TV script. Don't identify what you can see, but give it some other kind of interest. For example, a picture of a chief executive could say: *Chief Executive Mr Wong*, or it could better say:

Accountable . . . while emphasizing the business side of the Jockey Club, chief executive Lawrence Wong seeks openness, transparency and accessibility.

Further examples include:

Memorial . . . tourists in Beijing visit a tunnel used in the war against Japan.

Punting for tourists . . . life along the Sepik is changing.

All alone . . . the days when the elderly could look forward to twilight years surrounded by their children and grandchildren have gone as families fragment and move apart.

In a photostory, there has got to be a better way of describing a picture than: *Jane (left) and Joyce check a diamond for a client.* In the picture you see the client and the two shop assistants, with one of them clearly checking a diamond. A much better caption with more interest would be a quote from the story: *A diamond is forever, so it's got to be right*, which adds a lot to the picture of the woman checking the diamond. Over another picture of a woman checking a diamond: *It takes an expert to find the best.*

The problem with writing text to go with the photostory is that you should have only enough words, and not too many. Again, think of your script as a TV script to go with the pictures. You don't describe and tell the listener what's there on the screen in a TV script; the same applies in a good text for a photopage. Sometimes a very few words might be enough to provide a context, set the story up or to provide some colour or emotion to go with the pictures. You will certainly have to explain why you are running these pictures (where they were taken etc.).

Sometimes, only clever captions will be enough or you might need a lot of words; that is, make a story for which the pictures are further explanation. You, the photojournalist, must make these decisions. However, always try to write in a way that is different, creative and complements the picture story. Your photopage is a picture story, first and foremost. The words are secondary. If the words are the main part of the photopage, there is something wrong with the pictures and they should not be a two-page spread. Just as you write a news story differently from a feature, so you write a photopage story differently from anything else.

A good story idea for a photopage should be aimed at providing the pictures that will best show the idea you have. Try to have pictures that are interesting and say something in their own right. They should provide the reader with some additional information, interest, emotion that words can't give. They should also, wherever possible, show something that has movement in it, although a picture of a beautiful bowl of fruit or flowers can also provide all the elements of a good photopage.

The photos should provide easily recognizable links for the theme. The pictures can tell the story from beginning to end; they can compare, say, various historical and modern temples in Hong Kong; they can show the various stages of kicking a soccer ball; ballet lessons. The story ideas are limitless. Be creative and use your imagination to construct a theme that only pictures can tell, and the words will then write themselves.

INFORMATION GRAPHICS

Get used to thinking visually for your difficult data and statistics. People read charts on two levels:

- the visual (a quick scan that picks up the trends or relationships)
- the closer look (when the reader comes back to the graphic and looks at the numbers, the trends and the deeper levels of meaning provided by the graphic information).

Readers understand data better in graphics than in text, and remember the information presented pictorially and visually better than in text. Readers don't like difficult artwork. The visual must never distract, distort or make understanding more difficult; the simpler the better. As a reporter, you need to ask yourself: 'what's the best way to tell my story?' The answer will be one of several: inverted pyramid; narration; lists; sidebars; graphics. Or, more usually, a combination of these and other ways. Often the story will be better told in pictures, graphics, illustrations or maps rather than in words.

Types of graphic

1 Pie charts. Think of these as pies cut into different size slices. Each slice shows the relationship of that part to the whole. In an election, for example, if 25 per cent of people vote for party X the the X slice will be a quarter of the pie.
2 Line charts. Think of these as video. They show motion; lines rise or fall (like on a hospital temperature chart). They emphasize trends.
3 Bar charts. Think of these as a still picture. They freeze the numbers so readers can look at the comparisons. They can show trends, but they are most useful for comparing numbers at a given moment.
4 Tables. Tables help organize lots of data that do not necessarily have a mathematical relationship. A voting chart will show how the people in each area voted etc.

Remember: numbers don't mean much until they are compared to something else.

FURTHER READING

Anderson, D. (1994). *Sports Reporting*. McGraw-Hill.

Barnhurst, K. (1994). *Seeing the Newspaper*. St. Martin's Press.

Davis, A. (1998). *Magazine Journalism Today.* Focal Press.

Dobson, C. (1994). *The Freelance Journalist*. Focal Press.

Fischer, H. D. (1995). *Sports Journalism at its Best*. Nelson-Hall.

Gaines, W. (1994). *Investigative Reporting for Print and Broadcast*. Nelson-Hall.

Giles, V. and Hodgson, F. W. (1996). *Creative Newspaper Design*. Focal Press.

Harris, G. and Spark, D. (1993). *Practical Newspaper Reporting*. Focal Press.

Hennessy, B. (1997). *Writing Feature Articles*. Focal Press.

Hodgson, F. W. (1993). *Modern Newspaper Practice*. Focal Press.

Hodgson, F. W. (1998). *New Subediting: Apple Mac, QuarkXpress and After*. Focal Press.

Keene, M. (1995). *Practical Photojournalism*. Focal Press.

Kobre, K. (1996). *Photojournalism*. Focal Press.

Appendix

Below are two examples of reporting technique as a result of a big local Hong Kong story in 1996 and 1997: the Diaoyu islands, which were disputed territory between China and Japan. This story raised much anger in Hong Kong, where there were demonstrations and several attempts by activists to land on the disputed islands. The first time such an attempt was made, there was one death among the protesters. The third attempt, in May 1997, saw most accompanying reporters on a separate boat, rather than on the main protesters' boat, which was now judged to be too subjective for good reporting, and also too dangerous. Ho Wing-hong went on the first trip, but did not go on the second. He did return, this time on a separate press boat, for attempt three. He covered the story with in-depth and colour reporting. The piece below appeared first in the Chinese daily, *Singtao*, and was the next day reprinted in translation without any editing in the English daily *Hong Kong Standard*, a member of the same press group. The interesting thing about the English translation of this story is that the style was not changed to make it more 'English language'. It is therefore a most interesting example of the personal reporting style of the Chinese language newspapers, and how it looks in unedited simple translation.

Safe return after depths of despair on high seas

by Ho Wing-hong in Keelung

Is bloodshed a must for success? Or is everyone's safe return more worthy of celebration?

It was a big relief when I learnt that the two reporters thought to have drowned during the confrontation near the islands were safe.

When the radio blared out the news they had fallen from the boat into the rough waters, my body shivered and my heart pounded. The dying face of drowned Diaoyu activist David Chan Yuk-cheung last September flashed in my mind.

My God, not again . . . not something like this happening to reporters, I kept telling myself.

Against the background of the dark skyline our boat started to head back to Keelung – while my mind was obsessed with fears for the worst.

I was in absolute despair.

The clock struck eight as we waited desperately at the dockyard. But soon we saw the little shadow of a boat getting closer and closer. It was them – the reporters' boat. Thank God, they were safe and the radio message earlier was wrong. I realized what was meant by 'no news is good news'.

Good news or bad news, the Diaoyu protest has stirred up passions across Taiwan and Hong Kong since last year – sometimes with bloodshed, other times glory.

But the Diaoyu fever has cooled down this time. It seemed no one cared about the protests any more: the *Diao Yu Tai* set sail on a lonely trip.

But no matter if the protesters failed to land on the islands this time. I sensed the importance, value and preciousness of life.

It is easy to lose reason and go mad when seeing the islets. Of course the protesters want to land on them again.

But even if they cannot, it is not a failure. The fact that they can return safely is what counts most in the fight for the islands.

(Ho Wing-hong is a *Singtao* reporter travelling on a press boat accompanying the *Diao Yu Tai*)

Below is another example of personal colour reporting, this time by Hong Kong columnist, Tim Hamlett, a writer of brilliance and intelligent sensitivity. This piece is reprinted from the *Sunday South China Morning Post* the other English newspaper in Hong Kong.

The dangers of a pointless voyage

by Tim Hamlett

Reporting can be a dangerous business. Every year the casualty figures, world-wide, run to several tens. The number of journalists in prison for work-related reasons is usually about 400.

There is always a temptation for young people to 'seek the bubble reputation in the cannon's mouth'. The press corps in Vietnam suffered a higher loss rate than any of the military formations. So it goes.

I did not myself suffer anything more strenuous than the odd moment of anxiety at an English football ground. But we have all seen colleagues go off to wars, riots, disturbances, hazardous expeditions or dangerous pursuits.

Most of us can remember one or two who didn't come back.

What makes these tragedies easier to bear is the thought that the world needs news. It may not be a 'sweet and gentle thing' to die collecting it but at least the loss is not totally meaningless.

I am though, increasingly depressed by the likelihood that someone I know and like is going to make the supreme sacrifice for the purpose of covering an event as unnecessary, ill-organised and unreasonable as last week's sham battle for the Diaoyu islands.

I do not dispute for a moment that the islands belong to China. That does not explain the baleful influence which they seem to exert on otherwise sane people, depriving laymen of the most elementary common sense and turning master mariners into dodgem drivers.

It cannot just be patriotism because the illness is interestingly selective. There are plenty of disputed islands. But there is no such thing as a Nansha activist. No protest flotillas perpetrate monkey business at Mischief Reef. There are no suicidal swimming parties at the Scarborough Shoal.

It seems the problem with the Diaoyus is not that they ought to be Chinese but that the illegal occupant is Japan.

And indeed one of the frustrated island-hoppers could be heard on the news last Tuesday evoking the spectre of Japanese militarism. This argument will not wash. Its sell-by date passed years ago. No reasonable observer of Japan believes it is on the brink of a militaristic revival.

Clearly the problem is not Japan's past but its present: modern, prosperous, democratic and respected. All the things that China isn't.

This problem will not be remedied by the sort of events we saw last week. I knew it was not going to be a dignified voyage when the protesters turned up in Taiwan complaining that the trip so far had been unpleasant because the sea had waves on it. This is a surprisingly common occurrence.

The actual 'confrontation', as all television viewers could see, consisted of a Hong Kong vessel ramming a Japanese police launch. If this was not deliberate then the pilot was displaying a most reckless disregard for the likelihood of a collision.

At about the same time the boat carrying the *Post*'s correspondent was also in a collision with a Japanese vessel, whereupon the captain dived into the sea and swam to the other boat. We may charitably suppose that he was intent on the nautical equivalent of exchanging names, addresses and insurance companies. But this left his passengers bobbing about in the open sea with nobody on board qualified to drive them back to Taiwan.

Elsewhere it seems two reporters fell overboard but were recovered. Rumours that people had been drowned turned out to be just rumours. Next time they may not be so lucky.

The upshot of this episode is that the disputed islands remain as they were, legally, politically and geographically. The reckless behaviour of a few activists has endangered the lives of a large number of people, some of them Chinese and some of them Japanese.

And to what purpose? One of the Chinese newspapers said the action had 'galvanised the patriotic spirit of Chinese people world-wide' (a preposterous claim – how would they know?) but pollsters found the majority of Hong Kong people more embarrassed than inspired.

Perhaps this is because they knew what they were watching. This was not an oriental Trafalgar and the self-styled 'commander' who led it was not qualified to run the pedal boat fleet in the Wong Nei Chong Reservoir.

The whole sordid spectacle was devoted to the application of some political powered rhino horn to the wilting public potency of fading politicians.

Where but the Diaoyu Islands can paunchy middle-aged district board members pose as the heirs to Nelson?

There must be a thousand possible ways of protesting about the status of the Diaoyu islands and this must be the stupidest. Consider the potential for an 'own goal'.

Can you imagine any Japanese government giving up the disputed archipelago if seamen and coastguards have died in its defence?

Glossary

A/B roll	editing process using two separate rolls (cassettes or reels) of tape; each cassette contains alternate shots of the sequence, enabling the editor to use transitions other than straight cuts between shots
Absolute privilege	the right of legislators, judges and government officials to speak without threat of libel when acting officially
Acoustics	the science of sound; the way sounds behave
Active voice	structure in which the subject acts on the object of a sentence; news stories should be written in the more forceful active voice
Actuality	recording of an actual event, or someone speaking
Ad	abbreviation for an advertisement
Ad lib	unscripted comment
Anchor	a person in the television studio who ties together the newscast by reading the news and providing links between stories
Anecdotal lead	a newspaper story that uses some interesting incident to start the story
Angle	an item of information emphasized as the most important point in a story; it may be a 'new angle', giving the latest developments, or a 'local angle', giving the point of relevance for a local audience
AP	Associated Press newsagency
Assemble edit	recorded material arranged in sequence in a linear manner; may be done on raw tape without previously recording a control track

GLOSSARY

Atmos	background noise or music, often achieved by a special microphone placed to get the best natural sound of the event
Attribution	the source of a news story
Audience ratings	the percentage of people watching a programme at a specific time; usually measures the people who are in the room with the set switched on. Household ratings or set ratings refer to the percentage of households with a set tuned to the programme
Audio	sound material
Autocue	mechanical or electrical device that allows television presenters to read a script while looking at the camera
Back announcement	a final sentence giving extra information to be read by the anchor at the end of a report
Back bench	senior editorial executives of a newspaper
Background	information that can be attributed to an unnamed source
Back timing	the timing of the final part of a broadcast to help the newscaster and producer finish on time
Back projection	pictures projected on a screen behind the newsreader
Beat	a reporter's assigned area of responsibility; a beat may be an institution, a geographical area or a subject
Betacam	the half-inch video format developed by Sony and widely used in television
Bi-directional microphone	a microphone that will pick up sound in front and behind only
Blow up	a portion of a photograph enlarged so as to bring out the best or most interesting part
Boil	tight editing of a story done to reduce length or to streamline it by deleting minor details
Boom mike	microphone held on a long boom

Breaking news	unexpected events that cannot be anticipated, such as fires or crimes; often the event is still continuing when the story deadline is reached, and continues afterwards
Bridge	words that connect one piece of narration or soundbite to another
Brief	instructions for a reporter covering a story
Broadsheet	newspaper page size used to describe the quality press
Byline	reporter's name appearing with a story
C-band	the frequencies used by most communication satellites, specifically 4–6 gigaHertz
Camcorder	hand-held camera and videocassette recorder combined
Cartridge	self-contained and enclosed recording tape that is slipped on to a special playback machine; it does not need spooling
Character generator	electronic caption machine
Chromakey (colour separation overlay, CSO)	method of electronically replacing a single colour with a second picture or image (usually the colour replaced is blue)
Classified	small ads
Close-up (CU)	camera framing showing intimate detail; often a tight head shot
Commentary	a verbal description of an event as it happens
Continuity	(1) the orderly progression from one programme to another; (2) announcements filling intervals between programmes
Control track	synchronizing signal recorded onto videotape to align the heads for proper playback
Copy	typed news
Copy flow	the route along which copy moves in a newsroom
Copyright	the exclusive right of an author, composer, pictorial artist or assignee to dispose of work for publication, performance, etc.

Cue	a pre-arranged signal to a studio or other programme source to start or stop
Cue-light	light on top of the camera to tell the anchor the camera is live
Cue pulse	inaudible pulse recorded on tape just before the start of audio or pictures; when the recorder finds the pulse it will stop and the tape will be cued ready to play
Cultural imperialism	the tendency for one country's mass culture to be dominated by that of another country
Current affairs	see public affairs
Cutaway	the insertion of a shot in a picture sequence that is used to mask an edit
Dead air	silence during a broadcast because of some technical error
Deadline	the time at which copy is required
Delayed lead	keeping the most important information until later in the story to achieve added interest and mystery
Digital audio broadcasting (DAB)	a proposed system for over-the-air broadcasting utilizing digital encoding and decoding that will not work with present broadcasting equipment
Digital recording	the storage of sound and/or pictures that have been encoded as a series of numbers; playback translates those numbers back without the noise or distortion of conventional analogue recording techniques
Direct broadcast satellite (DBS)	the transmission of a television signal by satellite to a small receiving dish
Dissolve	where one picture is faded out and another is faded in at the same time
Documentary	programme on a given subject seeking to bring out the facts necessary to understand the subject better; can be news, information or entertainment (music)
Down link	transmission path from a satellite to a ground station; sometimes used to describe the ground station capable of receiving a satellite signal

Dub	make a copy of a programme or piece of material already recorded elsewhere
Editing	the process of cutting, rearranging, adaptation and selection of material
Editor	the most senior editorial executive; in newspapers, the person legally responsible for the newspaper content
Editorialize	inject the reporter's opinion into a news story; most newspapers and all broadcast stations only allow opinion in analysis stories, columns and editorials
Embargo	prohibition on publishing before a specified time; press releases are often distributed beforehand and then embargoed for release later
ENG	electronic news gathering with portable video cameras
Establishing shot	a wide shot of a scene, usually used at the beginning of a news story on television
Executive producer	the executive in overall charge of a radio or television programme or newscast
Feature	programme on a given theme or subject composed and presented according to certain techniques for print or broadcast
Fibre optics	the conversion of electrical signals into light waves sent through glass fibres
Flash	headline used by newsagencies to describe news of an extreme nature
Focus group	a research method in which a small number of people take part in a discussion on some specific important issue (used in TV and radio for audience research)
FX	shorthand for sound effects
Graphics	titles and other artwork used in programmes, newscasts and promos
Handout	free copy (a printed news release) of some event – usually put out by a firm's advertising or publicity department; it is invariably 'good news' that makes the company appear in the best possible light

Hard news	daily factual reporting of national, international or local events, especially focused on fast-breaking stories
Headline	the heading to text in news
High definition television (HDTV)	TV system of more than a thousand lines, resulting in excellent quality
Human interest	news value element; aspects of a story, usually about people, that appeal to the reader's or viewer's emotions
Input	keyboard data (story) into the computer (to input); also, the data itself (the input)
Insert	(1) short item or sequence to be inserted into a broadcast news bulletin to form part of it (a recorded item in a live programme; live insert from the studio or an outside source into a bulletin or programme); (2) portion to be included in a story already written
Invasion of privacy	breaching an individual's right to be left alone
Inverted pyramid	the organization of a news story in which information is arranged in descending order of importance
Investigative reporting	finding out information that has been concealed
In vision (IV)	instruction on script to indicate anchor or reporter should be on camera at this point
Jog mode	in hard disk, non-linear editing, reproduces samples of the sound in direct relation to the movement of the cursor over the defined region being listened to or edited
Jump cut	an edit in a sequence of shots that has the subject jerking from one position to another
Ku-band	frequencies used for transmitting some high-powered satellite signals; refers to the band between 11 and 14 gigaHertz; requires smaller receiving dishes than C-band
Layout	the design of a newspaper page
Lead	(1) a fresh introduction to a story ('new lead'); (2) the first sentence of a news story

Leading question	question asked during an interview that tries to elicit information the reporter wants to hear
Lead story	the most important news item in a bulletin or on the front page of the newspaper
Leak	information by an anonymous source, often a member of a public body, which was intended to be secret (to leak); information obtained in this way (a leak)
Libel	damage to a person's reputation caused by a false written statement that brings the person into hatred or contempt or injures their business or profession
Links	narrative linking or bridging interviews in a report, summarizing or giving additional information
Live	not pre-recorded; not edited
Long form	longer than the usual length for a news feature; a longer 60-minute plus news documentary or a documentary in-depth series
Master shot	extended wide shot establishing the scene and often running the entire length of the sequence; intended to be broken up during the editing process
Microwave	system for relaying audio and video signals on very short wavelengths
Middle managers	those responsible for the co-ordination of activities designed to help the organization achieve its overall goals and targets
Minidoc	a short news feature or documentary
Mix	the product of a re-recording session in which several separate sound tracks are combined through a mixing console
Mixdown	the point, usually in post-production, when all the separate audio tracks are combined into a complete final version
Medium close-up (MCU)	relative average framing for a shot; often framed from the waist up

Medium shot (MS)	wider than an MCU, often framed from head to toe
Mobile unit	A car, van or truck equipped to produce programme material
Modem	electronic device to send a story through telephone lines, usually from a portable computer at the scene of a news event to the newsroom
Monitor	check the technical quality of a transmission
Montage	an impressionistic sequence or combination of sounds
More	word centred at the bottom of a hard copy page to indicate that another page (take) follows
Multiplexing	simultaneously transmitting (via subcarriers) one or more television or radio signals in addition to the main channel; utilizes digital compression to fit a 6-mHz signal into a narrower band; in radio carries RBDS signals
Natural sound on film (NAT SOF)	location sound recorded on the tape as the footage is recorded
Negative lead	a lead sentence that contains the word 'not'; to be avoided
News judgement	ability to recognize the importance of various news stories
News peg	the current event or central aspect about which a news story is written
News values	elements that constitute news; consequence, prominence, proximity, timeliness, action, novelty, human interest, sex, humour
Nib	paragraphs of news, usually in a column (comes from news in brief)
Noddies	shots of the reporter nodding or listening carefully, which are recorded separately and usually after an interview and will be used when doing the final edits
OB	outside broadcast: a broadcast originating outside the studios

Obit (obituary)	story about a person's death; appears in a column of such stories and is written in a very specific manner
Off mike	sound directed away from the sensitive face of a microphone; it gives the impression of a distant speaker in a drama. In normal broadcast journalism it can sound wrong
Off-the-record	usually means 'don't quote me'. Some sources and reporters use it to mean something different: 'Don't print this'
Ombudsman	person who is paid by a media outlet to critique the job it is doing; the public can complain to this person, who will then investigate
Omni-directional mike	microphone with a circular pickup area
Output	(1) typeset version of a story that is printed out of the computer; (2) in broadcasting, the programme or newscast
Package	report comprising edited interviews separated by narrative links
Pagination	number of pages
Paintbox	electronic graphics machine
Panel	the control, on a studio control panel
Paraphrase	this puts a quotation into different words, usually those of the reporter, to give a clearer or more interesting meaning; quotation marks are not used
Piece	usual journalese for a story
Piece to camera (stand-upper)	information given by a reporter on location while facing the camera
Plagiarism	the use of any part of another's writing without attributing it; passing it off as your own work

Post-production	the third stage in the production process, when the recorded material is edited, sometimes re-recorded and mixed
Pre-production	the first stage in the production process, during which the creative, technical and business planning takes place
Production	(1) the middle stage in the production process, during which recording takes place; (2) the material that is produced
Profile	story intended to reveal the personality or character of a person or organization
Promo	broadcast advertisement for a new programme, or encouraging viewers and listeners to stay with the station rather than switch to another
Public affairs	programmes dealing with topical issues of public concern (political, economic, social)
Public journalism	the new approach to journalism that emphasizes connections with the community rather than being separated from it
Q & A	question and answer; interplay between source and reporter after opening statements at a press conference; also a form of story presentation designed to give verbatim query and response; the interview in a broadcast
RBDS	Radio broadcast data systems, a recently developed radio technology using FM subcarriers to multiplex a visual display (such as a station ID) and limit electronic scanning of stations to those channels with a required format; used extensively for traffic information to override the programme being listened to
Remote	live production from locations other than the studio
Rewrite	process of improving a story by making extensive revisions such as a new lead, a different sequence to the paragraphs or changing the story structure; a rewrite might even involve extra new information

Rough cut	first rough edit of a piece
Running story	one that is developing and constantly changing, giving new information, which makes it necessary to revise and update the story
Sampling	process in which a section of digital audio representing a sonic event is stored on disk or into the computer memory
Scrubbing	in hard-disk editing, moving the cursor through the defined region at any speed to listen to the sound being prepared for editing; this is the hard-disk equivalent of rocking a tape by moving the spools by hand in cut-and-splice editing, and the jog mode in electronic editing
Segue	cutting from one effect to another with nothing in between, or playing two recordings one after another with no live announcement in between
Shield laws	legislation giving journalists the right to protect the identity of sources
Short form	usually programme material in less than 30-minute lengths on television; typically up to 5 minutes for radio
Sidebar	a secondary story intended to be run with a major story on the same topic
Slant	emphasis or focus of a story; may also indicate that the story has a particular bias or over-emphasizes one aspect at the expense of other pieces of information
Slug	one or two words at the top of the story indicating the subject so it can be identified as it is processed through the newsroom
Soft lead	a lead that uses a quote, story or some other soft literary device to attract the reader
Soft news	opposite of hard, fast-breaking stories; consists of less topical features and reports that do not depend on happening news (for example, medical reports, entertainment stories, lifestyle, leisure, human interest etc.)

SOT	abbreviation for sound-on-tape; used on the video side of a split script page to indicate the tape has sound. Usually followed by the instruction, UPSOT
Soundbite	portion of an interview or 'grab' of actuality selected for broadcast
Sources	people or records from which a reporter gets information
Split page	the standard TV news script; the left side of the page is used for video directions and the right side is for the script and audio cues
Splitter box	device used to feed one input signal to more than one output; commonly used at news conferences to avoid a jumble of microphones by splitting the feed from one mike to all those covering the event
Spot news	an up-to-the-minute news report of an event that is happening at the same time
Spot story	an item of breaking news, such as a fire or air crash
Stand-upper	news story by a reporter in the field standing in front of the camera
Stet	editor marks copy for a change then decides to keep the original; it means 'let it stand as it was'
Sub-editor	journalist who checks, corrects and prepares copy for printing or broadcast
Summary lead	the first paragraphs of a news story in which the writer presents a synopsis of several actions rather than focusing on one specific angle
Super (caption)	title or caption mechanically superimposed or electronically generated on the picture; mostly used for the names, addresses and titles of people being identified in a news package or newscast
Tabloid	page size used to describe the 'down-market' popular press
Tag (outro)	ending segment of a story; often the anchor adds a line or two after a report

Take	(1) one page of copy; (2) one attempt at recording
Talking heads	discussion programme with two or more named participants in a studio, where the camera mainly focuses on the heads of those concerned; in radio, a studio discussion
Text	the main printed material in a newspaper, as distinct from headlines or graphics
Time code editor	a device that uses the time code recorded on a tape as the reference for editing
Transition	writing device that takes the reader smoothly from one aspect of a story to another loosely-related topic area
Transponder	one of several units on a communication satellite that both receives up-linked signals and retransmits them as down-linked signals; currently most satellites have 24 transponders, and digital compression of video signals has greatly increased transponder capacity
Two-shot	shot at a wide enough angle to include two people (usually the reporter and the person being interviewed)
Typo	typographical error
U-Matic 3/4"	videotape format created by Sony in the 1970s, which revolutionized video news gathering; has since been upgraded by a compatible U-matic SP format
Update	a type of follow-up story that gives newer developments to an earlier story
UPI	United Press International
Up link	transmission path from an earth station up to a satellite; sometimes used to describe the ground station capable of sending a satellite signal
Vertical interval time code (VITC)	time code that is recorded vertically on videotape within the video signal but outside the picture area so it is not visible
Video-on-demand (VOD)	system that will be able to deliver entertainment and information to users on demand; will work in conjunction with a set-top computer storage device to hold programming in memory for instant recall

Videotape	plastic coated tape with slanted magnetic particles used to record video and audio signals
Visuals	visual element of a TV report
Voiceover (v/o)	commentary recorded over pictures by an unseen reporter or reader
Voice report (voicer)	details and explanation of a story by a reporter; a report in a reporter's own voice – either in the studio or from elsewhere by phone or satellite
Vox pop	Latin *vox populi*; refers to street interviews conducted to poll public opinion and edited to give short comments
VTR	videotape recording
Web offset	printing process
Wildtrack	recording of ambient sound for dubbing later as background to a report
Wipe	crossing from one picture to another, giving the impression that one is wiping the other off the screen
World Wide Web	part of the Internet of computer networks; allows for the integration of text, voice and video data in the creation of various home pages of information, which can then be accessed by consumers
Wrap	finish shooting; also, the combination of three or more stories linked with a wipe between each and usually v/o'd by the anchor
Wraparound	news story consisting of at least two parts; an intro/outro and a centre portion reported by a second person
Zoom	special lens system with variable focal length enabling it to zoom from a wide angle to a closer shot and *vice versa*

Bibliography

A Future in Broadcast Journalism? Your Questions Answered (1993). NCTBJ leaflet.

Abbot, Waldo and Rider (1957). *Handbook of Broadcasting*. McGraw-Hill.

Abercrombie, D. (1990). *Elements of General Phonetics*. Edinburgh University Press.

Adams, R. C. and Fish, M. J. (1987). TV news directors' perceptions of station management style. *Journalism Quarterly*, **64**, 154–62

Aitchison, J. (1981). *Language Change: Progress or Decay*. Fontana.

Aitchison, J. (1981). *The Articulate Mammal*. Hutchison.

Akwule, R. (1992). *Global Telecommunications*. Focal Press.

Albarran, A. (1997). *Management of Electronic Media*. Wadsworth.

Alexander, S. (1976). *Talking Women*. Delacorte Press.

Alten, S. (1996). *Audio in Media*. Wadsworth.

Altschull, J. H. (1984). *Agents of Power: The Role of the News Media in Human Affairs*. Longman.

Anderson, D. (1987). How managing editors view and deal with ethical issues. *Journalism Quarterly*, Summer, 341–5.

Anderson, D. (1994). *Sports Reporting*. McGraw-Hill.

Armstrong, M. (1995). *Media Law in Australia*. OUP.

Auman A. (1995). Seeing the big picture: the integrated editor of the 1990s. *Newspaper Research Journal*, **16(1)**, 35–47.

Baggaley, J. and Sharpe, J. (eds) (1979). *Proceedings of the Second International Conference on Experimental Research in Televised Instruction*. Memorial University of Newfoundland.

Bagnell, N. (1993). *Newspaper Language*. Focal Press.

Bailey, R. (1984). *English as a World Language*. Cambridge University Press.

Bainbridge, C. and Stockdill, R. (1993). *The News of the World Story*. HarperCollins.

Baldwin, M. and Bates, B. (1992). Uses and values for news in cable television. *Journal of Broadcasting and Electronic Media*, **36(2)**, 225–33.

Bantz, C., McCorkle, S. and Baade, R. (1980). The news factory. *Communication Research*, **7**, 45–68.

Barnett, S. (1989). Broadcast news. *British Journalism Review*, **1**, 49–56.

Barnhurst, K. (1994). *Seeing the Newspaper*. St. Martin's Press.

Barnouw, E. (1966). *A Tower in Babel*. Oxford University Press.

Barrett, G. (1984). Job satisfaction among newspaperwomen. *Journalism Quarterly*, **61**, 593–9.

Barrett, M. (ed.) (1982). *Broadcast Journalism: 1979–1981*. Everest House.

Barwise, P. and Ehrenberg, A. (1994). *Television and its Audience*. Sage.

Baugh, A.C. and Cable, T. (1983). *A History of the English Language*. Oxford University Press.

Bayley, A. (1758). *An Introduction to Languages, Literary And Philosophical, Especially to the English, Latin and Greek*.

Becker, L. (1979). Reporters and their professional and organisational commitment. *Journalism Quarterly*, **56**, 753–63, 770.

Bell, A. (1984). Language style as audience design. *Language in Society*, **13(2)**, 145–204.

Bell, A. (1991). *The Language of the Media*. Blackwell.

Belsey, A. and Chadwick, R. (1992). *Ethical Issues in Journalism and the Media*. Routledge.

Bergen, L. A. and Weaver, D. (1988). Job satisfaction of daily newspaper journalists and organisation size. *Newspaper Research Journal*, **9**, 1–13.

Berkman, D. (1993). Is production overemphasised in broadcast studies? *Journal of the National Association of Educational Broadcasters*, **23(5)**, 44–51.

Biani, S. (1992). *Interviews that Work: A Practical Guide for Journalists*. Wadsworth.

Bjork, U. (1996). The European debate in 1894 on journalism education. *Journalism and Mass Communication Educator*, **51(1)**, 68–77.

Blainey, G. (1982). *The Tyranny of Distance*. Melbourne.

Blanchard, R. O. and Christ, W. G. (1985). In search of the unit core: commonalities in curricula. *Journalism Educator*, **40(3)**, 28–33.

Blankenburg, W. B. (1982). Newspaper ownership and control of circulation to increase profits. *Journalism Quarterly*, **59**, 390–98.

Bliss, E. and Patterson, J. (1971). *Writing News for Broadcast*. Columbia University Press.

Bliss, E. Jr, (1991). *Now the News*. Columbia University Press.

Blumler, J. (ed.) (1994). *Television and the Public Interest*. Sage.

Bolinger, D. (1980). *Language: The Loaded Weapon*. Oxford University Press.

Boyd, A. (1994). *Broadcast Journalism: Techniques of Radio and TV News*. Heinemann.

Braithwaite, N. (ed.) (1995). *The International Libel Handbook*. Butterworth-Heinemann.

Breed, W. (1960). Social control in the newsroom. In *Mass Communications* (W. Schramm, ed.), pp. 178–94. University of Illinois.

Breen, M. (ed.) (1998). *Journalism Theory and Practice*. MacLeay Press.

Briggs, A. (1967–9). *The History of Broadcasting in the United Kingdom*. Vols 1–4. Oxford University Press.

Brobrow, D. and Collins, A. (eds). (1986). *Representations and Understanding*. Academic Press.

Brody, E. W. (1991). *Managing Communication Processes: From Planning to Crisis Response*. Praeger.

Bromley, M. (1994). *Teach Yourself Journalism*. Hodder and Stoughton.

Brook, G. L. (1979). *Varieties of English*. Macmillan.

Brooks, B. S. (1996). *News Reporting and Writing*. St. Martin's Press.

Brosius, H.-B. (1996). How do text–picture relations affect the informational effectiveness of television newscasts? *Journal of Broadcasting and Electronic Media*, **40**, 180–95.

Burchfield, R. (1981). *The Spoken Word: A BBC Guide*. BBC.

Busterna, J. (1988). Trends in daily newspaper ownership. *Journalism Quarterly*, **65**, 831–6.

Calder, A. (1981). *Revolutionary Empire: The Rise of the English-Speaking Empires from the 15th Century to the 1780s*. Oxford University Press.

Carey, J. (1992). Where journalism education went wrong. Speech at Columbia University, New York, October 14.

Carey, P. (1998). *Media Law*. Sweet and Maxwell.

Carroll, R. (1993). *Electronic Media Programming: Strategies and Decision Making*. McGraw-Hill.

Chan, J. Man, Lee, P. S. N. and Lee, C.-C. (1996). Hong Kong journalists in transition. *Research Monograph*, **25**, Hong Kong Institute of Asia-Pacific Studies.

Chantler, P. and Harris, S. (1992). *Local Radio Journalism*. Focal Press.

Chippindale, P. and Franks, S. (1990). *Dished: the Rise and Fall of British Satellite Broadcasting*. Simon and Schuster.

Christ, W. G. (1990). The broadcast model curriculum project: developing national models. Paper presented at the 76th Speech Communication Association Convention, Chicago.

Clayton, J. (1994). *Interviewing for Journalists*. Piatkus.

Coldevin, G. (1979). The effects of placement, delivery format and missed cues on TV presenter ratings. In *Proceedings of the Second International Conference on Experimental Research in Televised Instruction*. (J. Baggaley and J. Shape, eds), pp. 73–90. Memorial University of Newfoundland.

Cook, B. and Banks, S. (1993). Predictors of job burnout in reporters and copy editors. *Journalism Quarterly*, **70**, 108–17.

Cooke, A. (1977). *America*. BBC.

Coupland, N. (1980). Style-shifting in a Cardiff work-setting. *Language in Society*, **9(1)**, 1–12.

Crissell, A. (1994). *Understanding Radio*, 2nd edn. Routledge.

Crissell, A. (1998). *An Introductory History of British Broadcasting*. Routledge.

Crone, T. (1995). *Law and the Media*. Focal Press.

Crook, T. (1998). *International Radio Journalism*. Routledge.

Cryle, D. (1994). Historical research in progress: a disreputable elite? Journalists and Journalism in colonial Australia. *Australian Studies in Journalism*, **3**, 130.

Crystal, D. (1971). *Linguistics*. Penguin.

Crystal, D. (1983). *Prosodic Systems and Intonation in English*. Cambridge University Press.

Czech-Beckeman, E. (1991). *Managing Electronic Media*. Focal Press.

Davies, C. L. (1994). The journalism industry award, arbitration and the universities. *Australian Studies in Journalism*, **3**, 80–1.

Davis, A. (1998). *Magazine Journalism Today*. Focal Press.

Dean aims to put law back into law studies. *Campus Review*, November 6–12, 1996.

Demers, D. (1991). Corporate structure and emphasis on profits and product quality at US daily newspapers. *Journalism Quarterly*, **68**, 15–26.

Demers, D. P. (1995). Autonomy, satisfaction high among corporate news staffs. *Newspaper Research Journal*, **16(2)**, 91–111.

Denning, Lord (1980). *The Due Process of Law.* Butterworth.

Denning, Lord (1982). *What next in the Law.* Butterworth.

Dillard, J. L. (1985). *Towards a Social History of American English.* Hawthorne.

Dillard, J. L. (1976). *American Talk.* Oxford University Press.

Dimbleby, J. (1975). *Richard Dimbleby: A Biography.* Hodder and Stoughton.

Dixon, F. (1975). *Inside the ABC: A Piece of Australian History.* Hawthorne.

Dobson, C. (1994). *The Freelance Journalist.* Focal Press.

Dodge, J. and Viner, G. (1965). *The Practice of Journalism.* Heinemann.

Downing, J. (1990). *Questioning the Media: A Critical Introduction.* Sage.

Dracos, T. (1989). News directors are lousy managers. *Washington Journalism Review,* September, 39–41.

Ducey, R. and Sapolsky, B. S. (1994). The future of broadcasting: entering the age of media convergence. *BEA Directory of Media Programmes in North American Universities and Colleges.*

Eastman, S. (1993). *Broadcasting/Cable Programming.* Wadsworth.

Eldridge, J. (ed.) (1993). *Getting the Message.* Routledge.

Ellis, A. J. (1889). *On English Pronunciation. OED.*

Erlich, M. (1996). The journalism of outrageousness: tabloid television news vs investigative news. *Journalism and Mass Communication Monographs,* **115**.

Fairbanks, G. (1986). *Voice and Articulation Handbook.* Harper.

Fairbanks, G. and Miron, W. (1957). Auditory comprehension in relation to listening rate and selective verbal redundancy. *Journal of Hearing and Speech Disorders,* **27**, 23–32.

Fang, I. E. (1972). *Television News.* Hastings House.

Feeler, F. (1989). *Reporting for the Print Media.* Harcourt.

Ferguson, C. and Heath, S. B. (eds) (1981). *Language in the USA.* Cambridge University Press.

Ferguson, M. (ed.) (1991). *Public Communication: The New Imperatives.* Sage.

Fiedler, F. (1974). *Leadership and Effective Management.* Scott, Foresman.

Findahl, O. and Hoijer, B. (1981). Media content and human comprehension. In *Advances in Content Analysis* (K. E. Rasangren, ed.), pp. 111–32. Sage.

Fischer, H.-D. (1995). *Sports Journalism at its Best*. Nelson-Hall.

Fischer, J. L. (1958). Social influences on the choice of a linguistic variant. *World*, **14**, 32–40.

Fisher, H. A. (1978). Broadcast journalists' perceptions of appropriate career preparation. *Journalism Quarterly*, **55(1)**, 140–44.

Fiske, J. (1987). *Television Culture*. Methuen.

Fiske, J. and Hartley, J. (1978). *Reading Television*. Methuen.

Flexner, S. (1976). *I Hear America Talking*. Longman.

Floridi, L. (1995). Internet: which future for organised knowledge, Frankenskin or Pygmalion? Paper delivered at the first UNESCO Philosophy Forum, Paris, March. (Seen at: www. unleyhs. schools.sa.edu.au/issues/floridi, html)

Foulke, E. (1978). Listening comprehension as a function of word rate. *Journal of Communication*, **18**, 198–206.

Fowler, G. and Shipman, J. (1982). Pennsylvania editors' perceptions of communication in the newsroom. *Journalism Quarterly*, **61**, 822–6.

Fowler, H. W. (1923). *The Split Infinitive*. S.P.E. Tract No. XV.

Fowler, H. W. (1978). *Modern English Usage*, 2nd edn. (revised by Sir Ernest Gowers). Clarendon Press.

Franklin, B. (1994). *Packaging Politics: Political Communications in Britain's Media Democracy*. Arnold.

Franklin, B. (1997). *Newszak and News Media*. Arnold.

Franklin, B. and Murphy, D. (1997). *What News? Market, Politics and Local Press*. Routledge.

French, D. and Richards, M. (1994). *Media Education across Europe*. Routledge.

Friend, C. (1994). Daily newspaper use of computers to analyse data. *Newspaper Research Journal*, **15(1)**, 35–48.

Fulton, K. (1996). A tour of our uncertain future. *Columbia Journalism Review*, March/Apr. (Seen at: www.crj.org/html)

Funkhouser, E. and Savage, A. L. (1987). College students' expectations for entry-level broadcast positions. *Communication Education*, **36(1)**, 23–7.

Gage, L. (1999). *A Guide to Commercial Radio Journalism*. Focal Press.

Gaines, W. (1994). *Investigative Reporting for Print and Broadcast*. Nelson-Hall.

Galtung, J. and Ruge, M. (1965). The structure of foreign news. *Journal of Peace Research*, **2**, 64–91.

Gans, H. (1980). *Deciding what's News*. Vintage.

Garrison, B. (1989). *Professional Feature Writing*. Erlbaum.

Gaziano, C. and Coulson, D. C. (1988). Effect of newsroom management styles on journalists: a case study. *Journalism Quarterly*, **65**, 869–80.

Gersh, D. (1993). Inverted pyramid turned upside down. *Editor and Publisher*, May 1, 22.

Gibbons, E. (1953). *Floyd Gibbons, Your Headline Hunter*. Exposition Press.

Gibson, R. (1991). *Radio and Television Reporting*. Simon and Schuster.

Gieber, W. and Johnson, R. (1961). The city hall beat: A study of reporter and source roles. *Journalism Quarterly*, **38**, 289–97.

Giles, H. and Powesland, P. (1975). *Speech Style and Social Evaluation*. Academic Press.

Giles, H., Mulac, J., Bradac, J. and Johnson, P. (1987). Speech accommodation theory: the first decade and beyond. In *Communication Yearbook 10* (M. L. McLaughlin, ed.), pp. 13–48. Sage.

Giles, R. (1995). *Newsroom Management*. Media Management Books.

Giles, V. and Hodgson, F. (1996). *Creative Newspaper Design*. Focal Press.

Gitling, T. (1985). *Inside Prime Time*. Pantheon Press.

Gladney, G. (1990). Newspaper excellence: how editors of small and large papers judge quality. *Newspaper Research Journal*, **11**, 59–71.

Glasgow Media Group (1976). *Bad News*. Routledge.

Glasgow Media Group (1980). *More Bad News*. Routledge.

Goffman, E. (1981). *Forms of Talk*. Harper and Row.

Golding, P. and Elliot, P. (1979). *Making the News*. Longman.

Granato, L. (ed.) (1998). *Newsgathering on the Net*. Macmillan.

Green, K. (1994). Computer-assisted reporting – sources from cyberspace. *Australian Studies in Journalism*, **3**, 83–96.

Greenbank, S. (ed.) (1984). *The English Language Today*. Oxford University Press.

Gross, L. S. (1996). *The International World of Electronic Media*. McGraw-Hill.

Gunning, R. (1968). *The Technique of Clear Writing*. McGraw-Hill.

Gunter, B. (1987). *Poor Reception: Misunderstanding and Forgetting Broadcast News*. Erlbaum.

Haas, M. R. (1990). Interlingual word taboos. *American Anthropologist*, **53**, 338–44.

Habermas, J. (1989). *The Structural Transformation of the Public Sphere*. MIT Press.

Hamlett, T. (1994). Mass communication education: a plastic Rolex? *Journal of the Association of Communication Administrators*, **2**, 124.

Hamlett, T. (1996). *The TYR Stylebook*. Department of Journalism, HKBU.

Hansen, J. (1994). *Connections: Technologies of Communication*. HarperCollins.

Hansen, K. (1987). Role of the newspaper library in the production of news. *Journalism Quarterly*, **66(3)**, 714–20.

Hao Xiaoming, Kewen Zhang and Huang Yu (1996). The Internet and information control: the case of China. *The Public*, **3(1)**, 125.

Harris, S. and Spark, D. (1993) *Practical Newspaper Reporting*. Focal Press.

Hartley, J. (1982). *Understanding News*. Methuen.

Hatchen, W. (1981). *The World News Prism: Changing Media of International Communication*. Iowa University Press.

Hausman, C. (1992). *Crafting the News for Electronic Media*. Wadsworth.

Hazinski, D. C. (1989). Equal time. *Feedback*, **30(1)**, 16–18.

Head, S. W. and Martin, L. A. (1956). Broadcasting and higher education: a new era. *Journal of Broadcasting*, **1**, 9–46.

Head, S., Sterling, C. H. and Wimmer, R. D. (1989). *Broadcasting in America: A Survey of Television, Radio and New Technologies*, 6th edn. Houghton Mifflin.

Hennessy, B. (1997). *Writing Feature Articles*. Focal Press.

Henningham, J. (1994). A suggested core curriculum in journalism education. *Australian Journalism Review*, **16(1)**, 88–93.

Herbert, J. (1976). *The Techniques of Radio Journalism*. A. and C. Black.

Herbert, J. (1981). Broadcast speech and the effect of voice quality on the listener: a study of the various components which categorise listener perception of vocal characteristics. PhD thesis, University of Sheffield.

Herbert, J. (1982). Journalism education and academia. *Media Reporter*, Winter.

Herbert, J. (1995). Hitch your typewriter to Cyberspace. Paper presented at the *International Improving University Teaching Conference*, Hong Kong, July.

Herbert, J. (1996). Truth and credibility: the sound of the broadcast journalist. *Australian Studies in Journalism*, **5**, 123–40.

Herbert, J. (1996). Broadcasting legislation and the convergence of media technology. Paper presented at the *Asian Mass Communication Institute Conference*, Singapore, July.

Herbert, J. (1996). Cascade learning approach to broadcast journalism education. *Asia Pacific Media Educator*, **1(1)**, 50–64.

Herbert, J. (1997). Journalism students need role models. Paper presented at *Journalism Education Conference*, Sydney, December 2.

Herbert, J. (1997). The broadcast voice. *English Today*, April, 18–23.

Herbert, J. (1997). Journalism education at the tertiary level. *Australian Journalism Review*, **9(1)**, 7–19.

Herbert, J. (1998). Broadcast journalism: format and language. In *Journalism Theory and Practice* (M. Breen, ed.). MacLeay Press.

Herbert, J. (1998). Towards a practical theory of broadcast journalism. *Asia Pacific Media Educator*, **5**, 137–43.

Hilliard, R. (1997). *Writing for Television and Radio*. Wadsworth.

Hilt, M. L. and Lipschultz, J. H. (1994). Broadcast manager concern about newsroom career preparation. *Feedback*, **35(3)**, 16–18.

Hilt, M. L. and Lipschultz, J. H. (1996). Broadcast newsroom hiring and career preparation. *Journalism and Mass Communication Educator*, **51(1)**, 36–43.

Hirsch, A. (1991). *Talking Heads: Television's Political Talk Shows and Star Pundits*. St. Martin's Press.

Hodgson, F. W. (1993). *Modern Newspaper Practice*. Focal Press.

Hodgson, F. W. (1998). *New Subediting*. Focal Press.

Holland, P. (1998). *The Television Handbook*. Routledge.

Hong, J. (1995). China's satellite technology: developments, policies and applications. *Telecommunications Policy*, **95(2)**, 117–33.

Hosley, D. and Yamada, G. (1987). *Hard News: Women in Broadcast Journalism*. Greenwood Press.

Hough, G. (1994). *News Writing*. Houghton Mifflin.

Howard, P. (1980). *Words Fail Me*. Hamish Hamilton.

Hunter, F. (1984). Grub Street and academia: the relationship between journalism and education 1880–1940 with special reference to the London University diploma for journalism 1919–1939. PhD thesis, City University, London.

Hyde, S. W. (1991). *TV and Radio Announcing*, 6th edn. Houghton Mifflin.

Inglis, A. F. (1991). *Satellite Technology: An Introduction*. Focal Press.

Ippolito, A. (1985). Databases in newspaper libraries. *Editor and Publisher*, 11 May, 60e–62e.

Itule, B. and Anderson, D. (1997). *News Writing and Reporting for Today's Media*. McGraw-Hill.

Jacoby, J. and Hoyer, W. D. (1987). *The Comprehension and Miscomprehension of Print Communications: An Investigation of Mass Media Magazines*. Erlbaum.

Jernow, A. L. (1994). China: the tight leash loosens; broadcast and press freedom. *Columbia Journalism Review*, **32(5)**, 31.

Johnston, C. (1995). *Winning the Global TV News Game*. Focal Press.

Johnstone, J. W. C. (1976). Organisational constraints on newswork. *Journalism Quarterly,* **53**, 5–13.

Joseph, T. C. (1983). Television reporters and managers preferences on decision-making. *Journalism Quarterly*, **60**, 476–9.

Karpf, A. (1985). News with the miracle ingredient. *The Guardian*, July 22, 13.

Keeble, R. (1998). *The Newspaper Handbook*. Routledge.

Keene, M. (1995). *Practical Photojournalism*. Focal Press.

Kemble, F. (1939). A Journal of Residence on a Georgia Plantation in 1838–9. Quoted in *Towards a Social History of America* (J. Dillard). Hawthorne.

Kemp, J. A. (1972). *Grammar of the English Language*, with Introductory Treatise on Speech by John Wallis. Longman.

Key, M. R. (1972). Linguistic behaviour of male and female. *Linguistics*, **88**, 15–31.

Klopfenstein, B. (1991). VCR attitudes and behaviours by length of ownership. *Journal of Broadcasting and Electronic Media*, **35(4)**, 487–504.

Knowledge Transfer and Usage in Communication Studies (1983). Asian Mass Communication Research and Information Centre, Singapore.

Kobre, K. (1996). *Photojournalism*. Focal Press.

Koss, S. (1984). *The Rise and Fall of the Political Press in Britain*. UNC Press.

Kumar, K. (1975). Holding the middle ground: the BBC, the public and the professional broadcaster. *Sociology*, **9(1)**, 67–88.

Laakaniemi, R. (1995). *Newswriting in Transition*. Nelson-Hall.

Labov, W. (1987). The case of the black English trial in Ann Arbor. In *Language & Society* (H. Dell, ed.), pp. 43–57. Cambridge University Press.

Lacy, S. (1990). A model of demand for news: impact of competition on newspaper content. *Journalism Quarterly*, **66**, 40–8.

Lacy, S., Sohn, A. and Wicks, J. (1993). *Media Management: A Casebook Approach*. Erlbaum.

Lee, P. and Wang, G. (1995). Satellite TV in Asia: forming a new ecology. *Telecommunications Policy*, **19(2)**, 135–49.

Lehmann, W. P. (ed.) (1967). *A Reader in Nineteenth-Century Historical Linguistics*. Indiana University Press.

Leichti, H. (1979). Towards a new paradigm: teaching the future of telecommunications. *Public Telecommunications Review*, **7(3)**, 42–6.

Lent, J. (1989). Mass communications in Asia and the Pacific: recent trends and developments. *Media Asia*, **16(1)**, 16–24.

Leonard, M. and Ricks, C. (eds). (1980). *The State of the Language*. Berkeley.

Limburg, V. (1994). *Electronic Media Ethics*. Focal Press.

Linton, B. (1987). Self-regulation in broadcasting revisited. *Journalism Quarterly*, **64**, 483–90.

Lloyd, C. (1985). *Profession: Journalist*. Hale and Iremonger.

Lloyd-James, A. (1935). *The Broadcast Word*. Kegan Paul.

Lloyd-James, A. (1936). Broadcast, *English*, **7**.

Lloyd-James, A. (1938). *Our Spoken Language*. Nelson.

Long, M. The Asia-Pacific region as a 'frenetic testbed' for communications development. *Intermedia*, **23(4)**, 40.

Luchsinger, R. and Arnold, G. E. (1965). *Voice–Speech–Language Clinical Communicology: Its Physiology and Pathology*. Belmont.

Mali, P. (1981). *Management Handbook: Operating Guidelines, Techniques and Practices*. Wiley.

Marckwardt, A. and Dillard, J. L. (1980). *American English*. Oxford University Press.

Matheson, H. (1933). *Broadcasting*. Thornton Butterworth.

Mayer, M. (1993). *Making News*. Doubleday.

McArthur, T. (ed.) (1992). *The Oxford Companion to the English Language*. Oxford University Press.

McCormick-Pickett, N. (ed.) (1984). *American Women in Radio and Television*. Women's Bureau, Department of Labour.

McCrum, R. (1986). *The Story of English*. Faber and Faber.

McLeish, R. (1999). *Radio Production*. Focal Press.

McNair, B. (1994). *News and Journalism in the UK*. Routledge.

McNair, B. (1998). *Sociology of Journalism*. Arnold.

McNichol, T. (1987). Databases: reeling in scoops with high tech. *Washington Journalism Review*, July/August, 28.

McQuail, D. (1969). *Towards a Sociology of Mass Communications*. Macmillan.

McQuail, D. (1969). Uncertainty about the audience and the organisation of mass communications. In *The Sociology of Mass Media Communicators* (P. Halmos, ed.), pp. 75–84. Sociological Review Monograph 13, University of Keele.

McQuail, D. (1992). *Mass Communication Theory: An Introduction*. Sage.

McQuail, D. (1992). *Media Performance*. Sage.

Medsger, B. (1996). *Winds of Change: Challenges confronting Journalism*. Freedom Forum.

Mencher, M. (1991). *News Reporting and Writing*. Brown.

Mencken, H. L. (1979). The *American Language*, 4th edn. Faber and Faber.

Merican, A. M. (1996). The relevance of philosophy in the journalism curriculum: the wisdom of journalism schools? Paper presented at the *Asian Communications: The Next 25 Years AMIC Conference*, June 1–3, Singapore.

Merrill, J. (ed.) (1995). *Global Journalism*. Longman.

Mickelson, S. (1972). *The Electronic Mirror*. Dodd, Mead.

Mickelson, S. (1989). *From Whistlestop to Soundbite*. Praeger.

Miller, T. (1988). The database revolution. *Columbia Journalism Review*, September/October, 35–8.

Millerson, G. (1993). *Effective TV Production*. Focal Press.

Mody, B. (1986). The receiver as sender: formative evaluation in Jamaican radio. *Gazette*, **38**, 147–60.

MPT (1992). Grand scale construction of optical cable system. *China Telecommunications Construction*, **4(5)**, 7–10.

Musburger, R. (1991). *Electronic News Gathering: A Guide to ENG*. Focal Press.

Nelson, H. E. (1948). The effect of variation of rate on the recall by radio listeners of 'straight' newscasts. *Speech Monographs*, **15**, 173–80.

Neuzil, M. (1993). Gambling with databases: a comparison of electronic searches and printed indices. *Newspaper Research Journal*, **15(1)**, 84–91.

Niven, H. (1961). The development of broadcast education in institutions of higher learning. *Journal of Broadcasting*, **5**, 241–50.

O'Donnell, L., Benoit, P. and Hausman C. (1993). *Modern Radio Production*. Wadsworth.

Oliver, W. J. (1978). Documenting training need. *Feedback*, **20(3)**, 5–7.

Orton, L. (1993). *Media Courses UK*. British Film Institute.

Pearson, M. (1993). Electronic mail as a news medium. *Australian Journalism Review*, **15(2)**, 131–8.

Pearson, M. (1997). *The Journalist's Guide to Media Law*. Allen & Unwin.

Pease, E. (1991). Blaming the boss: newsroom professionals see managers as public enemy No. 1. *Newspaper Research Journal*, **12**, 2–21.

Pease, E. (1992). Newsroom 2000: not my kid! Journalists leery of industry's future. *Newspaper Research Journal*, **13** 34–53.

Pease, E. (1993). Professional orientation equals second-class status in academe. *Journalism Educator*, **48(3)**, 38–45.

Peck, L. (1991). Anger in the newsroom. *Washington Journalism Review*, **13**, 22–7.

Petersen, N. (1993). *News Not Views: The ABC, The Press and Politics, 1932–1947*. Hale and Iremonger.

Picard, R. (1985). *The Press and the Decline of Democracy*. Greenwood Press.

Polansky, S. H. and Hughes, D. W. (1986). Managerial innovation in newspaper organisations. *Newspaper Research Journal*, **8**, 1–12.

Pollard, G. (1995). The impact of social attributes on professionalism among radio announcers. *Gazette*, **56**, 59–71.

Porter, M. (1979). Preparing students for careers in non-broadcast media. *Public Telecommunications Review*, **7(3)**, 52–4.

Porter, M. J. and Szolka, P. (1991). Broadcasting students' perspectives of broadcasting as liberal arts education. *Feedback*, **32(2)**, 18–21.

Pringle, P. K. (1995). *Electronic Media Management*. Focal Press.

Quirk, R. (1978). *The Use of English*. Longman.

Rampal, K. R. (1994). Post-martial law media boom in Taiwan. *Gazette*, **53**, 78–9, 87.

Ransom, W. S. (ed.) (1970). *English Transported*. Canberra.

Read, A. W. (1933). *British Recognition of American Speech in the Eighteenth Century*. Dialect Notes.

Reith, J. C. W. (1924). *Broadcast Over Britain*. Hodder and Stoughton.

Reith, J. C. W. (1949). *Into the Wind*. Hodder and Stoughton.

Renz, B. B. (1991). Yes to announcing. *Feedback*, **32(2)**, 22–4.

Reus, G. and Lee, B. B. (1993). The European community and professional journalism training. *Journalism Educator*, **47(4)**, 5.

Roberts, St. J. (1967). *Encyclopaedia of Radio and Television Broadcasting*. Cathedral Square Publishing.

Robertson, G. and Nicol, A. (1992). *Media Law*. Penguin.

Robinson, J. and Levy, M. (1986). *The Main Source: Learning from Television News*. Sage.

Rosenbaum, J. (1984). Revising telecommunications curricula. *International Television*, March, 66–9.

Rosengren, K. E. (1981). *Advances in Content Analysis*, pp. 111–32. Sage.

Ross, S. (1997). Columbia Journalism School survey of online media (seen at: www.mediasource.com/study/cont.htm).

Rubin, B. R. (1993). New technologies breach the five barriers of media control. *Intermedia*, **21(1)**, 22–8.

Rumbelhardt, D. E. (1986). Notes on a schema for stories. In *Representations and Understanding* (D.G. Bobrow and A. Collins, eds), pp. 211–36. Academic Press.

Ryan, M. (1995). The use of a writing model for print or on-line. *Journalism Educator*, Winter, 74–7.

Samuelson, M. (1962). A standardised test to measure job satisfaction in the newsroom. *Journalism Quarterly*, **39**, 285–91.

Scannel, P. and Cardiff, D. (1991). *A Social History of British Broadcasting, Vol. 1. 1922–1939*. Blackwell.

Scannell, P. (ed.) (1991). *Broadcast Talk*. Sage.

Schlesinger, P. (1978). *Putting 'Reality' Together*. Constable.

Schramm, W. (1954). *The Process and Effects of Mass Communication*. University of Illinois Press.

Schramm, W. (1964). *Mass Media and National Development*. University of Illinois Press.

Schramm, W. (1988). *The Story of Human Communication*. Harper and Row.

Scott, S. (1995). The technological challenge for curriculum and instruction. *Journalism and Mass Communication Educator*, Summer, 30.

Self, C. (1994). University industry task force finds complex alliance activity. *Journalism Educator*, Spring, 32–8.

Servaes, J. (1993). Beyond 'Europe 1992': communication and cultural identity in small nation states. *Telematics and Informatics*, **10(4)**, 321–43.

Seymour-Ure, C. (1997). *The British Press and Broadcasting since 1945*. Blackwell.

Sherman, B. (1995). *Telecommunications Management*. McGraw-Hill.

Shingler, M. and Wieringa, C. (1998). *On Air: Methods and Meanings of Radio*. Arnold.

Shoemaker, P. (1987). Building a theory of news content. *Journalism Monographs*, **103**.

Shoemaker, P. and Reese, S. (1991). *Mediating the Message: Theories of Influences on Mass Media Content*. Longman.

Siebert, F., Peterson, T. and Schramm, W. (1956). *Four Theories of the Press*. University of Illinois Press.

Sinai, P. (1979). Training of communication professionals in Asia. Asian Mass Communication Research and Information Centre, Singapore.

Smith, A. (1974). *The Shadow in the Cave: Study of the Relationship between the Broadcaster, Audience and the State*. Allen and Unwin.

Smith, A. (1979). *The Newspaper: An International History*. Thames and Hudson.

Smith, A. (1980). *Goodbye Gutenberg*: *The Newspaper Revolution of the 1980s*. OUP.

Smith, J. R. and McEwan, W. J. (1974). Effects of newscast delivery rate on recall and judgement of sources. *Journal of Broadcasting*, **18**, 73–83.

Sparks, C. and Dahlgren, P. (1993). *Communication and Citizenship: Journalism and the Public Sphere*. Routledge.

Stamm, K., Underwood, D. and Gifford, A. (1995). How pagination affects job satisfaction of editors. *Journalism and Mass Communication Quarterly*, **72(4)**, 851–62.

Sterling, B. and Sapolsky, B. S. (eds) (1994). Trends and changes in broadcast education. *BEA Directory of Media Programs in North American Universities and Colleges*, 8–9.

Stevenson, R. (1994). *Global Communications in the Twenty-First Century*. Longman.

Sticht, T. G. (1969). Comprehension of repeated time-compressed recordings. *Journal of Experimental Education*, **37**, 60–83.

Stone, G. (1992). *Newswriting*. HarperCollins.

Stone, V. A. (1989). J-grad quality and entry-level hiring surveyed. *Communicator*, **53(9)**, 58–9.

Straubhaar, J. and LaRose, R. (1996). *Communications Media in the Information Society*. Wadsworth.

Taylor, P. (1982). *Australia: The First Twelve Years*. Sphere.

Thakerar, J. N., Giles, H. and Cheshire, J. (1982). Psychological and linguistic parameters of speech accommodation theory. In *Advances in the Social Psychology of Language* (C. Fraser and K. R. Scherer, eds), pp. 205–55. Cambridge University Press.

Thomas, L. (1939). *Magic Dials*. Lee Furman.

Thomas, L. (1957). *History as You Heard It*. Doubleday.

Thomas, L. (1977). *So Long Until Tomorrow*. Morrow.

To Yiu-Ming and Ting Wai (1992). Journalism education and social/political development: a case study of the speciality curriculum of the communication department at Baptist College. In *Communication and Societal Development* (L. Chu and J. Chan, eds), pp. 465–80. Journalism and Communication Department, Chinese University of Hong Kong.

Trager, G. (1958). Paralanguage: a first approximation. *Studies in Linguists*, **13**, 1–12.

Trudgill, P. (1980). Sex, covert prestige and linguistic change in the urban British English of Norwich. *Lingua*, 179–97.

Trudgill, P. (1974). *Sociolinguistics*. Pelican.

Tuchman, G. (1978). *Making News: A Study in the Construction of Reality*. Free Press.

Tunstall, J. (1970). *Media Sociology*. Constable.

Tunstall, J. (1970). *The Westminster Lobby Correspondents*. Routledge.

Tunstall, J. (1971). *Journalists at Work*. Constable.

Tunstall, J. and Palmer, M. (1991). *Media Moguls*. Routledge.

Tunstall, J. (1996). *Newspaper Power*. OUP.

Twelow, J. (1993). Newspapers and media convergence. *Editor and Publisher*, June, 1–23, 96.

Underwood, D. (1988). When MBAs rule the newsroom. *Columbia Journalism Review*, March/April, 23–40.

Upped, K. Journalism education in India: a question of commitment. *Journal*, **4**, 110–12.

Utterback, A. (1990). *Broadcast Voice Handbook: How to Polish Your On-Air delivery*. Bonus Books.

Van Dijk, T. and Kitsch, W. (1983). *Strategies of Discourse Comprehension*. Academic Press.

Van Ginneken, J. (1998). *Understanding Global News*. Sage.

Wakelin, M. F. (1987). *English Dialects*. Athlone.

Walker, R. R. (1973). *The Magic Spark*. Hawthorne Press.

Wallis R. and Baran, S. (1996). *The Known World of Broadcast News*. Routledge.

Walters, R. (1994). *Broadcast Writing*. McGraw-Hill.

Weaver, D. and Wilhoit, C. (1986). *The American Journalist*. Indiana University Press.

Webster, J. (1989). Media study in a time of technological change. *Feedback*, **30(3)**, 20–3.

Weinberg, A. and Weinberg, L. (eds) (1961). *The Muckrakers*. Putnam's Sons.

Wells, J. C. (1982). *Accents of English*, Vols. 1–3. Cambridge University Press.

Welsh, T. and Greenwood, W. (1999). *McNae's Essential Law for Journalists*. Butterworth.

White, D. (1950). The gatekeeper: A case study in the selection of news. *Journalism Quarterly*, **27**, 383–90.

White, E. (1996). *Broadcast News Writing, Reporting and Producing*. Focal Press.

Whitman, W. (1855). *An American Primer*.

Wilby, P. and Conroy, A. (1994). *The Radio Handbook*. Routledge.

Wilkinson, A. (1965). Spoken English. *Educational Review Supplement*, **6**, 17.

Williams, F. and Pavlik, J. (eds) (1994). *The People's Right to Know: Media Democracy and the Information Highway*. Erlbaum.

Williams, R. (1965). *The Long Revolution*. Penguin.

Williams, R. (1974). *Television, Technology and Cultural Form*. Fontana.

Wodak, R. (1987). And where is the Lebanon? A socio-psycholinguistic investigation of comprehension and intelligibility of news. *Text* **7(4)**, 377–410.

Won, W.-H. (1993). The social and cultural impact of satellite broadcasting in Korea. *Media Asia*, **20(1)**, 15–20.

Yallop, R. (1982). Why Strine ain't English. *The Guardian*, 2 September.

Yancy, T. L. (1992). We must include skills courses in the broadcast core. *Feedback*, **33(2)**, 17–18.

Yoakam, R. D. and Cremer, C. F. (1989). *ENG: Television News and the New Technology*, 2nd edn. Southern Illinois University Press.

Yu X. (1995). Dilemma in information management: STAR TV and Beijing's control of satellite broadcasting. *Issues and Studies*, **31(5)**.

Zelizer, B. (1993). Has communication explained journalism? *Journal of Communication*, **43(4)**, 80–8.

Zhou, C. (1991). Strengthening management and development of communication industry. *Telecommunications World*, **3(1)**, 3–4.

Index

INDEX

www.focalpress.com

Visit our web site for:
- the latest information on new and forthcoming Focal Press titles
- special offers
- our e-mail news service

Join our Focal Press Bookbuyers'Club

As a member, you will enjoy the following benefits:
- special discounts on new and best-selling titles
- advance information on forthcoming Focal Press books
- a quarterly newsletter highlighting special offers
- a 30-day guarantee on purchased titles

Membership is free. To join, supply your name, company, address, telephone/fax numbers and e-mail address to:
Elaine Hill
E-mail: elaine.hill@repp.co.uk
Fax: +44(0) 1865 314423
Address: Focal Press, Linacre House, Jordan Hill, Oxford OX2 8DP

Catalogue

For information on all Focal Press titles, we will be happy to send you a free copy of the Focal Press Catalogue.

Tel: 01865 314693
E-mail: carol.burgess@repp.co.uk

Potential authors

If you have an idea for a book, please get in touch:

Europe
Beth Howard, Editorial Assistant
E-mail: beth.howard@repp.co.uk
Tel: +44 (0) 1865 314365
Fax: +44 (0) 1865 314572

USA
Marie Lee, Publisher
E-mail: marie.lee@bhusa.com
Tel: 781 904 2500
Fax: 781 904 2620